57 West Vine Street
Hatfield PA 19440

Ball Identification Guide to

Greenhouse Pests and Beneficials

By Stanton Gill and John Sanderson

Ball Publishing

Batavia, Illinois USA

Ball Publishing
335 North River Street
Batavia, Illinois 60510 USA

©1998 Stanton Gill and John Sanderson. All rights reserved.
Printed in Hong Kong
03 02 01 00 99 98 5 4 3 2 1

No part of this book may be reproduced or transmitted in any form or by any means, electronic or mechanical, including photocopying, recording or any information storage and retrieval system, without permission in writing from the publisher.

Disclaimer of liabilities: Reference in the publication to a trademark, proprietary product, or company name is intended for explicit description only and does not imply approval or recommendation to the exclusion of others that may be suitable.

While every effort has been made to ensure the accuracy and effectiveness of the information in this book, Ball Publishing makes no guarantee, express or implied, as to the procedures contained here. Neither the author nor publisher will be liable for direct, indirect, incidental, or consequential damages in connection with or arising from the furnishing, performance, or use of this book.

Library of Congress Cataloging-in-Publication Data
Gill, Stanton, 1952–

Ball identification guide to greenhouse pests and beneficials / by Stanton Gill and John Sanderson.

p.   cm.

Includes index.

ISBN 1-883052-17-3

1. Plants, Ornamental—Diseases and pests—Identification. 2. Greenhouse plants—Diseases and pests—Identification.. 3. Arthropod pests—Identification. 4. Arthropod pests—Biological control. 5. Arthropoda as biological pest control agents.

I. Sanderson, John, 1955–   . II. Title.

SB608.07G35 1998   97-51312
635.9'265—dc21   CIP

Cover photo: Melon aphid, courtesy of Communication Services, New York Agricultural Experiment Station, Geneva, New York.

Acknowledgments

The authors would like to give special thanks to the following people for reviewing the text for this book:

John A. Davidson, Professor Emeritus, Department of Entomology, University of Maryland, College Park, Maryland.

Andrew Jensen, Systematic Entomology Laboratory, USDA-ARS, Beltsville, Maryland.

Frederic Miller, Cooperative Extension Service, University of Illinois, Champaign, Illinois.

Ronald Oetting, Department of Entomology, University of Georgia, Griffin, Georgia.

Michael Raupp, Department of Entomology, University of Maryland, College Park, Maryland.

Rondalyn Reeser, IPM Scout, Cooperative Extension Service, University of Maryland, Ellicott City, Maryland.

Bruce Steward, Technical Representative, Bayer Company, Kennett Square, Pennsylvania.

About the Authors

Stanton Gill is a principal extension regional specialist, with professor rank, at the University of Maryland Cooperative Extension Service stationed at the Central Maryland Research and Education Center, Ellicott City. He is also an adjunct professor with Montgomery College, where he teaches integrated pest management for greenhouse and nursery management classes.

He has many years of experience working in IPM with the greenhouse, nursery, and landscape industries. He received a Bachelor's degree in horticulture and a Master's degree in entomology from the University of Maryland. He currently leads the greenhouse IPM team that works with the greenhouse industry in Maryland. The major goals of the program are to have as many greenhouse operations as possible integrate biological control with judicious use of compatible pesticides and keep plant losses to a minimum level.

He has first-hand familiarity with proper identification through the IPM programs that he runs with Maryland greenhouse growers and nurserymen. He also conducts field research on biological control of greenhouse pests. He publishes articles on a wide variety of greenhouse and nursery pest control topics for both scientific journals and popular magazines and is a regular speaker at state and national greenhouse and nursery conferences.

Dr. John Sanderson is associate professor in the Entomology Department at Cornell University in Ithaca, New York. He has both research (50%) and extension (50%) responsibilities in the biology and management of greenhouse arthropod pests.

He received his B.S. degree in zoology at San Diego State University and both his M.S. and Ph.D. degrees in entomology at the University of California, Riverside. He then completed a postdoctoral appointment with Dr. Michael Parrella, University of California, Davis, where he first became involved in greenhouse pest management. John arrived at Cornell in 1987 and became an integral member of Cornell's Greenhouse IPM Team.

His research has included insect sampling programs, plant resistance, evaluation of biological control organisms, evaluation of insecticides, and the integration of chemical and biological control. He also lectures on greenhouse insect pest management in various courses at Cornell and currently serves as Entomology Department Extension Leader.

He was the convener of the Greenhouse Working Group of the Nearctic Regional Section of the International Organization for Biological Control and of the Northeast Greenhouse IPM Workgroup. He regularly contributes articles to industry magazines and speaks at state and national greenhouse conferences.

CONTENTS

INTRODUCTION

The primary purpose of this book and its more than 450 photographs is to help greenhouse managers, integrated pest management practitioners, educators, and extension and regulatory professionals to identify arthropod pests and their natural enemies on crops grown in United States greenhouses. An essential part of an IPM program and selection of control strategy is proper identification of pests and natural enemies. For many reasons, a given insect or mite species may vary tremendously in appearance.

HOW TO USE THIS BOOK

Part 1 of this book briefly covers establishing an IPM program in the greenhouse. In Part 2, the major greenhouse pests are grouped for identification. Each pest grouping follows the same format: **general description** of the pest group, **plant damage** caused by the pest, **group characteristics**, **biology, monitoring** methods, **identification** and life cycle information, and **biological controls** for the pest species described.

Part 3 focuses on pest damage to specific crops, such as leaf stippling by mites, leaf curling from aphids, and feeding injury of thrips, to help growers recognize various injuries to many greenhouse crops.

Pest and plant samples for identification

Photographs alone, however, will not provide species confirmation with absolute certainty. Samples of pests and sometimes plant parts should be sent to your state cooperative extension office or to a professional diagnostic laboratory to confirm your identification. For locations of diagnostic laboratories, contact your state cooperative extension office.

Collecting and submitting samples

Pests. To send samples to a professional diagnostic laboratory, collect a fairly large number of pest specimens and place them in 70% ethyl or isopropyl alcohol. In each of the major pest sections of this book, we discuss what life stage is best used for identification purposes. For example, in the case of aphids, multiple specimens from several plants should be collected whenever possible, because it is common to have several aphid species in the same greenhouse or even on the same plant.

Placing an insect in a freezer for one or two days usually kills it. Hard-bodied insects such as beetles, flies, bugs, small moths, or butterflies should be killed, then wrapped in layers of cotton or facial tissue and placed in a pillbox, film canister, or other sturdy container. It is best to kill caterpillars, maggots, and grubs by dropping them into boiling water for 30 seconds, then placing them into rubbing alcohol. Soft-bodied insects, such as aphids, caterpillars, grubs, mealybugs, thrips, and mites, can be preserved in vials containing rubbing alcohol and securely wrapped or placed in a small box to avoid breakage during shipping.

Scale insects can be sent on infested leaves or stems. Whitefly nymphs can be sent on infested leaves. Be sure to send whitefly pupae if you want the species identified. To collect thrips, tap infested leaves or flowers over a small amount of rubbing alcohol, then pour the alcohol containing the thrips into a small watertight container for shipping.

Plants. It can be helpful or absolutely necessary to know the plant material on which the insects were found. If you do not know the identity of the plant, collect a fresh sample, wrap it in several paper towels, punch a few holes in a plastic bag, and insert the wrapped plant specimen. Do not moisten.

To send leaves that display possible insect or mite damage, collect fresh leaves, wrap them loosely in one or two paper towels, punch a few holes in a plastic bag, and insert the wrapped leaf specimens. Do not moisten. Pack loosely with newspaper into a sturdy box for shipping. If insects are found in the vicinity of the damage, collect several insects or mites, if possible, in each sample and include them along with leaf samples.

Record keeping. For your records and for the laboratory, again, record the original colors of the pest specimens. Also record the presence of waxy filament of the live pests, which may lose their normal wax filaments in alcohol. Note where on the plants they were found (roots, stems, leaves, flowers). Always be sure to include the date, locations, and species of plants on which the pests were found.

Similarly thorough records should accompany plant samples.

Shipping. Ship only dead insects or mites. It is unlawful to mail living insects across state lines and between countries. Provide thorough collection data (host plant, how many insects were present, where they were on the plant, and a description of symptoms and damage).

All samples should be shipped in a box, tube, or any common shipping container acceptable to the postal service. Containers should be sturdy enough so that they do not tear or get broken in shipment. Make sure that samples arrive at the lab before Friday afternoon, or they will spend the weekend in a post office, where they could be ruined by excessive heat or cold. Samples sent by overnight or next-day couriers arrive in the best condition.

Part 1

IPM in the Greenhouse

CHAPTER 1

Greenhouse Insect Control Using Integrated Pest Management

Research by land-grant university experiment station and extension service specialists has shown integrated pest management (IPM) to be the most effective, economical, and environmentally sound strategy for controlling insect and mite pests in greenhouses. With IPM you identify pest problems early, isolate or destroy pest-prone plants before the problem spreads, develop treatment thresholds, integrate use of beneficial organisms where practical, and use spot treatment of pesticides. An IPM program relies on regular monitoring and accurate identification of both problem pests and beneficial organisms present. Applying a control tactic against a misidentified pest can be an ineffective waste of money and time.

Thresholds

Market demand has created the unrealistic goal of eliminating all pests from the greenhouse. The grower strives to produce quality crops with no pests or damage. The reality is that retail evaluation studies very often have shown plants sold in the retail market are not entirely free of pests or pest damage. In most traditional chemical control programs, elimination of all pests is rare. Pests are often present, but at levels so low that most customers do not notice them.

There are several reasons why it is difficult to determine a threshold that is uniform for all growers. There are many different crops grown, often simultaneously, in various combinations, and in the same greenhouse. Outdoor climate differences make pest migration into the greenhouse a problem in some regions but not others. Some growers and their customers are able to tolerate a few more pests than others. Finally, greenhouse structures vary tremendously in size, ventilation system, or crops grown on benches versus floors.

You as a grower should develop your own threshold for a pest. The goal of most greenhouse pest management programs should be to maintain pests below an economically damaging level and at a level that your customer or state agriculture inspector is willing to accept. This threshold may change as the crop grows. You can use your scouting records to determine your own thresholds. Record the number of pests that were found on sticky cards or foliar inspections at important times in each crop and whether the amount of damage and cost of control tactics were significant. Note whether you applied a control tactic and whether the finished crop was acceptable to you and your customers.

PREVENTION

Sanitation

Depriving insects and mites of food sources or places to live is one of the chief reasons that we practice sanitation. Sanitation means keeping your greenhouse weed free, eliminating excess piles of growing media, algae, and piles of plant debris. All these can provide various insects (and diseases) with food or a place to live. Keep the outdoor area around the greenhouse free of weeds and garden plants that can be other sources of pests and diseases. Compost or cull piles should be located well away from greenhouse doors or vents. Prior to starting a new crop, the greenhouse should be inspected for all existing pest problems, including stock plants and pet plants (those plants staying in the greenhouse year after year that are particular favorites and are rarely, if ever, sold), leftover hanging baskets, and weeds. Either the source of pests should be eliminated, or the pest problem should be controlled, before the new crop is started.

Exclusion by microscreening

Effective microscreening. A significant proportion of insect infestations can result from insects moving into greenhouses from surrounding areas. There is little impediment to the movement of small insect pests into the greenhouse from surrounding areas. Greenhouse structures provide easy access to insect pests via open ventilation inlet louvers and exhaust fan openings. Frequently, there are also openings along the ground and around doorways and closed vents.

Screening greenhouses to exclude pests can be an important part of your integrated pest management plan. If installed and used properly, microscreening covering vents and doorways can reduce the influx of insects and the need for insecticides.

Screening can help reduce the need for pesticide application and all the associated costs and entry restrictions. Worker protection standards are encouraging many growers to look for alternatives to pesticide applications to control pests. Microscreening can help to fight resistance to pesticides in insects by reducing the number of applications being used in the greenhouse.

To prevent insects from entering the greenhouse, it is important that the grower installs tight-fitting entrance doors, seals spaces around vents, and closes openings at ground level around the perimeter of the greenhouse. Educate employees about the importance of keeping doors closed. Immediately repair any tears in the screening fabric. Regular cleaning of the screens to prevent buildup of dust, insects, or debris is essential to the performance of the system. Do not wash screens while the ventilation fans are running. The capillary action of water on the screen will effectively block airflow. Also, inspect plants for insects before they are moved into a screened greenhouse. Insect-infested plants must not be brought into a screened greenhouse.

Maintaining adequate ventilation. Many greenhouse growers comment that installing microscreening will cause cooling problems and is more trouble than it is worth. There is some truth to the first part. Improperly sized microscreening can reduce airflow, causing fan burnout, and in its short history of use in the United States, there have been some greenhouses where poorly designed microscreening systems have created cooling problems.

Application of screening presents two problems to the greenhouse. First, the screening must be fine enough that the target insects can not crawl through the openings. Second, a large screened surface area must be provided to get the necessary ventilation air into the greenhouse. Screening materials must have openings through them that are as small as or smaller than the insect to be excluded, such as troublesome thrips and much larger leafminers, aphids, and whiteflies (fig. 1.1). A hole about 192 microns (less than 0.0075 inch) in size is small enough. Finer materials will restrict airflow even more.The screening material should be resistant to ultraviolet (UV) radiation and physical damage.

Microscreening materials have a lot of mesh material that will block airflow. Mesh material is made out of uniform threads, *mesh* referring to the number of threads per inch in each direction. A 60-mesh material has 60 threads per inch (2.5 cm) in each direction. Each thread has a thickness or diameter that partially blocks the formerly open space. When the thickness of the thread is accounted for, the free open area for air passage through the screen is greatly diminished, perhaps only a small fraction of what it was before the screening was applied.

The screening causes resistance to air movement. Open area restriction causes a higher air velocity and a higher static pressure loss. This translates into poor airflow and heat buildup in hot weather. As the fan tries to force air through the openings in the screening, the static pressure drop increases and the airflow decreases. The fan moves less air at high static pressures. To solve these problems, the screened area must be several times larger than the vent opening it protects (fig. 1.2).

Fig. 1.1. Correctly installed microscreening can effectively exclude insect pests from the outside. *Photo: Stanton Gill*

Fig. 1.2. Microscreening should cover all intake vents to keep out migrating insects. *Photo: Stanton Gill*

Obtaining more information on microscreening. Several land-grant universities have created fact sheets on microscreening, including calculations on the area of microscreening needed. Microscreen factsheets are available from: University of Maryland Cooperative Extension Service, "Insect Screening for Greenhouses," FACTS 186, Biotechnology Resource Engineering Department, College Park, MD 20742; and from Jim Baker, Department of Entolomogy, P.O. Box 7613, North Carolina State University, Raleigh, NC 27695-7613. Ask for "Insect Screening," by J.R. Baker, M.L. Bell, and E.A. Searin, 1997 (rev); North Carolina Cooperative Extension Service, Department of Entolomogy Ornamentals and Turf; Information Note 104, 4pp.

MONITORING

Monitoring is the backbone of any IPM program. Knowing whether pests are present, their location, severity, and in many cases the life stage composition provides a knowledge base on which to make pest management decisions. Such information provides great peace of mind and eliminates the "spray and pray" uncertainty.

Monitoring must be done on a year-round, routine basis, usually weekly. Successful monitoring routines often make use of one or more employees who have these responsibilities in their job descriptions. Other greenhouse personnel may provide occasional input on pests, but the routine will work best if it is coordinated through someone designated to do the job. Such a person should not be pulled away from the scouting routine when things get busy, or "unexpected" pest problems may result. There are obvious advantages if a private scout is used, if available.

In many cases, a private IPM consultant may offer a big advantage. Having an independent IPM scout examine a greenhouse crop provides an objective viewpoint. The scout's weekly report helps the greenhouse manager make timely decisions concerning the health of the crop.

Thorough monitoring of a greenhouse may be done if it is divided into units of a size in which the crop can be inspected in a reasonable time, usually 2,000 to 4,000 square feet (186 to 372 m^2). It may be an entire 30- by 100-foot (3 by 9 m^2) greenhouse or one or several sections of a gutter-connected greenhouse. Each unit is scouted weekly, with records kept separately for each.

The scouting routine should include counts from several sticky cards and random foliage inspections to monitor nonflying pests. A few plants that have living pests can be flagged and used as sentinel plants. After sprays are applied or natural enemies released, they are reinspected to determine if control was achieved. Finally, during each scouting session the general health of the crop should be assessed and any other problems with the crop of greenhouse noted.

Foliage inspection

To monitor many of the pests, particularly nonflying ones, such as spider mites, many aphids, caterpillars, weevils, scales, and mealybugs, the plants must be inspected. Many pests live on the undersurfaces of leaves and may go unnoticed unless the leaves are turned over.

Some pests produce damage symptoms or other evidence of their presence, such as cast skins, fecal droppings, honeydew, and ants feeding on the honeydew. Tips for detecting and monitoring specific types or species of pests can be found in the insect chapters. The number of plants to inspect depends on the crop, the stage of crop, the pest complex, the labor costs, and the experience of the scout, among other things. In general, sample as many plants as you can afford to (1 to 10% of the crop is a very rough guideline). Plants should usually be selected randomly from throughout the growing area. Random plant selection is the best way to come across "hot spots" before they become obvious. Be sure to include hanging baskets, pet plants, and any weeds. Of course, if you know that certain crops, cultivars, or areas of the greenhouse are prone to have a given pest, be sure to inspect a few plants from these areas.

For general foliar scouting, select different individual plants each time the crop is inspected. Walk through the greenhouse and note any areas of the crops that are discolored, of different height or shape, drooping, or have other subtle differences.

To inspect a plant closely, look at both leaves and stems, and if there is wilting, inspect the roots. Inspect a few leaves from the bottom, middle, and top of the canopy. Look for damage symptoms on the upper surface of leaves, but also turn some leaves over to check for pests. The underleaf surface of a potted plant can often be easily inspected simply by holding the plant up and looking at it from below.

Recording the scouting results each week in some systematic way is important. A data sheet can be fashioned to keep track of weekly pest levels for each scouted area in the greenhouse. Data sheets for greenhouse IPM may be available from your Cooperative Extension Service. Include information on crop cultivar, crop stage, sticky card counts for each pest species, and counts from foliar inspections for each pest. Record the time required for scouting, pesticide applications, and other pest management tactics, and use the times to determine the costs of your pest management program. Also these records can be used to determine whether pest levels are declining and, compared with your spray records, to determine the best application method, pesticide, and time of application to gain the best control.

A routine, organized plan to get scouting results to the person responsible for making pest management decisions on a timely basis is critical. The plan should also include a follow-up mechanism to be sure that a control tactic was applied if needed and if control is being achieved.

Sticky cards for monitoring

Yellow and blue sticky cards should be standard greenhouse items for detecting pests and monitoring insect population trends. Yellow sticky cards attract most flying insect pests, such as fungus gnats, shore flies, winged aphids, whiteflies, leafminers, and thrips (fig. 1.3). Blue sticky cards are particularly attractive to thrips.

Sticky card monitoring. The number of each insect pest captured on sticky cards should be counted and recorded weekly. This way you will be able to detect whether an insect population is building or declining. Sticky cards can also detect whether certain insects are migrating into your greenhouse. If you quarantine incoming plant material in a separate greenhouse, you can use sticky cards, along with foliage inspec-

Fig. 1.3. Sticky cards generally end up with a mix of insects from which you must pick out the most important ones. *Photo: Stanton Gill*

tion, to evaluate whether the new plant material is infested. For general monitoring of most flying insect pests, place yellow sticky cards vertically on stakes or suspended from strings, maintaining the bottom of the card an inch (25 mm) or so above the top of the canopy. Use one card per 1,000 square feet (93 m^2), as a rule of thumb.

When first looking at a sticky card, it may seem to hold a jumble of twisted, distorted insect bodies. You must train your eye to distinguish the key pest insects from the insects that are not pests and the ones that are natural enemies. Often when an insect sticks to a card, it may appear different from a normal living, moving insect. To aid you in the identification of what insect pests and some of their natural enemies look like when they are entrapped on sticky cards, we have assembled the following pictures.

Winged aphid. The winged aphid may be easy to identify if the cornicles on the abdomen are visible. Cornicles are structures resembling tailpipes on either side of the abdomen. Aphid wings are much longer than the body, and wing veins are also distinctive (fig. 1.4).

Fungus gnat. A small, humpbacked, black fly, the fungus gnat has long legs and beaded antennae, a single pair of wings, and a characteristic forked vein on the wing (figs. 1.5, 1.6).

Synacra pauperi. This insect, a common parasitoid of fungus gnats, can be more numerous on sticky cards than fungus gnats themselves in unsprayed greenhouses (fig. 1.7). It is about the same size as a fungus gnat (fig. 1.8). It has a large and a small pair of

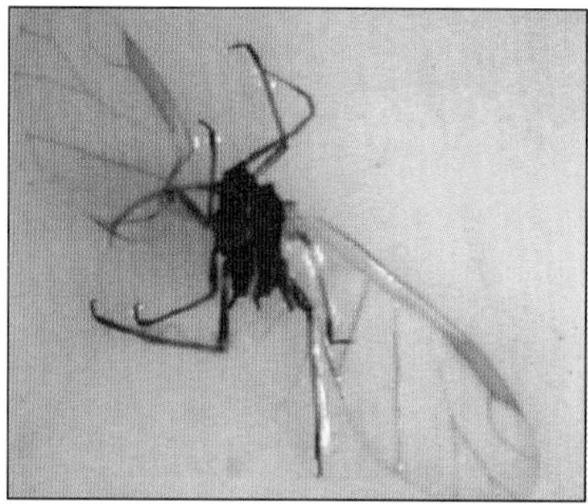

Fig. 1.4 Winged aphids have wings at least twice the length of the body with a distinctive pattern of wing veins. *Photo: John Sanderson*

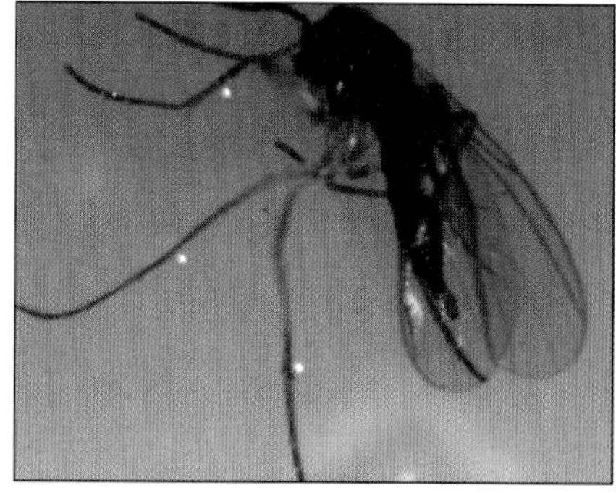

Fig. 1.5 Fungus gnat adults have beaded antennae and long gangly legs. *Photo: Stanton Gill*

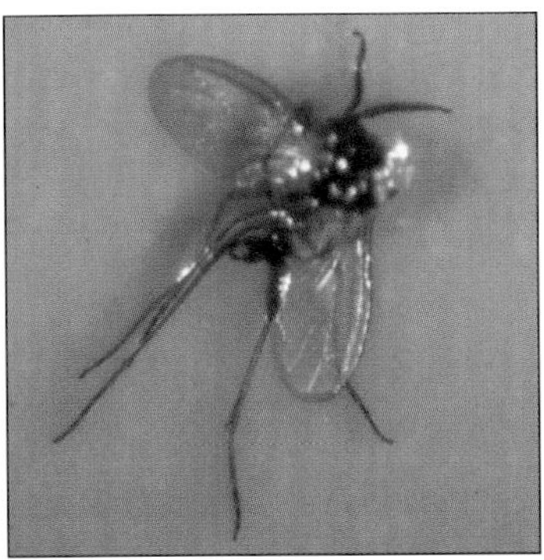

Fig. 1.6 The fungus gnat's wing vein forms a Y near the middle of each wing. *Photo: Stanton Gill*

Fig. 1.7 *Synacra pauperi*, is attracted to yellow sticky cards and can be numerous in unsprayed greenhouses. *Photo: John Sanderson*

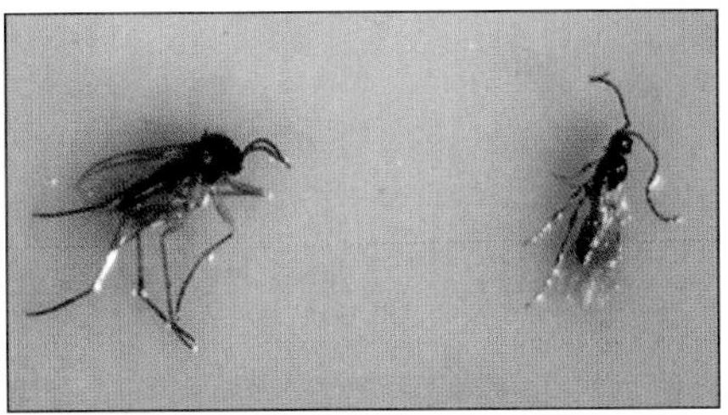

Fig. 1.8 *Synacra pauperi*, a parasitoid of fungus gnat larvae, next to a fungus gnat. *Photo: John Sanderson*

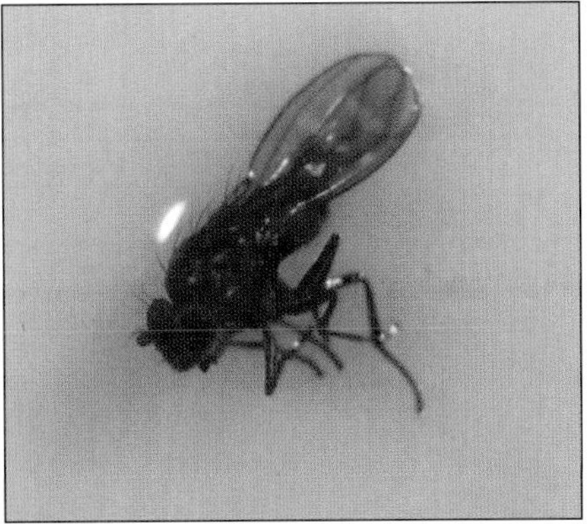

Fig. 1.9 Shore fly on a yellow card. Notice the clear spots on the gray wings. *Photo: John Sanderson*

wings, with reduced wing veins on the large forewing and no veins on the rear. There are noticeable constrictions between the head and the thorax and between the thorax and the abdomen. The abdomen tapers to a sharp tip. The female is brown to reddish brown, with black eyes. The antennae are elbowed, and near the tip the segments are darker and swollen. There are no noticeable antennal hairs. The male is black, with long antennae that are nearly the length of the body. The antennal segments are similar in size and shape, and each has several hairs.

Shore fly (*Scatella stagnalis*). A small, dark fly, the shore fly has short antennae and relatively short legs. The single pair of wings are dusty gray, but each has five large, distinctive spots without any gray (fig. 1.9). (A comparison of size of the drain moth, shore fly, and fungus gnat is shown in fig. 1.10)

Fig. 1.10 Here a moth fly (*top*), shore fly (*left*), and a fungus gnat are compared for size and appearance. *Photo: Stanton Gill*

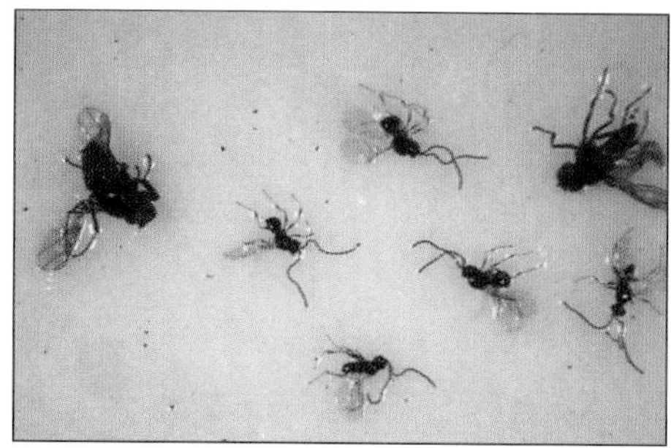

Fig. 1.11 Note the difference in size between *Hexacola hexatoma*, the shore fly parasitoid, and shore flies on a yellow sticky card. *Photo: John Sanderson*

Fig. 1.12 *Hexacola hexatoma*, the shore fly parasitoid, is attracted to yellow sticky cards. *Photo: John Sanderson*

Fig. 1.13 A moth fly on a yellow sticky card. Note that the body and wings are covered in hairs that give it a furry appearance. *Photo: John Sanderson*

Fig. 1.14 *Liriomyza trifolii* leafminer adults on a yellow sticky card. Note black and yellow body and large, black cannon-shaped ovipositor at the end of the abdomen. *Photo: John Sanderson*

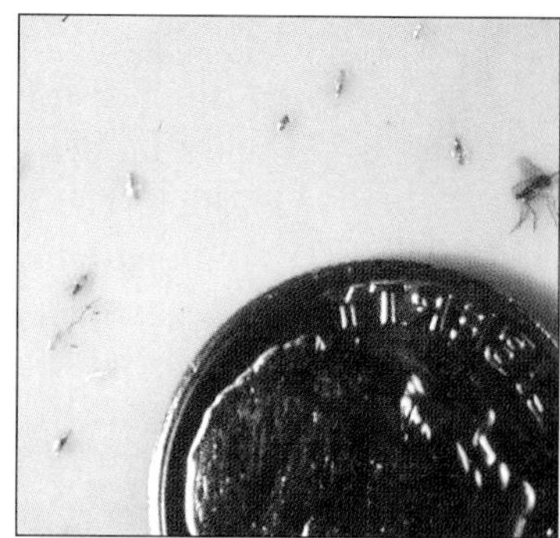

Fig. 1.15 Adult thrips. Note size comparison between a dime and a fungus gnat. *Photo: John Sanderson*

Hexacola hexatoma. A small parasitoid of shore flies, this insect is shiny black and about half the size of a shore fly (figs. 1.11, 1.12). It has long antennae about three-fourths the length of the body, made up of many tiny beads. There is a constriction between the thorax and the abdomen. The veins in the first pair of wings are very reduced, consisting mainly of dark veins near the leading edge of the wing. The hind wing is very reduced and without veins. In side view, the thorax and abdomen have very circular profiles.

Moth fly (*Psychoda* sp.). The moth fly is a short, small, gray insect with a single pair of very large, broad wings. The distinctive wings appear to be covered with scales that give a fringed, hairlike appearance similar to moth wings (fig. 1.13). The antennae are beaded, with several hairs arising from each bead.

Leafminer. This insect is a small, yellow-and-black fly. The leafminer has two transparent wings and short antennae. The female has a large, cannon-shaped, shiny black structure at the end of the abdomen, which it uses to puncture leaves and lay eggs (fig. 1.14).

Thrips. A thrips is tiny and often brown, black, or straw colored (figs. 1.15, 1.16). It is the same shape and size as a grain of peat and can be confused with it (fig. 1.17). A thrips has short antennae and very distinctive wings, made up mostly of fringes of tiny hairs (fig. 1.18).

Orius. *Orius* (minute pirate bug) is a predator of thrips that is occasionally attracted to yellow sticky cards. The adults are half the size of a shore fly. Adults are black and white in color, and there is a distinct enlarged triangle (scutellum) behind the head on the thorax. *Orius* nymphs are a bright yellow-orange color (fig. 1.19).

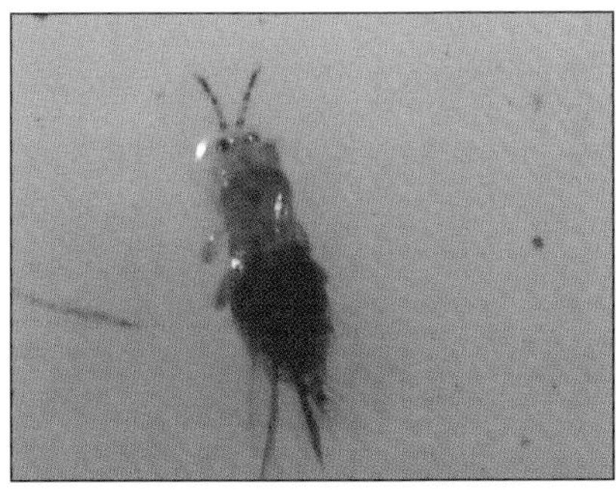

Fig. 1.16 Close-up of a thrips with its wings folded on a sticky card. *Photo: Stanton Gill*

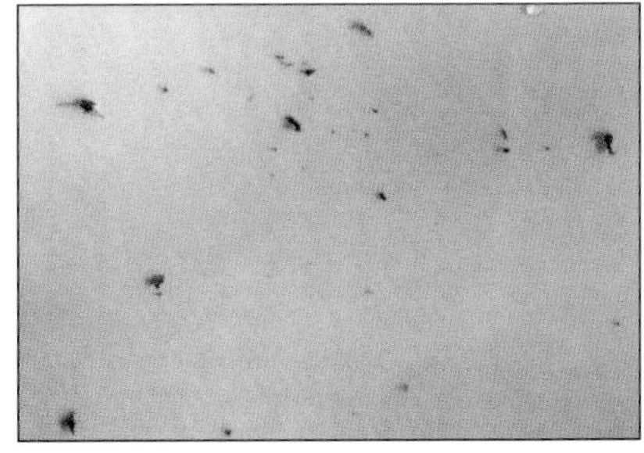

Fig. 1.17 Peat moss often falls onto sticky cards and appears, at first glance, to be an insect. *Photo: Stanton Gill*

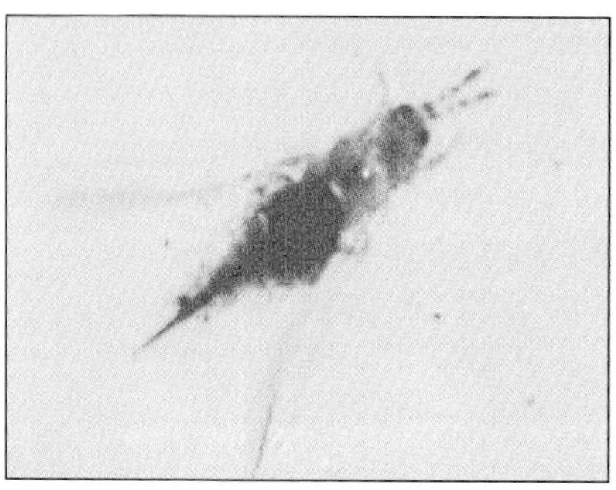

Fig. 1.18 This adult thrips on a sticky card has its wings sticking out showing the typical fringed wings. *Photo: Stanton Gill*

Fig. 1.19 *Orius* (minute pirate bug) nymphs are a bright yellow-orange color. All stages catch and feed on insects. *Photo: Robert Alde*

Fig. 1.20 On yellow sticky cards, whitefly appear as tiny white flakes, until their wings disappear into the sticky material. *Photo: John Sanderson*

Fig. 1.21 On sticky cards, the banded-winged whitefly is identified by the smoky gray bands on its wings. *Photo: Stanton Gill*

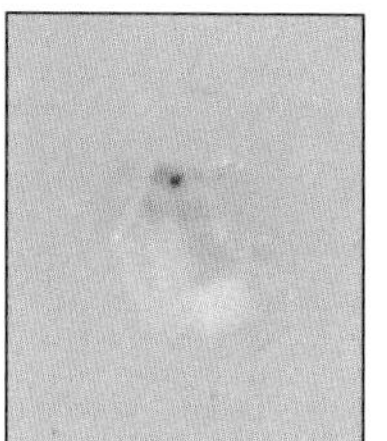

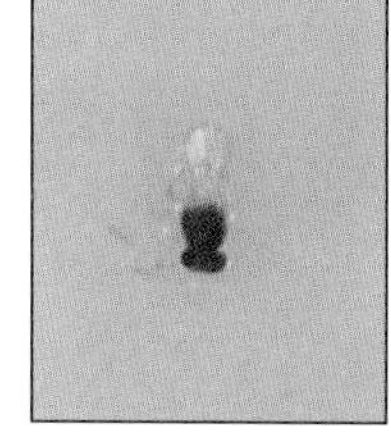

Fig. 1.22 *Encarsia formosa* adults (*right*), and *Eretmocerus eremicus* (*left*) are parasitoids of whiteflies. *Encarsia* is *somewhat* attracted to yellow sticky cards. *Photo: John Sanderson*

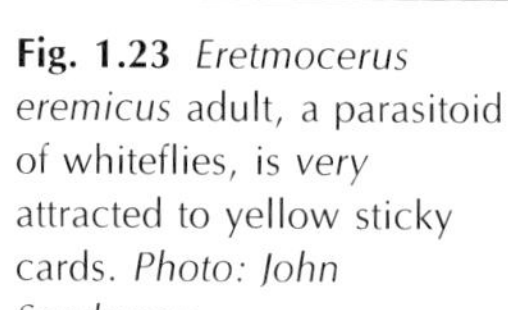

Fig. 1.23 *Eretmocerus eremicus* adult, a parasitoid of whiteflies, is *very* attracted to yellow sticky cards. *Photo: John Sanderson.*

Whitefly. This insect appears like a small, white speck for several days after being captured. Thereafter, its white wings lose all color as they blend into the sticky material (figs. 1.20, 1.21). Only the yellowish body remains, which may be mistaken for thrips, unless carefully examined.

Encarsia formosa **(Gahan).** A tiny wasp that attacks whiteflies, *Encarsia formosa* may be found on sticky cards either if they are being intentionally released for whitefly control or if they occur naturally in an unsprayed greenhouse. The adult has a black head and thorax and a yellow abdomen. On sticky cards they will appear as tiny, black dots and must be examined carefully to be accurately identified (fig. 1.22).

Eretmocerus eremicus **(Rose and Zolnerowich).** Another genus of common whitefly parasitoids, *Eretmocerus,* is generally yellow or straw colored. Some species, including *Eretmocerus eremicus (=californicus),* are very attracted to yellow, and, unfortunately, many may be captured on yellow sticky cards. They may be confused with some straw-colored thrips species if not examined carefully. Their wings are not as fringed as a thrips, and their antennae are elbowed (fig. 1.23).

Tarnished plant bug (*Lygus lineolaris*). Often found on yellow sticky cards, particularly in unsprayed greenhouses, the tarnished plant bug migrates into the greenhouse from outdoors. Greenhouses near farms growing forage crops may often suffer from invasion after crops have been harvested. The plant bug is small (6 mm, .236 inches) and fairly oval in outline, with large eyes and a pronounced beaklike structure for mouthparts. The adult is pale yellow with some black markings, or it may be reddish brown to black with a few pale yellow markings. There is sometimes a characteristic white triangle between its shoulders (fig. 1.24).

Four-lined plant bug (*Poecilocapsus lineatus*). Another plant bug that may be found on sticky cards is the four-lined plant bug (see fig. 11.23). The bug is similar in size and shape to the tarnished plant bug, but is distinguished by being yellow with four black stripes on the wing covers.

Leafhoppers. Leafhoppers are slender insects with short bristlelike antennae. Most of the species are wedge shaped, tapering to the rear,

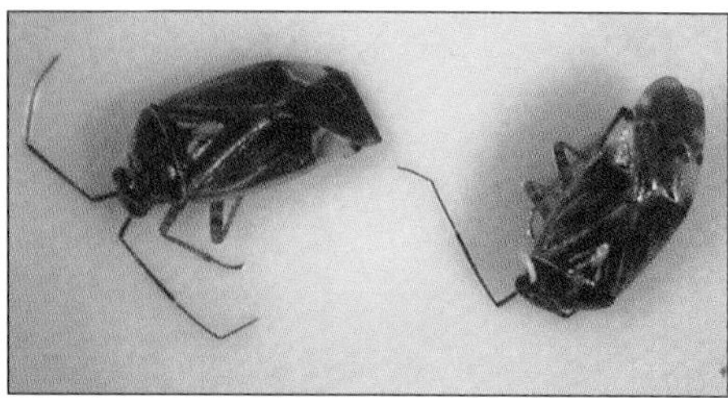

Fig. 1.24 Tarnished plant bugs are often tan and brown. The forewing area is leatherlike, and the wing tip is membranous. Note the whitish triangle between the shoulders. *Photo: John Sanderson*

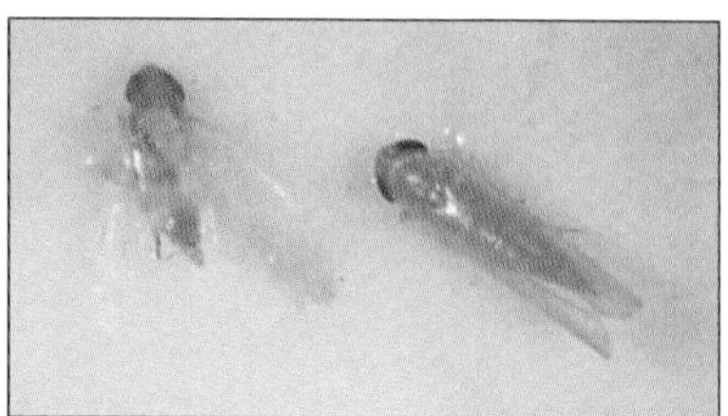

Fig. 1.25 The narrow, streamlined body shape of leafhoppers helps distinguish this insect on sticky cards. Wings may or may not be transparent as in the potato leafhopper pictured. *Photo: John Sanderson*

Fig. 1.26 The spotted cucumber beetle is greenish yellow with black spots. *Photo: John Sanderson*

Fig. 1.27 The striped cucumber beetle has alternating yellow and black stripes. *Photo: John Sanderson*

but they vary in coloration and size (fig. 1.25). Wings are held rooflike over the abdomen.

Cucumber beetles. Cucumber beetles are shiny black with black heads and about 6.3 mm (.248 inches) long. The spotted cucumber beetle adult is greenish yellow and has black spots on its back (fig. 1.26). The western and striped cucumber beetles are yellowish orange with black stripes (fig. 1.27).

Biological control

Biological control means using natural enemies that control insect and mite pests. The natural enemies that we will discuss in this book include predators, parasites, and pathogens of greenhouse pests. Recognizing biological control organisms and understanding how they attack their hosts is essential to evaluating their effectiveness in an IPM approach.

Predators

A predator is a mobile organism that feeds on more than one host to reach maturity. It sometimes consumes the host completely, and usually rapidly. Predators may attack prey as both immatures and adults.

Some predators are very active, with long legs that enable them to move quickly, such as predaceous mites (1.28). Winged forms of predators are generally good fliers, such as the *Orius* (minute pirate bug) (see fig. 1.19), enabling them to move from plant to plant searching for prey. The mealybug destroyer blends in with the mealybugs it feeds on by covering its body with long strands of white wax (fig. 1.29). These characteristics enable them to live by hunting.

In most cases, the predator is larger than the animals it eats. Many of the predators are generalists, feeding on several species of insects. Generalists include green lacewings (family Chrysopidae) (figs. 1.30, 1.31, 1.32), and assassin bugs (family Reduviidae) (fig. 1.33). Some, such as the mealybug destroyer, limit themselves to

Fig. 1.28 *Hypoaspis* adult has large, needlelike mouthparts (chelicerae) that it uses to pierce its prey. *Photo: Stanton Gill*

Fig. 1.29 Mealybug destroyer larvae have white waxy filaments that make them look similar to a mealybug. *Photo: John Davidson*

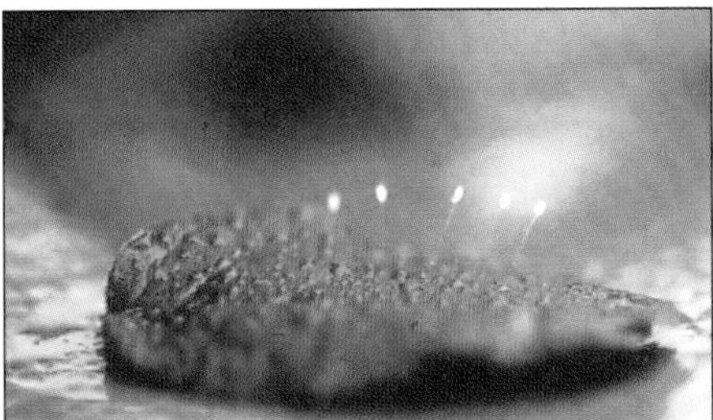

Fig. 1.30 Lacewing eggs look like tiny balloons on the end of a threadlike stick. Hatching larvae crawl down the thread to start feeding on insects. *Photo: Robert Alde*

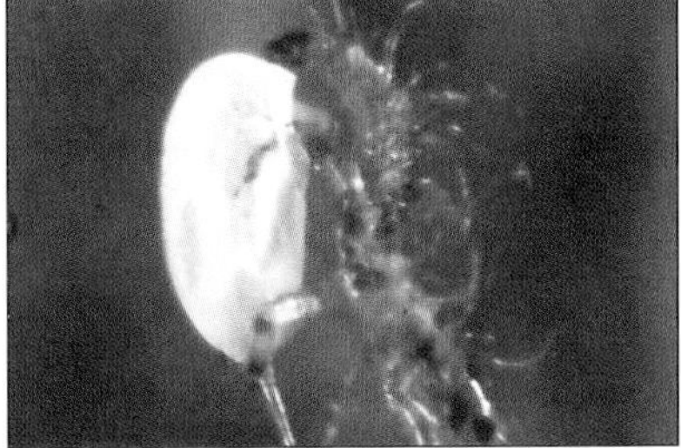

Fig. 1.31 Lacewing larvae look like miniature alligators with large, sickle-shaped mandibles. *Photo: Stanton Gill*

Fig. 1.32 Adult lacewings have gold eyes and lacelike wings that are longer than the body. *Photo: Stanton Gill*

Fig. 1.33 Assassin bug adults have a long piercing mouthpart (stylet) that they use to pierce other insects and feed. *Photo: Stanton Gill*

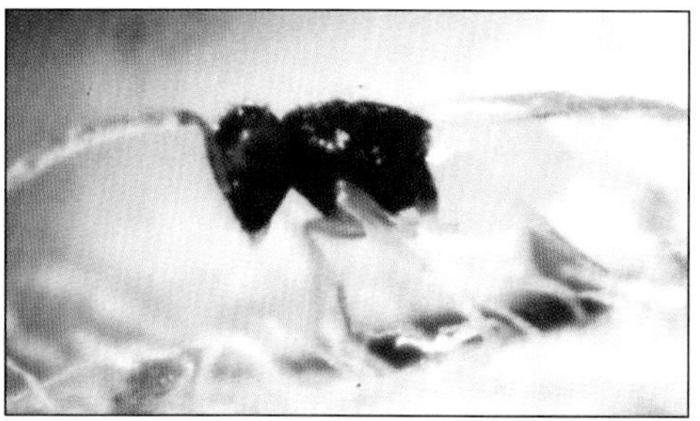

Fig. 1.34 *Encarsia formosa* adults attack settled (sessile) stages of whitefly by piercing and feeding or by ovipositing immature whiteflies. *Photo: John Sanderson*

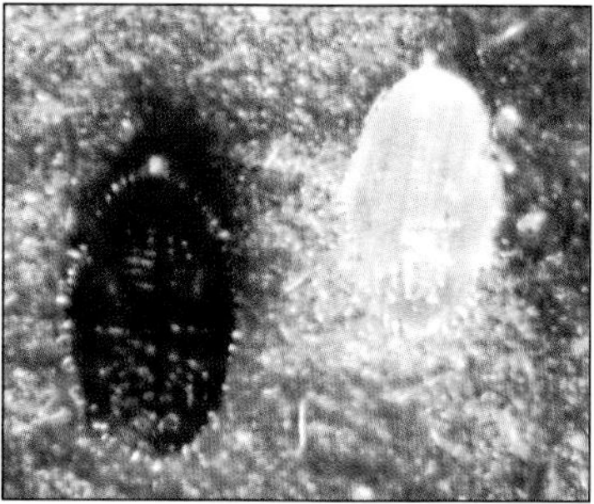

Fig. 1.35 Pupae of whitefly with *Encarsia* larvae developing inside the whitefly. *Photo: John Sanderson*

feeding on a specific order of insects. All predators kill their prey relatively rapidly, either eating the whole organism or sucking the internal contents from it.

Parasites

Parasites live in or on another organism. The parasite benefits, and the insect host is usually killed in the process. A parasite requires only one host to reach maturity. Adult parasites are generally smaller than their hosts.

A host that harbors a parasite is said to be parasitized. The immature whitefly can be parasitized by the wasps *Encarsia* (fig. 1.34) and *Eretmocerus*. Parasitized immature whiteflies and many other insect pests exhibit characteristic symptoms, such as change in color (fig. 1.35, 1.36). These symptoms can help in estimating the amount of parasitism in a pest population, which is important in determining whether additional control tactics or which control tactics will be used.

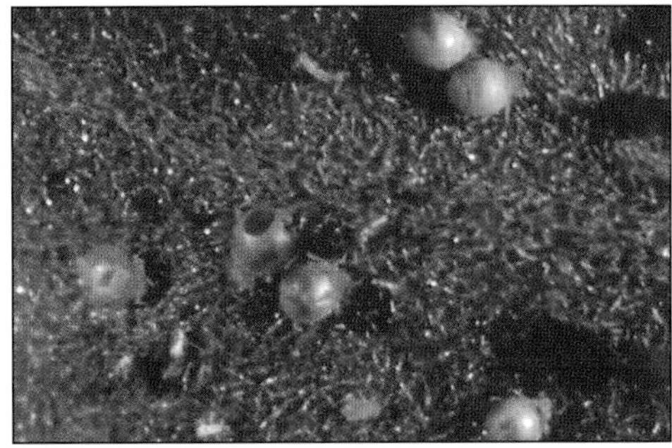

Fig. 1.36 Aphid mummies parasitized with *Aphidius* larvae appear swollen and turn brown. *Photo: Stanton Gill*

Parasites that feed and develop inside the host are called *endoparasites*. The *Encarsia* and *Leptomastix* wasps are examples of endoparasites. Usually, the eggs of endoparasites are inserted into their hosts where they also hatch. An insect parasite that kills its host may be called a *parasitoid* to distinguish it from parasites that do not kill their hosts.

Parasites that remain on the outside of the host and feed by sucking body contents through the host skin are called *ectoparasites*. Most ectoparasites are smaller than their hosts, and many are wasps and flies. Some of the scale insects are parasitized by ectoparasites, such as *Aphytis melinus*.

Not all death of the pest is caused by parasitism. In the case of *Encarsia* and other parasitoids, the adult female can cause puncture wounds with her ovipositor (stinger), killing the host. The female then takes in the fluids that exude from the wound, a predacious activity called feeding.

Parasitoids generally attack a few or only one insect species and are better at searching for their host than predators. A parasitoid life cycle is generally synchronized to its host's life cycle and works at lower pest densities. The parasite eggs or young are placed in or on the host, which eliminates the host searching required of newly hatched predator larvae.

Pathogens

Pathogens that attack and kill insects are called entomopathogenic. Pathogens of greenhouse pests include bacteria, fungi, and nematodes. Most pathogens enter insects or mites either through penetrating the exoskeleton or by being ingested.

Entomopathogenic nematodes. Insects that have life stages in soil, such as dark-winged fungus gnat larvae and weevil grubs, are

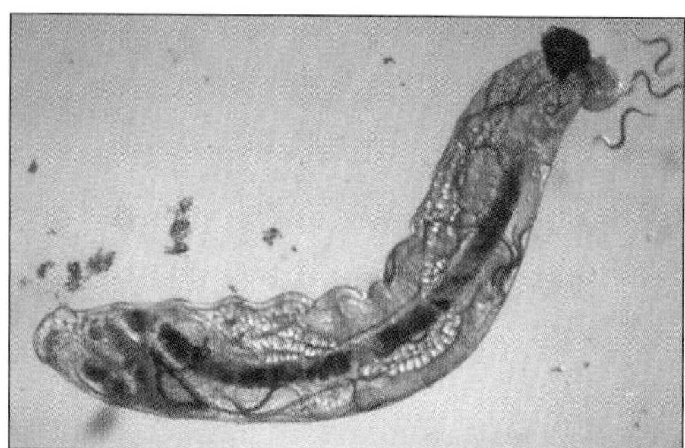

Fig. 1.37 Fungus gnat larvae infected with the entomopathogenic nematode, *Steinernema feltiae. Photo: George Poiner*

ideal candidates for biological control by entomopathogenic nematodes. These nematodes infect only insects or related arthropods, and the survival of these nematodes in moist soil is high.

The third-instar juvenile nematode travels through soil media and water and enters through an insect body opening, such as the mouth, spiracles, or anus. Once inside, the nematode releases *Xenorhabdus* bacteria. The insect dies of bacterial septicemia in 24 to 48 hours (fig. 1.37). If the soil environment is warm (50 to 85F, 10 to 29C) and moist, this nematode can complete its life cycle within the victim's body.

Several commercial companies are marketing juvenile-stage nematodes for controlling greenhouse soil insects. The species *Steinernema feltiae, S. glaseri, S. carpocapsae,* and *Heterorhabditis bacteriospora* are commercially available. Formulations include water-dispensible granules and alginate clay suspended on disposable sponges. All materials are mixed with water and applied as a soil drench to greenhouse growing media and areas under benches.

Bacteria. There are over 35 species and subspecies of the bacterium *Bacillus thuringiensis* (Bt) that have been identified. These pathogens are naturally occurring, soil-inhabiting bacteria that are safe to humans. *Bacillus thuringiensis* var. *kurstaki* is potent against several species of caterpillars. *Bacillus thuringiensis* var. *israelensis* (Bti) is toxic to fungus gnat and mosquito larvae.

The bacterium must be ingested by a young insect larva. Once the bacterium is in the gut of the insect, a toxic crystal dissolves. The crystal toxin causes holes in the insect's gut wall. A paralysis of the gut occurs, and feeding ceases. Death of the insect follows.

Bt and Bti are available in several formulations. Bti is applied as a drench for control of larval stages of fungus gnats. Bt is applied as sprays to foliage and stems for young caterpillars feeding on plant tissue above the soil level.

Fig. 1.38 Shore fly adult with hyphae of *Paecilomyces fumosoroseus* fungus growing from the body. *Photo: Stanton Gill*

Fungi. Over 500 fungi are associated with insects, yet very few have been used commercially as control agents. Fungi infect a wide range of soft-bodied insects and mites. The infective unit in entomopathogenic fungi is the conidium, a spore, which may penetrate the insect cuticle (skin) from a combination of mechanical pressure by the germ tube and enzymatic degradation of the cuticle. Once through the insect cuticle, the fungus proliferates as hyphal bodies. Insects that are infected with a pathogen may change color or in humid conditions (above 95% relative humidity) have mycelium growing from the body (fig. 1.38). The fungus spreads through the insect body, and the insect normally dies within two to 14 days after spore application. Death of the insect is either through action of a toxin or as a result of fungal growth within the insect's body cavity.

Strains of the fungus *Beauveria bassiana* have been shown to be pathogenic to aphids, whiteflies, thrips, leaf-feeding caterpillars, flea beetles, lygus bugs, and spider mites. Other species of fungal pathogens that may be useful against greenhouse pests include *Verticillium lecanii*, a pathogen that has demonstrated good control of green peach aphid and whitefly. *Paecilomyces fumosoroseus* may be a potential control for aphids, spider mites, and whiteflies. *Metarhizium anisopliae* is particularly promising for thrips and green peach aphid.

Pesticides

The grower should use pests' natural enemies as the first control method in an IPM program, saving pesticides as backup. When chemicals must be used to control plant-feeding pests, however, there are several ways to reduce the potentially adverse effects on beneficial organisms. First, select from the new chemicals receiving registration for use in greenhouses that have minimal impact on beneficial organisms.

Second, treat only plants or portions of plants requiring treatment rather than a whole greenhouse. Third, apply materials at the time when they will be most effective against the pest. For example, do not spray an insect pest when the majority of the population is in the egg or pupal stage. Many pests have specific times in their life cycles when they are relatively immune to control by pesticides. Pesticides should not be applied during these times. Fourth, select pesticides that are least disruptive to beneficial organisms you may be releasing in the greenhouse. Fifth, by selecting short residual pesticides, you can reduce pest populations and reintroduce natural enemies after a short interval. Sixth, natural enemies may be used for much of a crop's duration, saving pesticides for a final cleanup, if necessary. A list of the effects of pesticides against natural enemies is available from commercial insectories.

IPM programs in Maryland, New York, Massachusetts, Connecticut, and California have been developed for poinsettia crops, bedding plants, cabbage and kale, herbs, and herbaceous perennials. In most cases regular monitoring has been able to reduce pesticide use by over 50%.

Part 2

Identification of Major Pests

CHAPTER 2

Aphids

Knowing the species of aphid present in an infestation can be important in achieving control. Susceptibility to certain insecticides can change with species, and, more importantly, some natural enemies are much more effective on certain aphids than on others.

Aphids are among the most common pests of greenhouse crops. There are more than 4,400 known species of aphids worldwide, and as a group they attack a range of plant species. Though many aphids infest a limited number of plant species, the most common and problematic aphids found on greenhouse crops attack a very large number of plant species. On greenhouse crops in general, the two most common species by far are the green peach aphid, *Myzus persicae,* and the melon aphid, also known as the cotton aphid, *Aphis gossypii.*

Aphids that are at least fairly common to greenhouse crops in the United States are covered here, though many of these aphid species are found in greenhouses throughout the world. The species descriptions are intended to provide some characteristics that can be used for "field" identification by people who are not professional entomologists. However, aphid taxonomy is complex and is best left for experts.

General description

Plant damage

Aphids are commonly encountered on many floral crops. They can be found on all plant parts (figs. 2.1, 2.2, 2.3). A few species can

Fig. 2.1 Aphids can attack plant stems in large clusters. *Photo: Bob Alde*

Fig. 2.2 Aphids often feed on undersides of leaves and go unnoticed until large numbers develop. *Photo: John Sanderson*

Fig. 2.3 If not controlled in time, some aphids can infest flowers at time of sale. *Photo: John Sanderson*

Fig. 2.4 Aphid feeding injury can cause leaf distortion. *Photo: John Sanderson*

Fig. 2.5 Cast skins, honeydew, and sooty mold caused by an aphid infestation. *Photo: John Sanderson*

Fig. 2.6 White cast skins on leaf can be used to detect an aphid infestation. *Photo: John Sanderson*

even infest roots. Their presence can decrease the aesthetic value of a plant.

Aphids feed by inserting their stylet mouthparts through plant tissue directly into the phloem and sucking plant sap. Their feeding can cause plant stunting and leaf deformities (fig. 2.4). Large numbers of aphids can remove enough nutrients from a plant that its vigor is affected. Their excrement coats leaves with a sweet, sticky substance called honeydew, which in turn promotes the growth of unsightly gray, sooty mold (fig. 2.5). Aphids can reduce the salability of a floral crop by the accumulation of the white cast skins that they leave behind as they molt from one stage to another (fig. 2.6). The combination of honeydew and cast skins created by an aphid infestation can be ugly. Finally, aphids are responsible for the transmission of about 60% of all plant viruses on agricultural crops worldwide (fig. 2.7).

Group characteristics

Many different aphid species can occur on greenhouse crops, differing in size, coloration, location on a plant, and crop preferences. They are all generally small (1 to 4 mm, .039 to .157 inches), slow moving, soft bodied, and pear shaped, without obvious segmentation into head, thorax, and abdomen. Their legs and antennae are typically long and slender. Aphid nymphs resemble small, wingless adults (fig. 2.8). Adult aphids may or may not have wings (fig. 2.9). The unwinged form of an aphid is usually more common on green-

Fig. 2.7 Aphids transmitted this mosaic virus on calla lily. *Photo: Margery Daughtrey*

Fig. 2.8 Except for size, aphid nymphs and wingless adults generally look similar. *Photo: John Sanderson*

house plants than the winged form, though winged forms may be found on yellow sticky cards. Most notably, aphids have a pair of unique structures, called cornicles, resembling tailpipes on either side of the body near the end of the abdomen.

Biology

Under greenhouse conditions, aphids reproduce *parthenogenetically*, that is, all the insects present are females, and each female gives birth to more females without the need to mate (fig. 2.10). In the greenhouse, aphids are viviparous, wherein females give birth to living nymphs rather than lay eggs. In fact, in some species, an unborn aphid already contains a complement of developing nymphs, a phenomenon known as *paedogenesis.* In the outdoors, green peach aphids produce eggs only if the number of daylight hours drops below 10, under short-day conditions in the fall. (Aphids in the egg stage are immune to insecticides.)

Aphids' ability to reproduce without mating or egg production during most of the season causes their populations to increase almost explosively, especially because individuals can mature and begin to reproduce very rapidly. As an aphid colony increases in age and size on individual plants, the proportion of winged forms may increase.

Aphids can vary in their preference for host plants. For example, although green peach aphids infest chrysanthemums, melon aphids can develop much higher populations on this crop. Aphids often also prefer certain plant cultivars over others. Careful record

Fig. 2.9 Some adult aphids may have wings, which are longer than the body, and a wing vein pattern that is distinctive to aphids. *Photo: David Voegtlin*

Fig. 2.10 Under greenhouse conditions, aphids give live birth to female offspring and do not need to mate to reproduce. *Photo: John Sanderson*

keeping of aphid infestations by crop cultivar may reveal these differences and aid the grower in cultivar choice.

Aphids have a well-known capability to develop insecticide resistance. Strains of some species have documented resistance to carbamate, organophosphate, and pyrethroid insecticides. In green peach aphid, resistance can be conferred by increased production of an enzyme that provides immunity to insecticides from several chemical classes.

Pest Detection

Monitoring

Inspect a greenhouse thoroughly for sources of aphids before a new crop arrives. Then carefully inspect plant material brought into your growing areas. If possible, quarantine newly arrived plants, and inspect thoroughly before moving them into production areas. Avoid planting aphid-susceptible cultivars near doorways or vents, where they could be infested from an outside source.

Aphid control is much more successful when an infestation is detected and controlled early in a crop production cycle. Train workers to recognize signs of an aphid infestation, and incorporate their observations in your regular scouting effort. With experience, many aphids can be identified in the greenhouse using a 10× hand lens or, preferably, a dissecting microscope.

Stems and lower surfaces of leaves of various ages on each plant should be examined. The presence of white cast skins or honeydew on leaves may indicate an aphid colony on a plant (see figs. 2.5, 2.6).) Ants are attracted to the honeydew and can signal an infestation (fig. 2.11). Pay close attention to those plant varieties on which aphids seem to occur most frequently. Group aphid-susceptible plants or cultivars together to make intensive scouting and control efforts more efficient and to minimize the spread of aphids throughout the production area. Aphids can be spread on clothing, so plants located near walkways and doors should be examined.

Yellow sticky cards may provide an early indication of an aphid migration into the greenhouse, particularly in the spring, summer, and early fall (fig. 2.12). Winged aphids that are active outdoors during these times may invade the greenhouse. Yellow sticky cards may

Fig. 2.11 Ants forage for honeydew. Their presence on foliage may indicate an aphid infestation. *Photo: John Sanderson*

Fig. 2.12 Winged aphids are attracted to the yellow color of a sticky card. Once captured, the body may be too shriveled and distorted to identify as an aphid, but the wing vein pattern is distinctive. *Photo: John Sanderson*

alert you to their presence; but it is even more important to inspect plant foliage on at least a weekly basis for early detection and monitoring of aphid infestations.

To aid in evaluating insecticide efficacy, several plants infested with aphids can be marked with flags or flagging tape, and an estimate of the number of aphids on each should be recorded. A few days after insecticides are applied, the number of surviving aphids should again be recorded. Examine plants carefully and frequently to determine whether repeat applications are required (fig. 2.13).

Species identification

Several characteristics of an aphid can be used to tell species apart (fig. 2.14). These include the plant on which it is found, where it occurs on the plant, the body coloration, the length of the antennae, and the color and length of the cornicles.

The shape of the cauda is also important. The *cauda* is a structure at the extreme tip of the abdomen that may be thought of as a "tail." Some species have a pronounced cauda; in others it is very reduced. The cauda can be long or short; tapered, triangular, parallel-sided; or vary in yet other ways. The number of tiny hairs on the cauda can be important in identification, but they require a great deal of magnification to be seen.

Fig. 2.13 Aphids killed by insecticides may be discolored and shriveled. *Photo: Dan Gilrein*

In some species the presence and form of antennal *tubercles* (bumps) is important. If present, these tubercles are located on the inside of each antenna near the base, producing an apparent indentation in the aphid head between them (fig. 2.15). The size and shape of the aphid tubercles varies among certain species and gives these indentations different shapes.

The descriptions of aphids in this manual refer to the unwinged adult forms of each species *(apterae)* rather than the winged forms *(alatae)*, because the unwinged forms are the most likely to be encountered on greenhouse crops. Winged forms may be found on

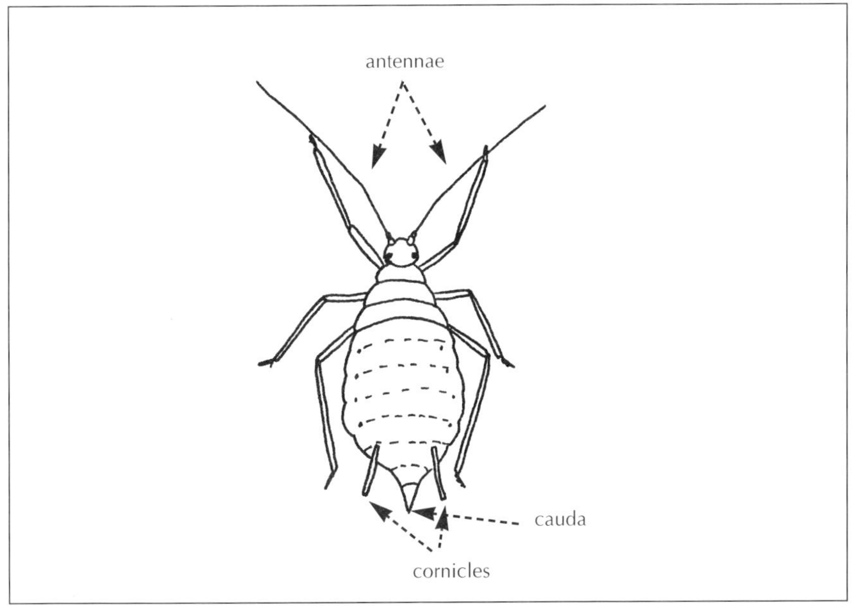

Fig. 2.14 Generalized aphid body as seen from above. Note the antennae, cornicles, and cauda. *Line drawing: John Sanderson*

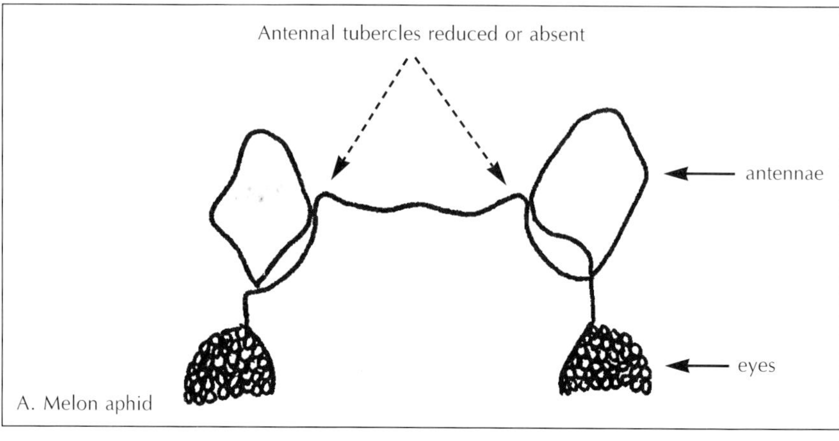

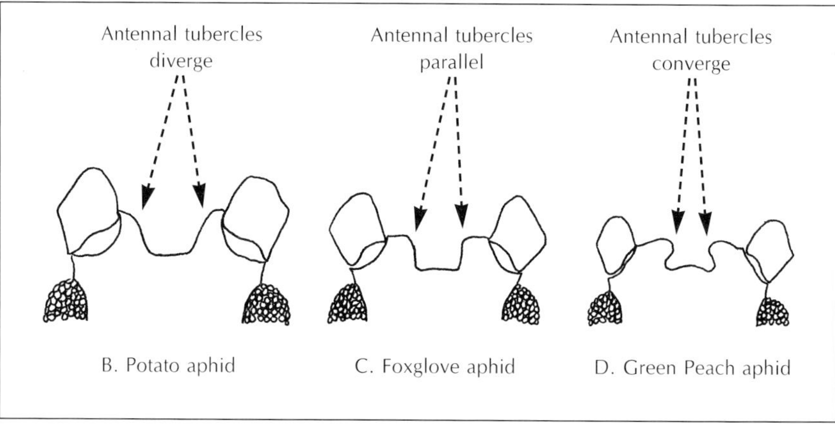

Fig. 2.15. (A) Aphid head with antennal tubercles reduced or absent (melon aphid). (B) Antennal tubercles well developed and diverging (potato aphid). (C) Antennal tubercles well developed and parallel (foxglove aphid). (D) Antennal tubercles well developed and converging (green peach aphid). *Line drawing: John Sanderson*

yellow sticky traps, but entrapment usually obscures the characters needed for identification.

Green peach aphid, *Myzus persicae* (Sulzer). The green peach aphid can infest a wide range of floral crops. It can also transmit over 100 plant viruses among at least 30 plant families. The color of green peach aphids can range from light green, light yellow, green, or gray-green to pink or reddish (fig. 2.16). It is usually a fairly large aphid. It can be winged or unwinged (fig. 2.17).

The green peach aphid has pronounced indentation between the bases of the antennae on the front of the head (see fig. 2.15-D), caused by the presence of a large tubercle on the inside base of each antenna. The sides of this indentation converge away from the head (figs. 2.18, 2.19). The cornicles are long, thin, and very slightly swollen in the middle. The color of the cornicles matches that of the rest of the aphid, except that the extreme tips of the cornicles are typically darkened and slightly flared (see fig. 2.16). The cauda is fairly long and tapered and has three hairs on each side.

Melon aphid, cotton aphid, *Aphis gossypii* Glover. The melon aphid is a cosmopolitan pest, attacking a wide range of plants and capable of transmitting over 50 plant viruses. It is generally a small

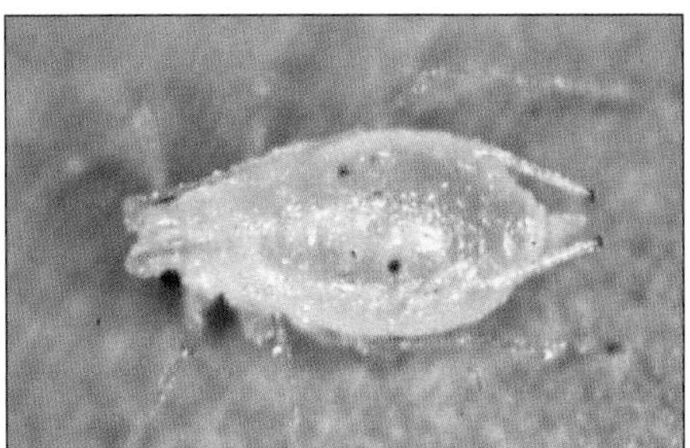

Fig. 2.16 Green peach aphids range in color from light green to gray-green, to pink or red. Note the darkened tips of the cornicles and the indentation between the base of the antennae. *Photo: Manya Stoetzel*

Fig. 2.17 Winged green peach aphids are often evident when populations have built up to high levels on the plant. Wings enable the aphid to fly to new plant sites. *Photo: Manya Stoetzel*

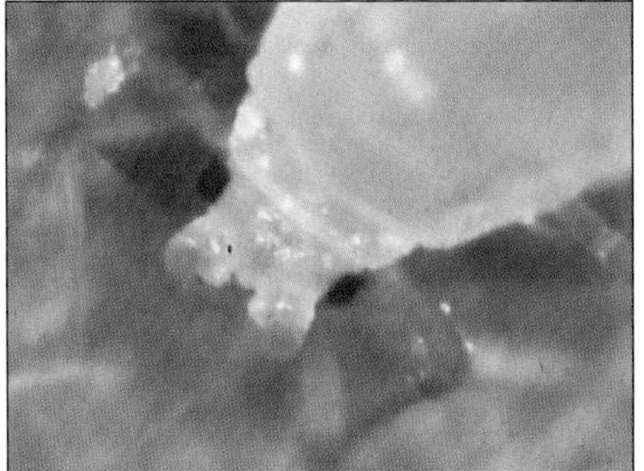

Fig. 2.18 A close-up view of the indentation in the head of a wingless green peach aphid. *Photo: Manya Stoetzel*

Fig. 2.19 This characteristic indentation is found on winged and wingless forms of green peach aphid. *Photo: Manya Stoetzel*

Fig. 2.20 A yellow form of the melon aphid. Note that the cornicles are uniformly dark. *Photo: Michael Hoffmann*

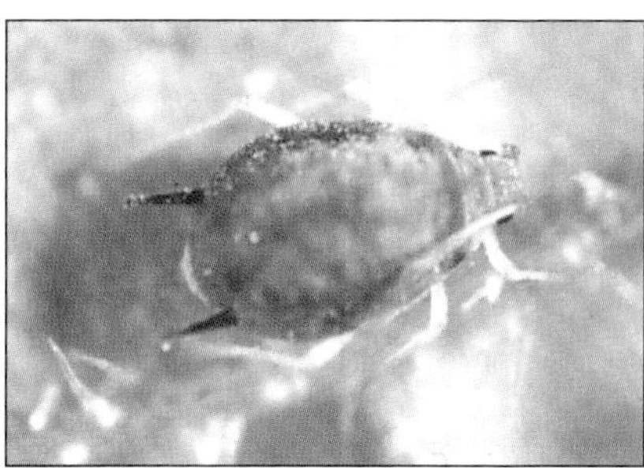

Fig. 2.21 A green form of the melon aphid. Note that the cornicles are dark, and there is no indentation in the head. *Photo: Michael Hoffmann*

Fig. 2.22 Some forms and life stages of the melon aphid can appear mottled green. *Photo: Michael Hoffmann*

Fig. 2.23 A very dark green form of the melon aphid. *Photo: Michael Hoffmann*

aphid (0.9 to 2.0 mm, .035 to .078 inches). Its color, often depending on food source and temperature, may vary from light yellow to very dark green (figs. 2.20, 2.21, 2.22, 2.23). Antennae are shorter than the length of the body, and there is no pronounced indentation between the bases of the antennae (fig. 2.23). The cauda is tapered and has two or three hairs on each side.

To distinguish it from the green peach aphid, note that the adult melon aphid is smaller; it has no pronounced indentation between the antennae bases; and the entire length of the cornicles is always very dark, regardless of body color.

Potato aphid, *Macrosiphum euphorbiae* (Thomas). This is a very restless, active aphid that readily drops off the plant when disturbed. The potato aphid has been recorded from many greenhouse crops, including abutilon, carnation, cineraria, lettuce, rose, tomato, and tulip. It can infest almost every crop that the melon aphid or green peach aphid can, including over 200 plant species in more than 20 families. It also can transmit over 45 viruses.

Because this is an extraordinarily variable species, the following statements describe this aphid's "normal" appearance, but much variation may occur. It is a very large aphid (1.7 to 3.6 mm, .066 to .141 inches). Its color can be yellow, pink, or green (fig. 2.24). Nymphs are paler than adults and often have a dark stripe down the length of the body (fig. 2.25). If the stripe is present, it is likely that the specimen is a potato aphid. The antennae are about as long as the body and are dark near the ends. The sides of the head indentation between the antennae bases diverge, getting wider away from the head. The legs are long and the same color as the body. The cornicles are long and very slender and the same color as the body, except darkened and reticulate at the tip. The cauda is very long and prominent, gradually tapering, with four to five hairs on each side and one or two tiny hairs on the top side near the tip.

Fig. 2.24 Potato aphids can be green, pink, or yellow. The dark stripe down the middle of the back is usually present and is a good indicator of potato aphid. *Photo: Ward Tingey*

Foxglove aphid, *Aulacorthum solani* (Kaltenbach). This aphid can infest anemone, arum, calceolaria, carnation, cineraria, dahlia, geranium, gloxinia, lettuce, and nasturtium. It is another aphid that has a very wide host

Fig. 2.25 Close-up of a potato aphid. Note the dark stripe down the back and the lighter colored cornicles with the darkened tips. *Photo: David Voegtlin*

range; it can infest nearly every plant that is attacked by the melon aphid or green peach aphid. It is reported to transmit about 40 plant viruses.

The adult is slightly larger than the adult green peach aphid (1.8 to 3.0 mm, .070 to .118 inches). The color is usually shiny, light green or yellow, and the head, thorax, and the part of the abdomen around the cornicle bases is often slightly darker than the rest of the abdomen (fig. 2.26). The head area at the antennal bases is also often a darker green than the rest of the body. The legs and antennae are pale but have dark joints.

The pronounced indentation between the antennal bases is similar to that of the green peach aphid, but the sides are slightly straighter and parallel to each other (fig. 2.27). The cornicle tips are flared and nearly black. The cauda is fairly long and tapered, with three to four hairs on each side and one tiny hair near the tip.

Rose aphid, *Macrosiphum rosae* (Linnaeus). Primary host plants of this species are typically in the Rosaceae family. The rose aphid can transmit at least 12 plant viruses, but it does not transmit rose mosaic or rose streak viruses.

This is a fairly large aphid (2.5 to 3.5 mm, .098 to .137 inches). The body is shiny, and its color can be pinkish, red-brown, light green, or dark green (fig. 2.28). The head is shiny black. The antennae and legs have dark areas near the joints. The top of the abdomen sometimes has black patches near the sides. The cornicles are long, slender, and dark. The cauda is pale, long, and slender, with five hairs on either side and one or two hairs on the top side near the tip.

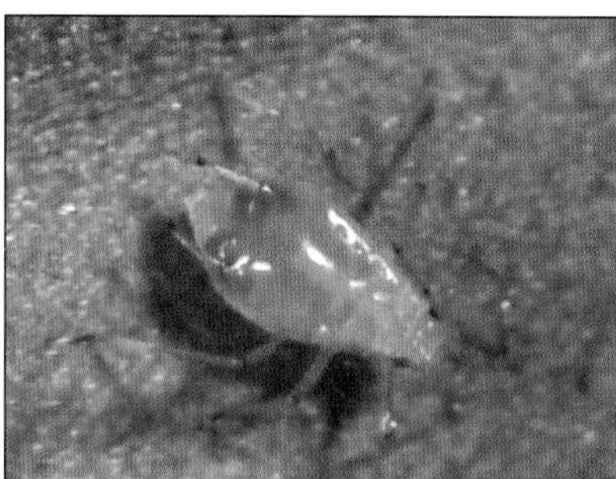

Fig. 2.26 The shiny body and dark patches on the abdomen at the bases of the cornicles are good indicators of foxglove aphids. *Photo: Dan Gilrein*

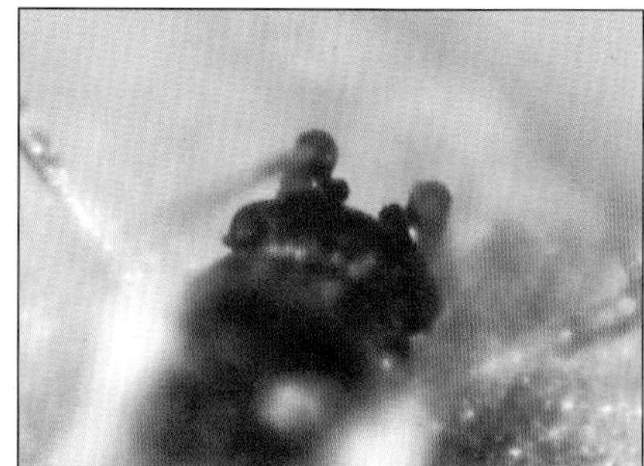

Fig. 2.27 Close-up of the indentation of a foxglove aphid head. *Photo: Dan Gilrein*

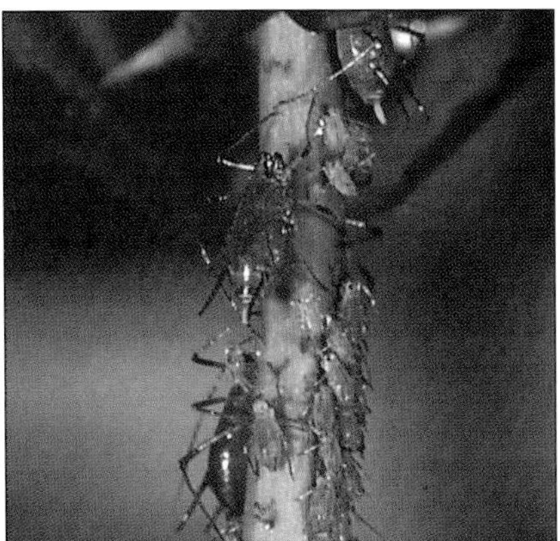

Fig. 2.28 Rose aphids can be red as pictured or pinkish, light green, or dark green. They are shiny, have long slender cornicles that are uniformly dark, and legs that are black near the joints. *Photo: David Voegtlin*

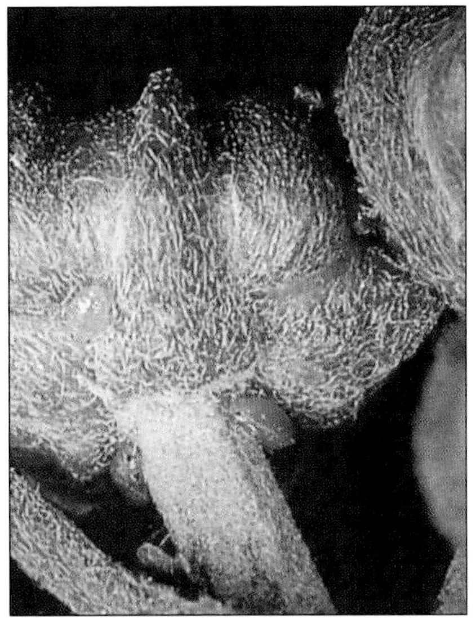

Fig. 2.30 Leaf-curling plum aphids can be found on mums and other composites. They can be green, pale yellow, or almost white. The cornicles are very short and cone shaped. *Photo: Glasshouse Crops Research Institute*

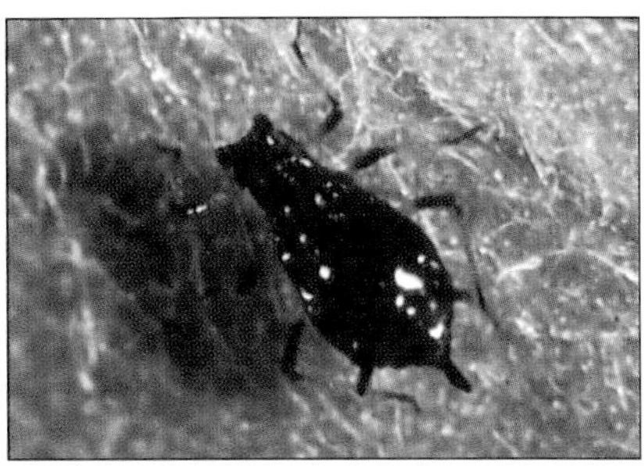

Fig. 2.29 Chrysanthemum aphids are only found on mums. They are shiny, reddish to blackish brown, with short, dark cornicles. *Photo: Manya Stoetzel*

Fig. 2.31 Oleander aphids can form dense colonies on younger stems. *Photo: John Sanderson*

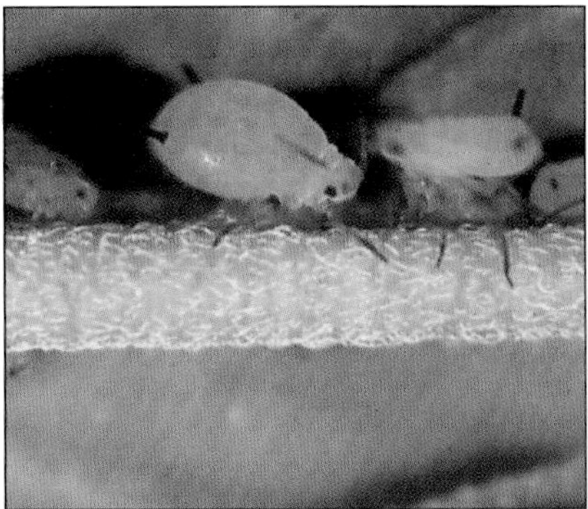

Fig. 2.32 Oleander aphids are bright yellow-orange with black cornicles. They are often found on tropical plants. *Photo: Lance Osborne*

The rose aphid can be distinguished from green peach aphid by its cornicles, which are long, slender, and completely black, and by the black areas on its legs.

Chrysanthemum aphid, *Macrosiphoniella sanborni* (Gillette). The chrysanthemum aphid is found only on chrysanthemum. It can transmit chrysanthemum vein mottle and chrysanthemum virus B.

It is a small to moderate-sized aphid (1 to 2.5 mm, .039 to .098 inches). It is shiny, and its color varies from reddish brown to blackish brown (fig. 2.29). The cornicles are short, stout, and black, enlarged at the base, and with a reticulated pattern on two-thirds of the cornicle from the tip. The cauda is long and black.

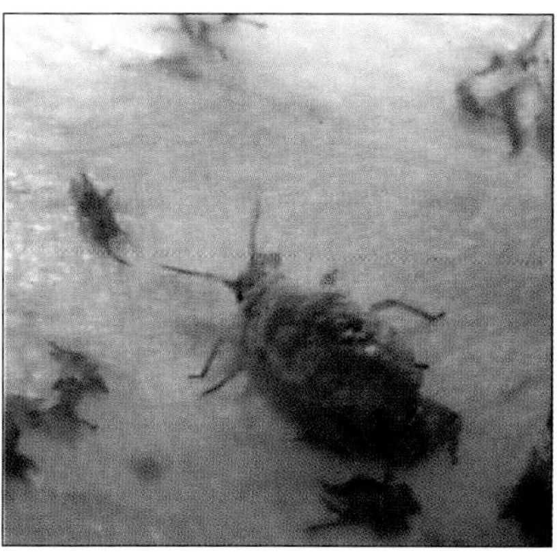

Fig. 2.33 Tulip bulb aphids infest tulip bulbs and corms of gladiolus and iris and may spread to leaves and shoots. They can be gray, pink, or pale green and are lightly covered with dusty wax. *Photo: Dan Gilrein*

Fig. 2.34 Bean aphids are olive green to black with light-colored legs. *Photo: David Voegtlin*

Fig. 2.35 The spirea aphid can occasionally be found on greenhouse crops. It is light green with dark cornicles and short antennae. *Photo: Ray Yokomi*

Fig. 2.36 Brown citrus aphids are occasionally found on greenhouse crops. Adults are shiny, reddish, brown to black, and have black and white banded antennae. Nymphs are brownish. *Photo: Ray Yokomi*

Leaf-curling plum aphid, *Brachycaudus helichrysi* (Kaltenbach). In the greenhouse this aphid has been found on Compositae hosts, including *Achillea* sp., chrysanthemum, *Senecio* sp., and *Ageratum* sp. It is able to transmit cucumber mosaic, dahlia mosaic, and cineraria mosaic viruses.

The leaf-curling plum aphid is a fairly small aphid (0.9 to 2.0 mm, .035 to .078 inches). The color can be shades of green, pale yellow, or almost white (fig. 2.30). Cornicles are very short, cone shaped, and with a flared tip.

Oleander aphid, *Aphis nerii* Boyer de Fonscolombe. Oleander aphid can infest plants in the Asclepiadaceae, Apocyanaceae *(Nerium oleander, Vinca),* and occasionally in the Euphorbiaceae, Compositae, and Convolvulaceae. It often forms dense colonies on younger stems (fig. 2.31) and may be found on plants from tropical regions.

It is bright orange-yellow with black cornicles and cauda, and the antennae and legs are dark (fig. 2.32). It is a moderate-sized aphid (1.5 to 2.6 mm, .059 to .102 inches). It does not have a deep indentation in the head between the bases of the antennae.

Tulip-bulb aphid, *Dysaphis tulipae* (Boyer de Fonscolombe). Colonies of this aphid can infest the outer skins of tulip bulbs and corms of gladiolus and iris. Infested bulbs can produce distorted growth or may fail to develop. When the bulbs or corms are forced, the aphids can spread to the leaves and flowering shoots.

They are 1.5 to 2.5 mm (.059 to .098 inches), gray, pink, or pale green, and lightly covered with wax (fig. 2.33). The cornicles are short, tapered, and dark. The cauda is short, about as long as it is wide, and tapered, with five hairs.

Bean aphid, *Aphis fabae* Scopoli. This is another aphid with a wide host range. It is recorded from citrus, carnation, dahlia, nasturtium, and tulip.

Size ranges from 2 to 2.5 mm (.078 to .098 inches). The body is dark olive green to black, and the legs are white (fig. 2.34). The bean aphid's antennae are shorter than its body. The cauda is tapered, bears many hairs (bushy), and is about as long as the cornicles, which are relatively short and slightly tapered.

Spirea aphid, *Aphis spiraecola* Patch. This aphid is most common on trees and shrubs, particularly citrus, chestnut, quince, pyracantha, spirea, tuliptree, and viburnum. It can occasionally be found on some greenhouse crops, also.

It is 1.5 to 2.0 mm (.059 to .078 inches) long and light green, with some faint dark patches on the sides of the abdomen, some leg joints, the "feet," and the bases of the cornicles (fig. 2.35). The antennae are shorter than the body. The spirea aphid has no pronounced indentation in the head between the bases of the antennae. The cauda is short and bushy, with about six pairs of hairs. The cornicles are longer than the cauda.

Brown citrus aphid, *Toxoptera aurantii* (Boyer de Fonscolombe). Occasionally found on greenhouse crops, the brown citrus aphid has been recorded from citrus, *Ficus, Camellia,* and *Gardenia.* The brown citrus aphid has been found on 120 plant species. It can transmit several viral diseases of citrus and coffee. This aphid may be found in dense colonies on the undersides of young leaves that may be deformed due to their feeding damage.

It is relatively small (.043 to .078 inches, 1.1 to 2.0 mm), and oval shaped. Adults are shiny, reddish brown, brown-black, or black. Antennae are black-and-white banded (fig. 2.36). Nymphs are brownish. Antennae are shorter than the body. The cornicles and cauda are black, and the cornicles are slightly longer than the cauda.

Cowpea aphid, *Aphis craccivora* Koch. This is another aphid with a wide host range, but it has a preference for leguminous plants. Able to transmit several plant viruses, it is commonly found infesting the young, growing parts of a plant.

It is a small (1.4 to 2.0 mm, .055 to .078 inches) aphid. Adults are shiny black, but their legs are white with black tips. Nymphs are lightly dusted with grayish white wax (fig. 2.37). Antennae are shorter than the body, and there is no pronounced indentation in the head between the base of the antennae. There are few (three or four pairs) hairs on the cauda. The cornicles are dark and longer than the cauda.

Cabbage aphid, *Brevicoryne brassicae* (Linnaeus). This aphid only infests cruciferous plants such as cabbage, cauliflower, Brussels sprout, kale, and broccoli and is not usually a pest in greenhouses.

It is about 1.4 to 2.5 mm (.055 to .098 inches) long. The antennae are shorter than the body. It has short, swollen, dark cornicles and a short, triangular cauda (fig. 2.38). The grayish green or dull

Fig. 2.37 Cowpea aphids are usually found on legumes. Adults are shiny black with white legs and antennae. Nymphs are covered lightly in whitish gray wax. *Photo: Manya Stoetzel*

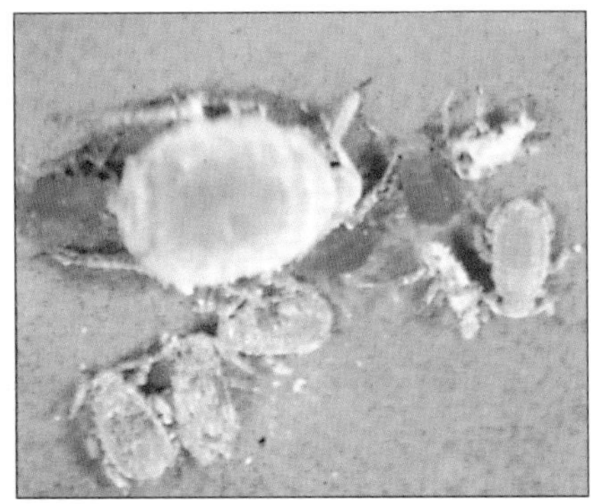

Fig.2.38 Cabbage aphids only infest cruciferous plants such as ornamental kale and cabbage. The body is light to midgreen and covered in light wax. Cornicles and antennae are short. *Photo: Dan Gilrein*

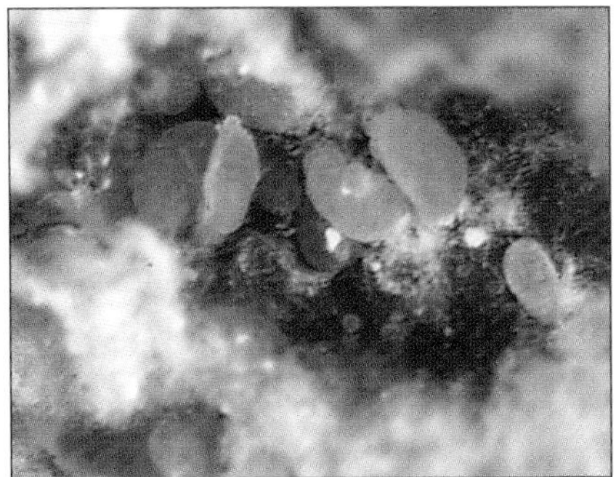

Fig.2.39 Root aphids can infest the roots of some greenhouse crops. They are grayish, covered with wax, and may be confused with small root mealybugs. Cornicles are reduced to rings on the abdomen. *Photo: David Voegtlin*

Fig. 2.40 The lady beetle, *Harmonia axyridis* (adult and eggs), is found throughout the United States. The adults overwinter and may be found in fall looking for a protected overwintering site. *Photo: John Davidson*

midgreen body is covered with grayish white wax. Wax may also be found on the plant surface during an aphid infestation.

Root aphid, *Pemphigus* spp. Hartig. Root aphids may be occasionally found attacking the roots of greenhouse crops, though certain *Populus* spp. (poplar) are their primary host plants. In aquatic greenhouses that produce pennywort, root aphids can be a major pest. They generally infest the leaves of their primary poplar host in winter and the roots of their secondary host plants in the summer.

They are small to medium sized and wax covered, somewhat resembling mealybugs. The cornicles are reduced to rings on the abdomen (fig. 2.39). The cauda is very reduced.

BIOLOGICAL CONTROL

Aphids have many natural enemies, including ladybird beetles, lacewings, parasitic wasps (e.g., *Aphidius colemani*), predaceous midge *(Aphidoletes aphidomyza),* and several insect-pathogenic fungi *(Verticillium lecanii, Beauveria bassiana, Metarhizium anisopliae)*. A number of these are available commercially.

Lady beetles (family Coccinellidae). Several species of lady beetles, or ladybugs, may occasionally be found in greenhouses (fig. 2.40). Adults are small, round to oval, dome-shaped beetles, usually colored bright red, orange, or yellow, and usually with black spots. Larvae look nothing like the adults. They are soft bodied, dark, long, and fairly thin and have three prominent pairs of legs (fig. 2.41).

The species most commonly sold commercially for aphid control is the convergent lady beetle, *Hippodamia convergens.*

Green lacewing, *Chrysoperla* (=*Chrysopa*) *carnea*, *C. rufilabris*. Adult green lacewings feed only on nectar or honeydew, but their larvae are voracious predators of a wide variety of insects, including aphids (fig. 2.42). Lacewing eggs are found at the tips of long, fragile stalks (see fig. 1.30). Newly hatched larvae are tiny (1 to 2 mm, .039 to .078 inches), elongate, and pinkish grayish brown,

Fig. 2.41 Ladybird beetle larvae are long, black, and orange, with spines covering the body. *Photo: John Davidson*

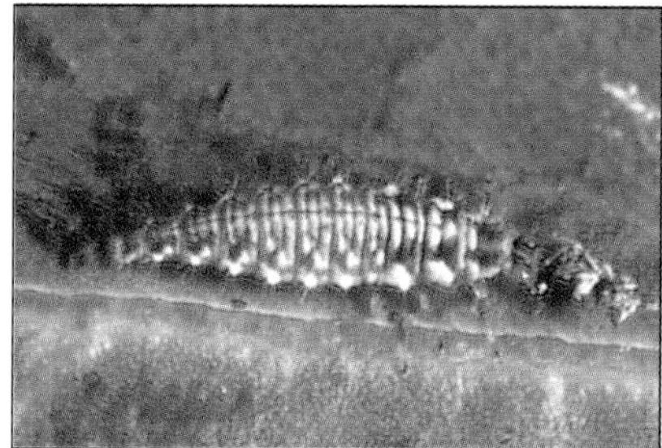

Fig. 2.42 Lacewing larvae are mottled pinkish gray with prominent, sickle-shaped mandibles. They are voracious predators of aphids and other pests. *Photo: NYSAES Communications Services*

Fig. 2.43 Adult *Aphidoletes* have long mosquito-like legs and bodies. *Photo: Linda Gilkeson*

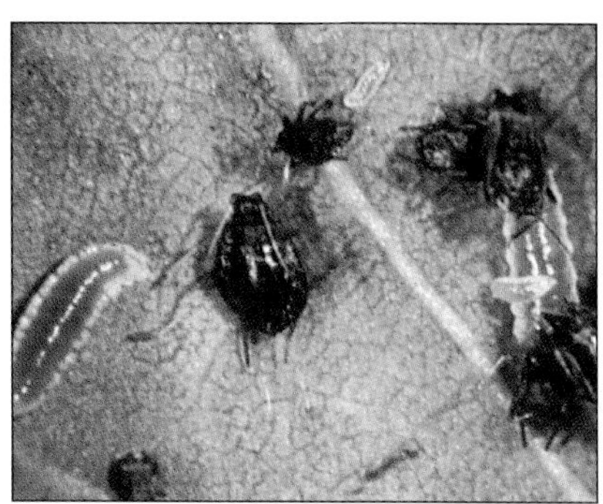

Fig. 2.44 Midge larvae attacking aphid. *Photo: Linda Gilkeson*

with well-developed legs and very prominent, sickle-shaped mandibles. They roam leaves fairly quickly, searching for arthropods to attack, sucking body fluids through their mandibles. They grow to about 8 to 10 mm (.303 to .314 inches) long as larvae.

In nature, pupation occurs within a round, parchmentlike cocoon attached to leaves or stems. Adults are large (12 to 19 mm, .50 to .75 inches long) and pale to bright green, with prominent golden eyes, long antennae, and delicate, lacy, transparent wings (see fig. 1.32). In greenhouses lacewings are usually released in the egg stage or as young larvae.

Aphid midge, *Aphidoletes aphidomyza*. This commercially available midge species only attacks aphids. The adults, which are small, delicate, mosquito-like flies (fig. 2.43), do not attack aphids, but lay eggs in aphid colonies. The resulting larvae are tiny orangish to reddish, legless maggots that crawl through the aphid colony. They bite their prey, paralyzing it before sucking it dry and leaving behind a shriveled aphid cadaver (fig. 2.44). After three instars they become as large or slightly larger than their aphid prey.

Parasitic wasps (family Aphidiidae, e.g., *Aphidius colemani*). Several species of these wasps are available commercially. Some parasite species only attack aphids. Adults are long, thin, shiny, black wasps slightly longer than an aphid. The presence of adults is not the most common sign that the wasps are active, however. Aphids that are parasitized usually turn into "mummies," become swollen and more spherical, and change to a straw color. Some parasites turn their aphid hosts black, but this is not common. When a

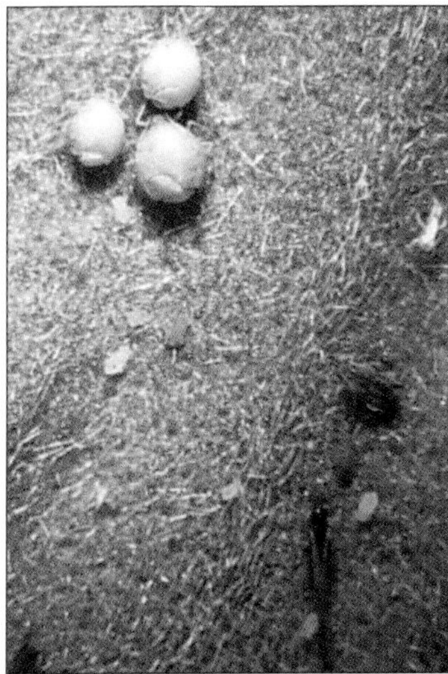

Fig. 2.45 Aphids that have been parasitized usually turn straw colored and are referred to as mummies. Round holes in the abdomen indicate the emergence of a parasitoid. *Photo: John Sanderson*

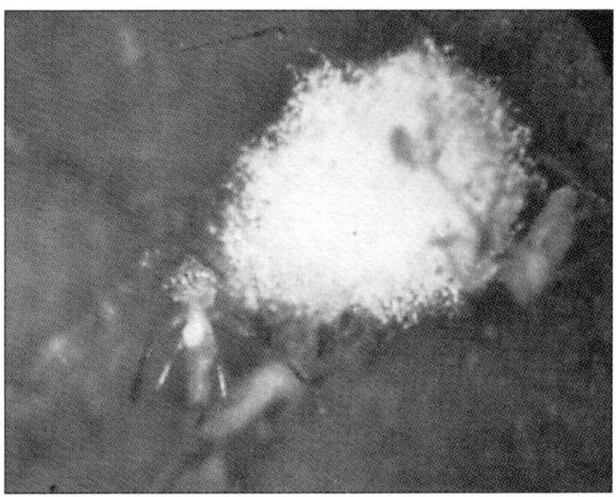

Fig. 2.46 Green peach aphid infected by *Beauveria bassiana* under humid conditions can become a mass of white fluff as the fungus sporulates. *Photo: D. McClean*

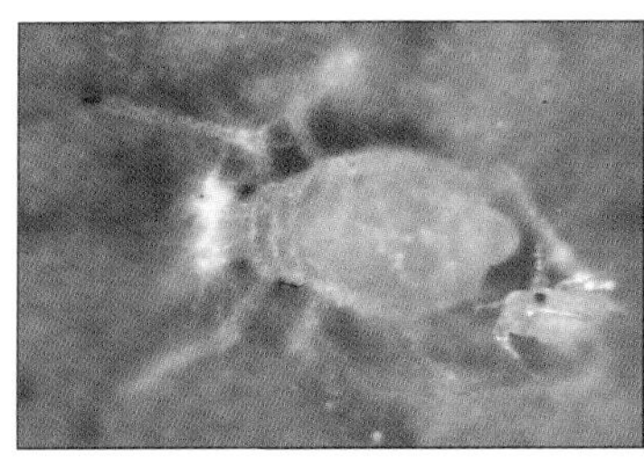

Fig. 2.47 Aphid infected with *Verticillium lecanii* fungus with hyphal structures growing from the body. *Photo: Lance Osborne*

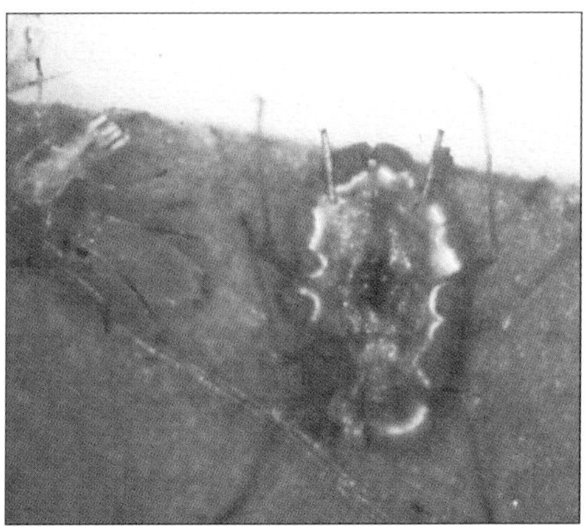

Fig. 2.48 Green peach aphid infected by *Metarhizium anisopliae* becomes discolored. *Photo: D. McClean*

wasp emerges from the mummy, it chews a round hole in the aphid's abdomen (fig. 2.45).

Entomopathogenic fungi *(Verticillium lecanii, Beauveria bassiana, Metarhizium anisopliae*). Entomopathogenic fungi that can infect aphids and have been in commercial development include various strains of *Beauveria bassiana* (fig. 2.46), *Verticillium lecanii* (fig. 2.47), *Paecilomyces fumosoroseus,* and *Metarhizium anisopliae* (2.48). Aphids infected by these fungi usually change color in some way and, under very humid conditions, may appear fuzzy or as tiny balls of fluff as the fungus sporulates outside the body. A discussion of the infection process and fungal life cycle appears in Chapter 1.

CHAPTER 3

Caterpillars

Caterpillars are the immature or larval stage of insects in the order Lepidoptera. Caterpillars of several species of moths and butterflies feed on greenhouse crops. Most moths and butterflies overwinter outdoors, and the adult moths migrate into greenhouses, particularly in spring through fall. Most adult female moths and butterflies are active laying eggs from spring through early fall, and plants infested with eggs or caterpillars may be brought into a greenhouse.

Screening is an effective method of excluding adult moths and butterflies. In some crops, such as pansies and ornamental cabbage and kale, the plants are started in the greenhouse, then moved outdoors for several weeks before shipping. Adult moths or butterflies often lay eggs on these unprotected plants.

Butterflies (families Pieridae, Papilionidae, and Nymphalidae) are day fliers and can be observed during daylight hours by alert greenhouse workers. Most of the moths, including the families Noctuidae, Tortricidae, Pyralidae, Arctiidae, and Crambidae, are night fliers and are often attracted to night lighting in or around a greenhouse operation.

General description

Plant damage

All caterpillars have chewing mouthparts called mandibles. The most common damage is the consumption of leaves and flowers

Fig. 3.1 This chewing injury to salvia foliage is caused by caterpillars feeding on the leaves. *Photo: Stanton Gill*

(fig. 3.1). A few species damage plants by rolling leaves with silken threads, while others bore or chew into stems and buds. Others, such as cutworms, cut off plants at the base.

Biology

All the caterpillars discussed in this section are the larval stages of moths or butterflies in the order Lepidoptera. Female moths or butterflies give off chemical attractant odors called *pheromones* to attract mates. After female moths or butterflies mate, they lay their eggs on the host plant. They can lay eggs singly, as the cabbage looper does, or in masses, like armyworms.

The eggs hatch, and larvae (called caterpillars) migrate either singly or in groups to feeding sites on the plant. Many caterpillars have appendages on the abdomen called *prolegs*. Prolegs have small hooks on the base that enable the caterpillar to hold onto surfaces. Caterpillars have chewing mouthparts that, depending on the species, chew holes in leaves or bore into stems of plants. Most caterpillars feed voraciously and grow rapidly, shedding their skins (molting) three to five times before entering a nonactive pupal stage.

Some species spin cocoons to pupate in; others do not. Most species have a characteristic location for pupation either on leaves, stems, or in soil. A butterfly larva forms a chrysalis, which is generally attached upright to plant material by silken threads. A butterfly emerges from the chrysalis, and a moth from the pupal case, after several days to several months, depending on the species and the season. Some moths and butterflies have one generation per year, while others have three or four.

Pest Detection

Monitoring

Many of the Lepidoptera prefer to feed on specific greenhouse crops. Regular monitoring of adult flight activity in your area will enable you to determine when to begin looking for newly laid eggs on foliage. Eggs and young larvae must be detected before damage is extensive. Butterflies, such as the variegated fritillary butterfly and the imported cabbageworm butterfly, are active during the day. Adults flutter around areas where they lay eggs. Observations of adult daylight activity should help pinpoint when and where to monitor in the crop for the presence of eggs and young larvae.

Pheromone traps are available to monitor for many lepidopterous pests. Use of pheromone traps outdoors or in open-sided greenhouses helps determine the moth activity in your crop area and narrows the time to check for egg laying and young larvae on plants. Pheromone traps can be hung just above the canopy of susceptible crops and monitored at regular (at least weekly) intervals (fig. 3.2).

Butterfly species identification

Imported cabbageworm, *Pieris rapae* (Linnaeus), family Pieridae. The imported cabbageworm is native to Europe but has spread to most temperate areas. The larvae are found damaging ornamental cabbage, kale, mint, parsley, and lettuce.

Fig. 3.2 To monitor for adult flight activity, pheromone traps can be placed among greenhouse crops that are moved outdoors. *Photo: Stanton Gill*

The imported cabbageworm adult is a white butterfly tinged with yellow on the undersides of the wings (fig. 3.3). Males can be distinguished from females by the black spots on their wings. The male butterfly has one spot on the top of the forewing, and the female has two black spots. The adults can be observed during the day fluttering over plants on which the female is laying eggs. Monitoring for adult activity is the easiest way to focus on which crop the larvae will be found.

Eggs are bullet shaped and generally laid on upper leaf surfaces (figs. 3.4, 3.5). They are stuck to the leaf, standing on end. Eggs are easily detected on the foliage of most plants. Close examination reveals that the eggs have fine, sculptured, parallel lines.

The larva is velvety green with a light green-yellow stripe running down its back (figs. 3.6, 3.30). The caterpillar has five pairs of prolegs on the abdomen, in addition to the three pairs of anterior legs. A behavioral characteristic of this caterpillar is that when prodded, it will swing its head from side to side. The larva generally feeds on the undersides of the leaves, and damage appears as holes in the leaves (fig. 3.7).

When a larva is fully grown, it frequently migrates some distance from the feeding site and attaches itself by silk to the underside of a leaf, where it changes into a chrysalis. The chrysalis is green at first but matures to a brown color. Multiple generations can occur during a growing season. In colder climates the imported cabbageworm overwinters in the chrysalis stage.

Fig. 3.3 The imported cabbage butterfly is white, with the undersides of its wings tinged with yellow. Males have one spot on the forewing, females have two dark spots. *Photo: Stanton Gill*

Fig. 3.4 The imported cabbage butterfly lays its eggs on leaf surfaces. *Photo: Stanton Gill*

Fig. 3.5 The imported cabbage butterfly egg has fine, sculptured, parallel lines. *Photo: Stanton Gill*

Fig. 3.6 Larvae of the imported cabbage butterfly are velvety green. *Photo: Stanton Gill*

Fig. 3.7 Typical feeding injury from the imported cabbage worm on ornamental cabbage. *Photo: Stanton Gill*

Fig. 3.8 The distinct black stripes of the parsley caterpillar are rather pleasing in appearance. *Photo: Stanton Gill*

Swallowtail butterflies, *Papilio* spp., family Papilionidae. *Papilio troilus* Linnaeus, the spicebush swallowtail, and *Papilio polyxenes* (= *joanae*) Stoll, the American swallowtail, do the most damage. The larvae of these two butterfly species feed on greenhouse-grown herbs and vegetables, including several oil-type herbs, such as rue, parsley, dill, and fennel. Both species are found throughout the Midwest and along the east coast of the United States.

Adults of all papilionids visit flowers. Adults of both *Papilio* species are active from spring through fall. Females are attracted to greenhouse crops, where they lay eggs on susceptible hosts. Eggs of *P. polyxenes* and *P. troilus* are cream white and laid singly on leaves and flowers of the host.

The larva lacks spines or horns but has a forked, brightly colored, foul-smelling, fleshy gland (called an osmeterium) that extrudes from behind the head to repel enemies when disturbed. The larva of *P. polyxenes* feeds on open leaves and flowers. The larva is green, yellow-green, bluish green, or whitish green, with black lines between segments and yellow spots (fig. 3.8). The black lines and bands are variable in thickness. The chrysalis is brown or green and often found on thick stems.

First and second instars of *P. troilus* live in a silken, bent-over flap of leaf. An older larva lives in a tube made by bringing two sides of a leaf upward and together with silk. The larva is green, with a broad, yellow, lateral band that is edged beneath with a fine black line. The larva pupates near the ground.

Variegated fritillary butterfly, *Euptoieta claudia*, family Nymphalidae. *Euptoieta claudia*, the variegated fritillary butterfly, is active in the southern regions of the United States in spring, spreading northward to Canada and west during the summer. Pansies are the primary greenhouse crop that fritillary caterpillars feed on. Pansies that are greenhouse grown for fall sales are fed on from July through October in the southeast. The growth of these plants outdoors coincides with the flight activity of the fritillary butterfly. The larva also feeds on portulaca and sedum.

The pale green or cream eggs are laid singly on leaves and stems of host plants. The first- through fifth-instar larvae feed openly on the foliage. The larvae are orange, white, and black, with six longitudinal rows of thick, sharp spines (fig. 3.9). The full-grown larva attaches itself by silk to the underside of a leaf and changes into the resting stage, which is called a chrysalis.

The butterfly is orange and black and has a wingspan of approximately 76 mm (3 inches) (fig. 3.10). The adults are active from July through the first heavy frost. The butterfly will enter through ventilation openings during daylight hours.

Moth species identification

Beet armyworm, *Spodoptera exigua* (Hübner), family Noctuidae. *Spodoptera exigua,* the beet armyworm, is native to Asia but has spread to most temperate and tropical areas. The beet armyworm infests a wide range of ornamental plants, including chrysanthemums, carnations, roses, and geraniums.

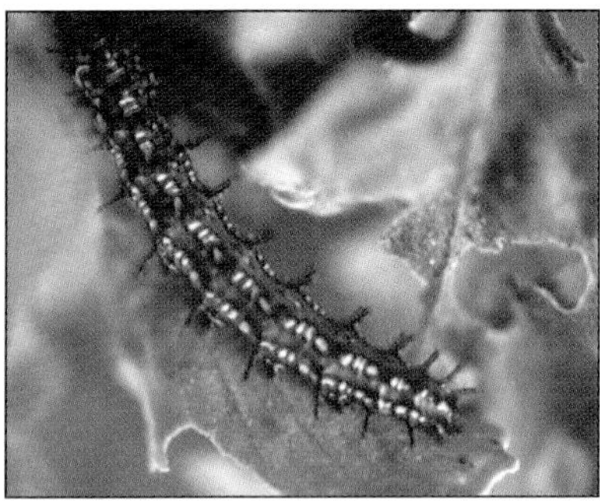

Fig. 3.9 The spined larva of variegated fritillary is orange white and black with six longitudinal rows of thick sharp spines. *Photo: Stanton Gill*

Fig. 3.10 The adult variegated fritillary butterfly is orange and black. *Photo: Stanton Gill*

The adult moth is grayish brown with a pale, circular spot near the middle of the forewing (fig. 3.11). The hind wings are white with dark edges. The moth is nocturnal, with mating and egg laying occurring at night. Pheromone traps can help monitor for moth flight activity. Female moths lay eggs in clusters on the undersides of leaves. Females often cover the eggs with a mat of body scales.

First- and second-instar larvae feed in groups, and they often web young, terminal leaves together and feed within the webbed area (fig. 3.12). The webbing protects the larvae from predators and insecticide applications. The third through fifth instars feed on old leaves as well as young leaves. The caterpillars are often cannibalistic. At the end of the larval development, individual beet armyworms tunnel into soil and form a cell in which they pupate (fig. 3.13). Beet armyworms can have multiple generations per year.

Fig. 3.11 Beet armyworm adult is grayish brown with a pale circular spot near the middle of the forewing. *Photo: Galen Dively*

Fig. 3.12 Beet armyworm larva feeds on old and new foliage. *Photo: Stanton Gill*

Fig. 3.13 The beet armyworm at the end of its development bores into the ground and forms a cell in which to pupate. *Photo: Galen Dively*

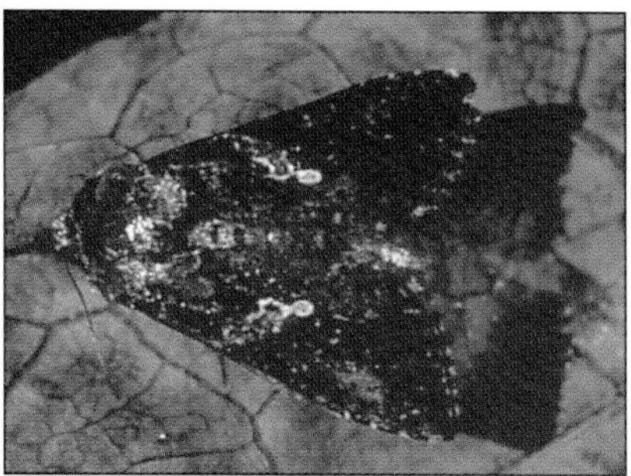

Fig. 3.14 Cabbage looper is dark brown with mottled wings and a silvery figure eight on each forewing. *Photo: Galen Dively*

Cabbage looper, *Trichoplusia ni* (Hübner), family Noctuidae. *Trichoplusia ni,* the cabbage looper, is dark brown with mottled wings and a silvery figure eight on each forewing (fig. 3.14). The female moth lays white, round eggs singly or in small groups on the leaves. The eggs have ornate ridges.

The first-instar caterpillar is light green, with faint white stripes running down each side and along the back. The body of the caterpillar is tapered, with the rear being wider than the front. The early-instar caterpillar feeds through most of the leaf, leaving a thin, transparent layer of plant tissue. The caterpillar feeds for 14 to 21 days and reaches a final length of 31 to 38 mm (1.25 to 1.5 inches). The caterpillar moves with a characteristic looping motion. This is done by holding onto the leaf with the front legs and arching the middle section to bring the rear prolegs forward (fig. 3.15). If the caterpillar is disturbed while on the plant, it will rapidly move in this looping method until it drops off the leaf or finds coverage on the plant. The caterpillar pupates in a loosely woven cocoon that is usually attached to a leaf.

Greenhouse ornamental cabbage and kale are the usual hosts for this caterpillar pest (figs. 3.16, 3.30), but it also feeds on carnation, snapdragon, nasturtium, tomato, and lettuce. Chrysanthemum foliage and flowers can occasionally be damaged by this caterpillar.

China mark moth, *Nymphuiella daeckealis,* family Crambidae. *Nymphuiella daeckealis* damages water lily foliage. The adult has forewings that are white, marked with dark gray. The hind wings are white. Adult females lay eggs on the upper leaf surface of the water lily.

Fig. 3.15 Cabbage looper larva moves with a characteristic looping motion. *Photo: Stanton Gill*

Fig. 3.16 Cabbage looper larvae are often found on ornamental cabbage and kale foliage. *Photo: Stanton Gill*

Fig. 3.17 China mark moth larvae are aquatic caterpillars that feed on water lilies. *Photo: Stanton Gill*

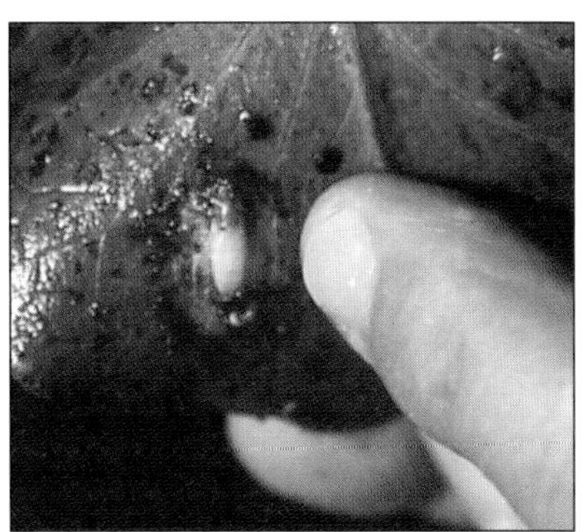

Fig. 3.18 The China mark moth, an aquatic moth, has a pupal stage on the underside of a water lily leaf. *Photo: Stanton Gill*

The larva cuts out a small section of the leaf (1 to 2 mm, .039 to .078 inches) and floats on this miniature boat. The larva then cuts an equal size leaf piece and webs it to the bottom piece. The larva is covered as it floats to the edge of the water lily leaf where it feeds by sticking its head out as it chews on the leaf surface (fig. 3.17). If disturbed, the larva will withdraw into the "leaf boat." For cultivated water lilies grown in the greenhouse or in aquatic pools the feeding injury can render a plant unattractive and unsaleable.

The larva is whitish to green and has branched tracheal gills. Mature larvae build silken cocoons and pupate on the leaf surface, sometimes anchored on the underside of the lily leaf (fig. 3.18).

Corn earworm, *Helicoverpa zea* (Boddie), family Noctuidae. The corn earworm feeds on plants throughout the world on a wide array of plants. It feeds on a variety of greenhouse crops, including ageratum, carnation, chrysanthemum, rose, dahlia, geranium, hibiscus, mint, nasturtium, phlox, sunflower, poppy, cleome, and morning glory. Adults have distinct green eyes. The wing coloration varies from light yellow to brown with irregular lines and dark areas near the tips on the forewings. The hind wings are white with irregular markings near the margins. The moths are nocturnal and are often attracted into greenhouses if night lighting is used.

The adult female moth lays eggs that are hemispherical and ridged (fig.3.19). Adult moths are attracted to nectar-producing plants and will often lay eggs on these flowering hosts. Females lay eggs, usually singly, on new foliage.

Larvae vary from pale green to dark brown, with alternating light and dark longitudinal stripes that run the length of the body (fig. 3.20). The head is yellow to orange. Corn earworm larvae have tiny, short spines covering large areas of the skin that can be seen with a 10× hand lens (fig. 3.21). The young larvae prefer to feed in still rolled or expanding foliage. All larval stages feed on flowers, leaves and fruit (if present). Fully developed larvae tunnel into the ground to pupate. Adult moths emerge from the ground. Adults are strong fliers and often migrate north from warmer regions.

Cross-striped caterpillar, *Evergestis rimosalis* (Guenée), family Pyralidae. The cross-striped caterpillar damages ornamental cabbage and kale. The adult is yellowish brown, with a dark zigzag marking on the forewings and five or six small, brown spots near the inner border of the hind wings. The eggs are yellow, thin, and flattened. The

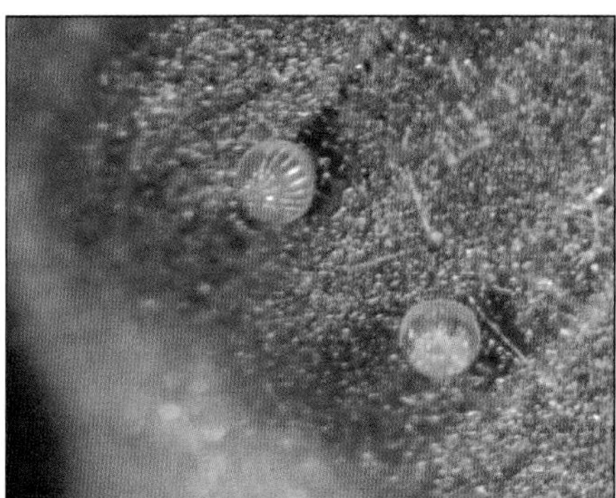

Fig. 3.19 Eggs of corn earworm are hemispherical and ridged. *Photo: Dan Gilrein*

Fig. 3.20 Corn earworm larvae vary in color from pale green to dark brown and have alternating light and dark longitudinal stripes. *Photo: Dan Gilrein*

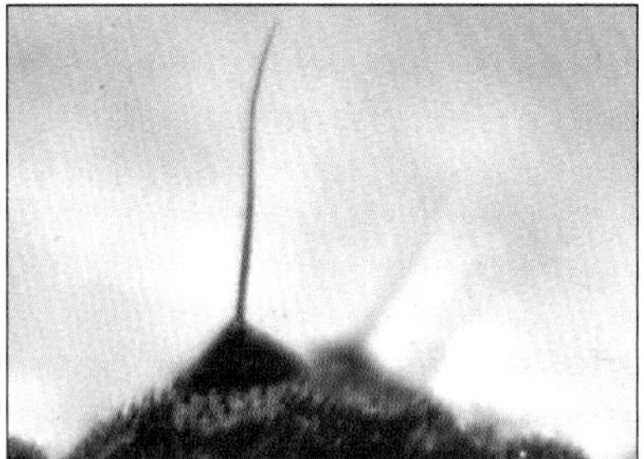

Fig. 3.21 European corn earworms have short spines covering large areas of the skin that can be seen with a 10× hand lens. *Photo: Dan Gilrein*

Fig. 3.22 The cross-striped caterpillar is blue-green with black stripes across the top of the body and black and yellow stripes along each side. *Photo: Galen Dively*

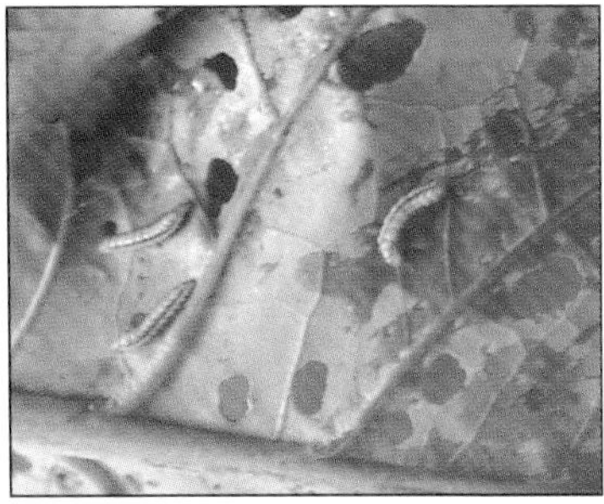

Fig. 3.23 Cross-striped caterpillars feeding on ornamental cabbage. *Photo: Stanton Gill*

Fig. 3.24 Black cutworm larvae are nocturnal. *Photo: Galen Dively*

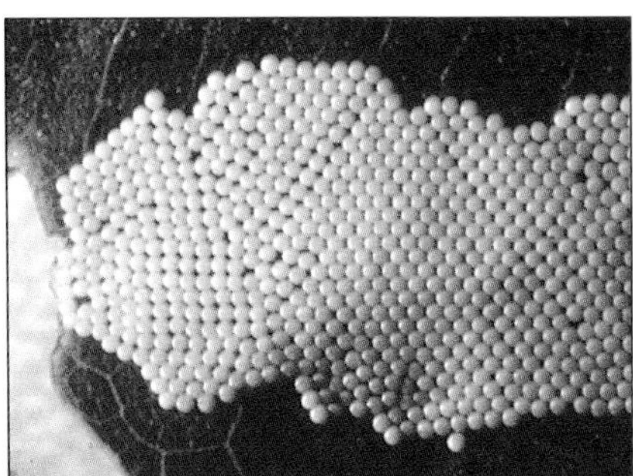

Fig. 3.25 Cutworm eggs are laid singly or in clusters. *Photo: Stanton Gill*

Fig. 3.26 Cutworm larvae have six instars and pupate in the soil. *Photo: Galen Dively*

eggs are laid overlapping like fish scales in masses of 20 to 30 eggs on the leaves.

The larva is blue-green, with black stripes across the top of the body and a black stripe with a yellow one underneath along each side (figs. 3.22, 3.23). The insect overwinters as a larva and pupates in the spring. There can be multiple generations per year.

Black cutworm, *Agrotis ipsilon* (Hufnagel); variegated cutworm, *Peridroma saucia* (Hübner), family Noctuidae. Cutworms feed on plant stems and leaves and frequently cut stems off at the soil line. There are several species of cutworms that damage plants, but two of the most destructive to greenhouse plants are *Peridroma saucia,* variegated cutworm, and *P. ipsilon* (fig. 3.24), black cutworm. Cutworm larvae attack pansy, marigold, nasturtium, zinnia, chrysanthemum, carnation, aster, and dahlia.

Adult moths are nocturnal, and females lay eggs singly or in clusters (fig. 3.25) during the night. The larvae are also nocturnal

Fig. 3.27 Black cutworm causing feeding injury. *Photo: Galen Dively*

Fig. 3.28 The light colors of the forewings of an adult diamondback moth fit together to form a diamond shape. *Photo: Galen Dively*

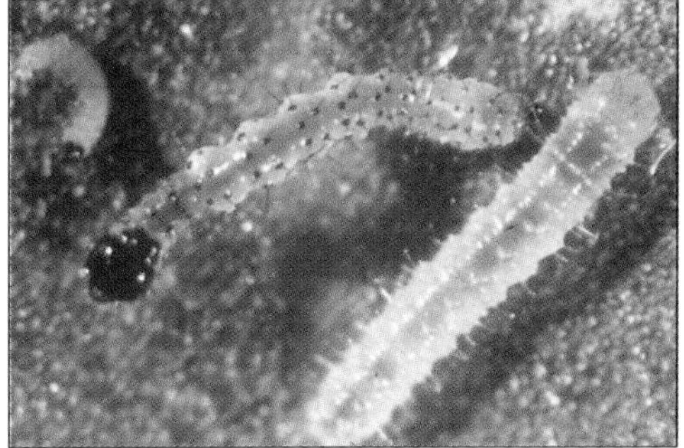

Fig. 3.29 Diamondback cabbage larva (*left*), next to imported cabbage butterfly and looper larva. All are early instars. *Photo: Galen Dively*

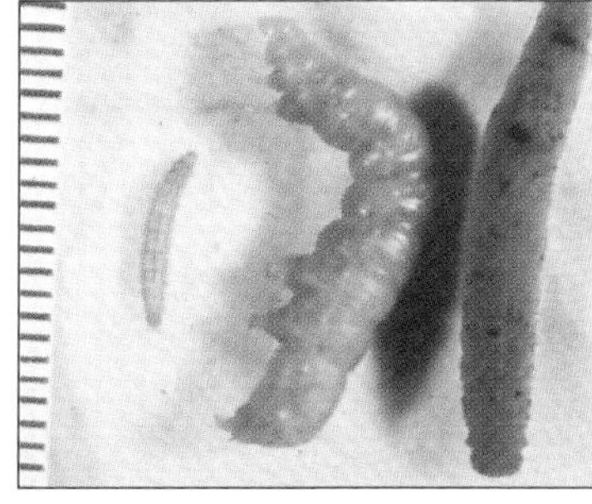

Fig. 3.30 Diamondback cabbage larva (*left*), next to looper larva and imported cabbageworm butterfly. These are later instars. *Photo: Galen Dively*

and feed through six instars (figs. 3.26, 3.27). The overwintering cutworm form occurs in the soil as either a pupa or a mature larva.

Diamondback moth, *Plutella xylostella* (Linnaeus), family Plutellidae. The diamondback moth is widespread in its distribution in North America. The adult, in its normal resting position, is a very small moth about 8 mm (.314 inches) long. When the moth is at rest, the light colors on the forewings fit together to form diamond-shaped spots (fig. 3.28). These moths overwinter, hibernate, or remain active through the winter, depending on the weather. Eggs are laid on the leaves of cabbage, kale, and other related hosts, such as mustard weed.

The young larva feeds mainly on the undersides of foliage. The early-instar larva is pale green in color (figs. 3.29, 3.30). The body is slender and pointed at both ends. There is a distinctive "V" formed by two prolegs at the rear of the larva. Larvae feed for two or three weeks, then spin a loose-mesh cocoon and pupate on the plant. Multiple generations, up to seven, can occur in a growing season. *Bacillus thuringiensis* is usually very effective against early-instar larvae. An ichneumon wasp, *Diadegma fenestrale* (Holmgren), is one of the more effective parasites of diamondback larvae.

European corn borer, *Ostrinia nubilalis* (Hübner), family Pyralidae. Native to Europe, the European corn borer was introduced to the United States at the beginning of the twentieth century and has spread throughout thc United States and Canada. European corn borer prefers to infest corn but will damage over 200 plant species, including chrysanthemums, sunflowers, daisies, peppers, and tomatoes.

The adult female moth is heavy bodied, pale yellow to light brown, and the outer third of the wing is crossed by zigzag lines (fig. 3.31). The male is slender bodied and darker colored than the female (fig. 3.32); the wings of the male are crossed by two zigzag streaks of pale yellow. Male flight activity can be monitored outdoors using a pheromone trap. Flight activity starts at sundown, and mating and egg laying occur during the night. Female moths lay an egg mass of 20 to 30 eggs, which are covered with a shining, waxy, protective material.

European corn borer larvae are cannibalistic, and only a few survive, but it does not take many to damage a plant. The first-instar larva has a black head, five pairs of prolegs, and a pale yellow body,

Fig. 3.31 Corn borer adults are pale yellow to light brown, and the outer third of the wing is crossed by zigzag lines. *Photo: Michael Hoffmann*

Fig. 3.32 Corn borer male is slender and darker colored than the heavy-bodied female adult. *Photo: Galen Dively*

which has several rows of small, black or brown spots (fig. 3.33). On most plants the larva begins feeding on the leaf surface. The larva is exposed for only two to three days before it bores into the stem of a plant. Frass and silk near the entrance hole are evidence that the borer has moved into the stem of the plant. The larva continues to develop through five instars.

Florida fern caterpillar, *Callopistria floridensis* (Guenee), family Noctuidae. The Florida fern caterpillar, *Callopistria floridensis*, occurs naturally in Florida and tropical America and can sometimes be found in greenhouses on ferns shipped from tropical regions. The caterpillars are active feeders and can rapidly defoliate a plant. The younger larvae are often found on tender new growth, but larger larvae will feed on older growth. The Florida fern caterpillar has been reported feeding on several species of ferns including Boston fern, sword fern, and maidenhair fern.

The adult moth has variegated wings and conspicuously tufted legs and flies at night. Female moths lay eggs under fern leaves, usually near tip growth. Females can lay 300 to 400 eggs.

The larva feeds through five instar stages over three to four weeks. The caterpillar has five color forms: a light green form; a green one; upper and lower white-and-black lines down each side (fig. 3.34); velvety, dark-striped or black; and a velvety, dark-striped or black form (figs. 3.35, 3.36). The larva spins a cocoon, which is covered with soil or plant material, and pupates on the surface of the potting soil or on the greenhouse floor.

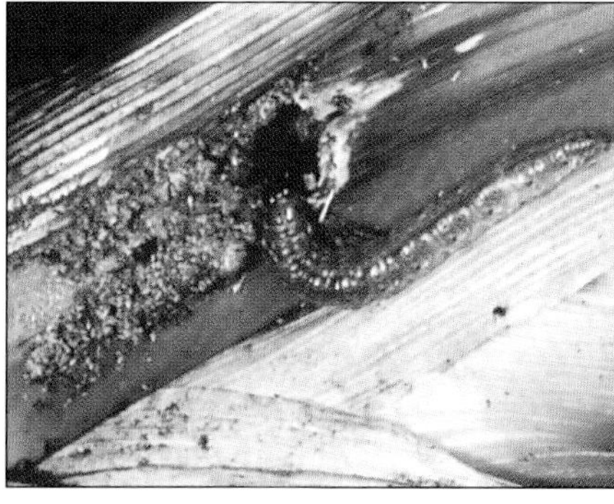

Fig. 3.33 The corn borer larva has a black head, five pairs of prolegs, and a pale yellow body that has several rows of small black or brown spots. *Photo: Galen Dively*

Fig. 3.34 The Florida fern caterpillar has five color forms. Note the stripe running the length of the body. *Photo: Stanton Gill*

Fig. 3.35 The Florida fern caterpillar has a color change in its later instar stage. This is the velvety black form. *Photo: Stanton Gill*

Fig. 3.36 The Florida fern caterpillar is seen here in one of its color forms. *Photo: Stanton Gill*

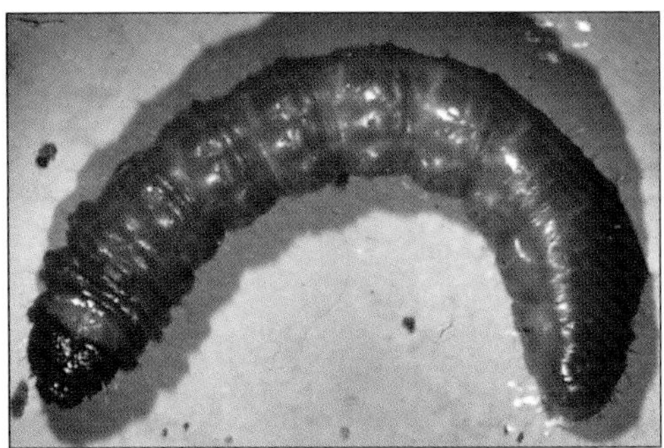

Fig. 3.37 The iris borer in the later instar stage is rather plump. *Photo: Stanton Gill*

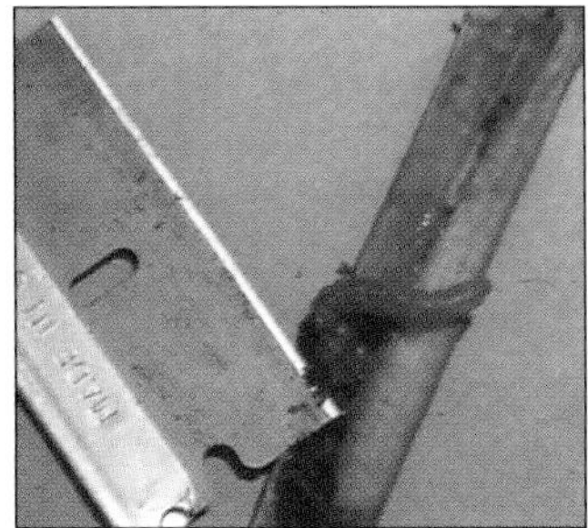

Fig. 3.38 Early instar iris borer larva that has been dissected from the stem. *Photo: Stanton Gill*

Iris borer, *Macronoctua onusta* Grote, family Noctuidae. The iris borer, *Macronoctua onusta,* is a serious pest of irises. It prefers Japanese, German, and blue flag irises, but it has also been recorded damaging blackberry lily.

The adult iris borer moths are mottled brown, with yellow-brown hind wings. Female moths mate and lay eggs in the evening and are active in late summer on the east coast of the U.S. A female can lay up to 1,000 eggs. The nearly spherical eggs are white with a slight green tinge. The eggs are laid on leaves of the plant before old foliage yellows and dies back. The eggs overwinter on the old foliage. The best physical control is to remove all old foliage before new growth emerges in the spring.

The first-instar caterpillar feeds on the iris leaves causing the leaves to appear ragged (figs. 3.37, 3.38). The larva then mines into the leaf and tunnels down to the rhizome (fig. 3.39). The larva feeds on the edge of the rhizome and will often mine into it. Often a root rot will then enter the wounded rhizome. The larvae pupate in the rhizome, and the adults emerge in late summer.

Leafrollers, *Choristoneura* spp., family Tortricidae. The oblique-banded leafroller, *Choristoneura rosaceana* (Harris), is found throughout the United States. The spotted fireworm, *Choristoneura parallella,* is found in the eastern United States and eastern Canada. Leafrollers are reported damaging poinsettias, gardenias, azaleas and roses in greenhouses.

The adult oblique-banded leafroller is a red-brown-colored moth with distinct bands on the forewings (fig. 3.40). The hind wings are yellow for the females and orange to yellow for the males.

Fig. 3.39 The darkened galleries are iris borer injury to the rhizome. *Photo: Stanton Gill*

Fig. 3.40 The adult oblique leafroller is reddish brown with distinct bands on the forewing. *Photo: Galen Dively*

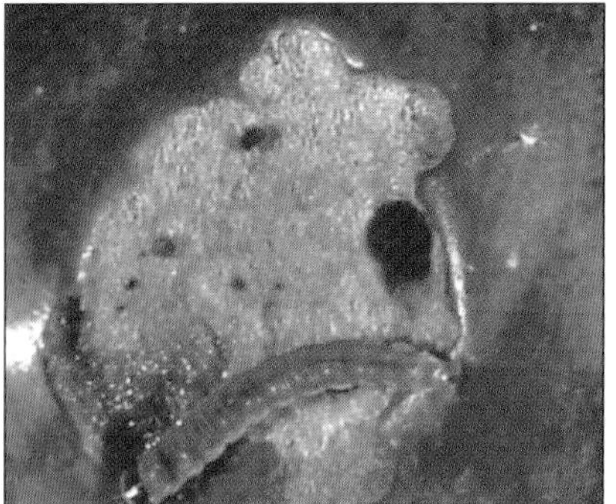

Fig. 3.41 The oblique leafroller larvae will often tie plant leaves together and feed in the clustered leaves. *Photo: Galen Dively*

Fig. 3.42 Early instar of saltmarsh caterpillar is light in color, and late instar of saltmarsh caterpillar is darker brown. *Photo: Dan Gilrein*

The spotted fireworm adult is red to orange, with two dark patches on the outer margins of the top wings. Female moths lay eggs in masses on the leaves of plants.

Newly hatched larvae disperse by crawling or by wind currents. The larval stage has seven instars. The larva of the spotted fireworm has two small, brown spots on the front margin of the thoracic shield (top area, just behind the head), and the anal shield (a plate at the posterior end of the caterpillar) is brownish. The larva of the oblique-banded leafroller does not have spots on the thoracic shield, and the anal shield is not brownish. The oblique-banded leafroller ties leaves together and feeds in the clustered leaves (fig. 3.41).

Saltmarsh caterpillar, *Estigmene acrea* (Drury), family Arctiidae. Saltmarsh caterpillars are very hairy, and the early instars may be yellowish white. In the early instars the caterpillars feed gregariously on the foliage of soybeans, cotton, and many greenhouse crops. Older larvae are reddish brown and over 5 cm (1.97 inches) in length (fig. 3.42). Pupae overwinter in brown, hairy cocoons in debris on the ground.

Adults appear in the spring. The female adults are white on the top of the wings and yellow on the underside. The males are similar, except the hind wings are yellow both on the top and underside. Both sexes have numerous black spots on the wings. The spherical eggs are laid in masses on plant foliage.

Saddleback caterpillar *Sibine stimulea* (Clemens), family Limacodidae. The saddleback caterpillar has a sluglike ventral side and is armed with venomous setae (hairs) on the front and rear dorsal side. The caterpillar has a bright green, blanketlike coloration in the middle of the back, with an oval, brown circle in the center. The venom from the setae can cause a very painful sting (fig. 3.43).

Fig. 3.43 The stinging saddleback caterpillar larva has a brown oval in the middle of a bright green blanket pattern. *Photo: Stanton Gill*

Biological control

***Bacillus thuringiensis* Berliner.** *Bacillus thuringiensis* (Bt) is a soil-inhabiting bacterium first identified in Japan in 1901. With regular monitoring and detection of early instars of caterpillars, Bt is a very safe, effective, biological material for the control of several species of greenhouse caterpillars. Bt is most effective against young larvae. The bacterium is applied to the foliage as a spray, and the larvae ingest the Bt.

***Cotesia glomeratus*.** *Cotesia glomeratus* is a small, braconid wasp that parasitizes the larval stage of the imported cabbageworm. The female inserts her eggs into the host, which may continue to live for some time. The parasite larva feeds internally in the cabbageworm larva, killing the caterpillar (fig. 3.44). The adult is a stout-bodied, dark-colored wasp 7 to 8 mm (.275 to .314 inches) in size. The antennae are relatively long and curved, but not elbowed (fig. 3.45).

***Trichogramma* spp.** These are among the smallest parasitic wasps. They attack the eggs of many species of moths and butterflies. Female wasps oviposit into the eggs of the moth or butterfly. The feeding parasite kills the egg. Eggs that have been parasitized by *Trichogramma* wasp usually turn black. Females lay 80 to 100 eggs and can destroy plant feeding insects' eggs by adult feeding activity. There are many species of *Trichogramma* available from commercial insectaries.

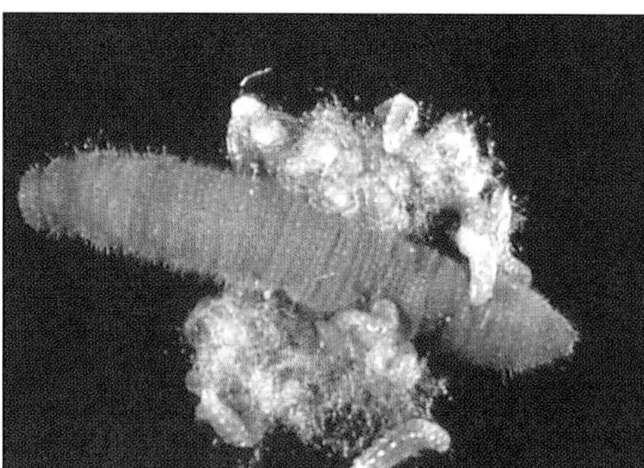

Fig. 3.44 *Cotesia* wasp attacking caterpillar. *Cotesia* females insert eggs into the host caterpillar. *Photo: Michael Hoffmann*

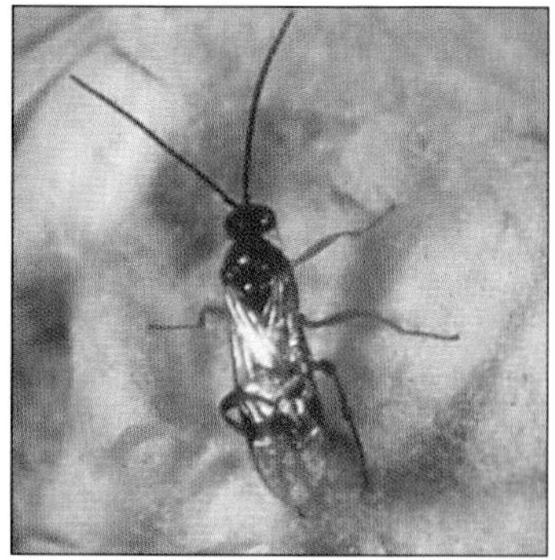

Fig. 3.45 The antennae of *Cotesia* wasp adult are relatively long and curved, not elbowed. *Photo: Michael Hoffmann*

CHAPTER 4

Fungus Gnats, Shore Flies, Humpbacked Flies, Moth Flies

The greenhouse environment is an ideal breeding site for several species of flies and gnats. The constantly wet conditions and high-humidity atmosphere of many greenhouses provide a very favorable environment for development of four fly families: fungus gnats, shore flies, humpbacked flies, and moth or drain flies. Adult gnats and other flies can be a major nuisance to workers and customers in greenhouses. In interior landscapes where low light and high soil moisture conditions exist, fungus gnat and shore fly adults often become a major nuisance to workers and the public.

During the adult stage, fungus gnats, shore flies, humpbacked flies, and drain flies do not feed on plant stems, leaves, or roots. As a group, most are weak fliers that are usually most noticeable when plant material is moved or disturbed and the adults flutter around. The adults of each of these flies and gnats are attracted to yellow sticky cards. During the larval stage, shore flies, humpbacked flies, and drain flies are not found feeding on plants but rather feed on algae, fungi, or decaying plant material. Only fungus gnat larvae feed directly on roots and bore into stems of susceptible herbaceous plants.

Plant damage

Previously, fungus gnats and shore flies were considered a minor nuisance problem in greenhouse production. Fungus gnat larvae can cause serious feeding injury to some greenhouse crops, however. Fungus gnat larvae feed on root hairs and tunnel into stems (figs. 4.1, 4.2, 4.3). Crops such as poinsettia are often damaged both while under misting systems and when growing in constantly wet

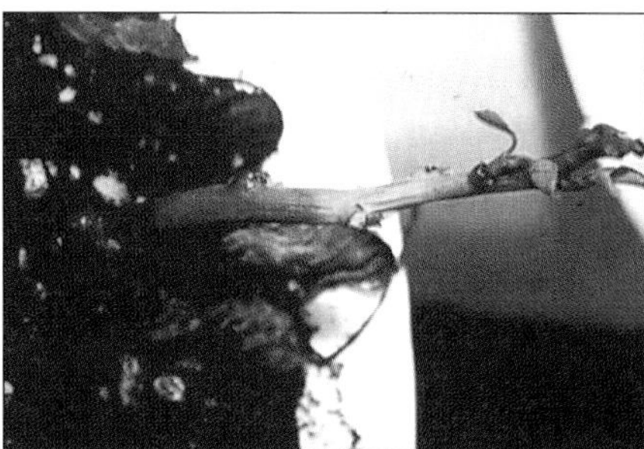

Fig. 4.1 Fungus gnat larvae injury to poinsettia. *Photo: Stanton Gill*

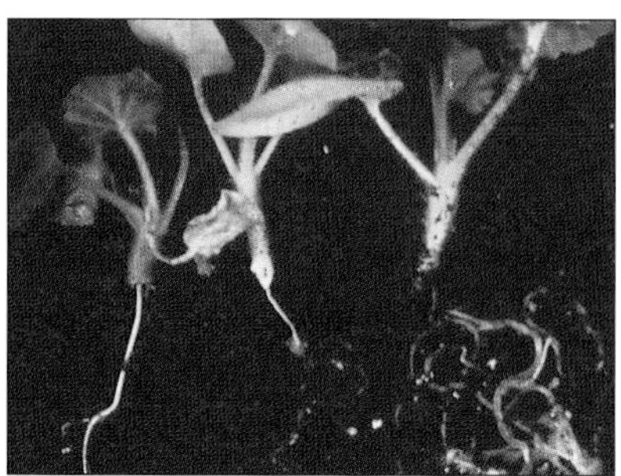

Fig. 4.2 Fungus gnat larvae have bored into the stem, causing injury to geranium. *Photo: Margery Daughtrey*

Fig. 4.3 Fungus gnat larvae bore in roots, often killing back tip growth of roots. *Photo: Margery Daughtrey*

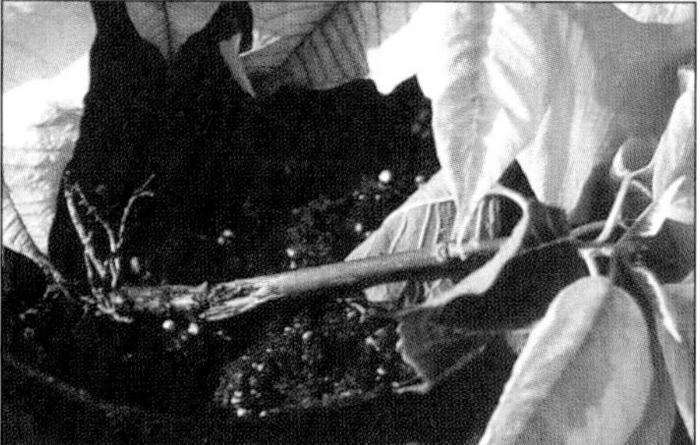

Fig. 4.4 Fungus gnat larva injury to poinsettia: The larva has bored into the stem causing the plant to collapse. *Photo: Stanton Gill*

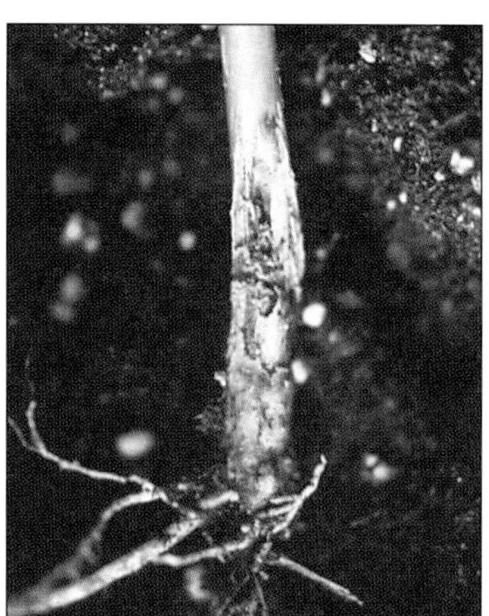

Fig. 4.5 A close-up of fungus gnat larva injury to poinsettia. *Photo: Stanton Gill*

Fig. 4.6 Fungus gnat larva feeds in the upper surface of the soil. The black head capsule and slightly translucent body help identify this soil pest. *Photo: Stanton Gill*

Fig. 4.7 The highest number of adult fungus gnats will be captured using a sticky card laying flat and parallel with the soil surface. Sticky cards that are placed upright will capture fewer fungus gnats but will have less dirt splashed on the surface. *Photo: Stanton Gill*

soils (figs. 4.4, 4.5). Two sciarid species of fungus gnats, *Bradysia coprophila* and *Bradysia impatiens*, have been associated with damaged roots and stems (fig. 4.6). The larvae of fungus gnats have been known to transmit *Pythium, Fusarium, Phoma,* and *Verticillium.*

Research has linked adult fungus gnat and shore fly activity in greenhouses with the transmission of *Pythium, Verticillium, Botrytis,* and *Fusarium.* It is believed that adult fungus gnats and shore flies can carry fungal spores from plant to plant as they migrate through the greenhouse. Fungal spores are also in fungus gnat fecal droppings found on plants and soil surfaces.

Although they may be nuisances to people, humpbacked and moth flies do not directly injure greenhouse plants. They are attracted to decaying plant material, however.

Pest detection

Monitoring

Monitor for fungus gnats, shore flies, humpbacked flies, and drain flies using sticky card traps. Yellow sticky cards laid flat (horizontally) near the plant pot surface generally attract twice the number of adult fungus gnats as sticky cards placed in a vertical position on a florist stake (fig. 4.7). The difficulty with placing sticky cards near pot surfaces is that soil substrates will splash onto the card during plant watering, making count taking difficult. Placing cards vertically may not catch as many adult fungus gnats, but it is generally easier to make an accurate count on cards free of soil particles, and they will reflect general population trends, which are apparent when the cards are monitored on a weekly basis.

Species identification

It is important to correctly identify fungus gnats from other greenhouse pests before attempting control strategies. Use a 10 to 15× hand lens for field identification. Adult fungus gnats are generally easy

Fig. 4.9 The Mycetophilidae adults have long legs and dark brown bodies. *Photo: John Davidson*

Fig. 4.8 Sciaridae adults have black bodies with veined wings. The thorax region is relatively large. *Photo: John Sanderson*

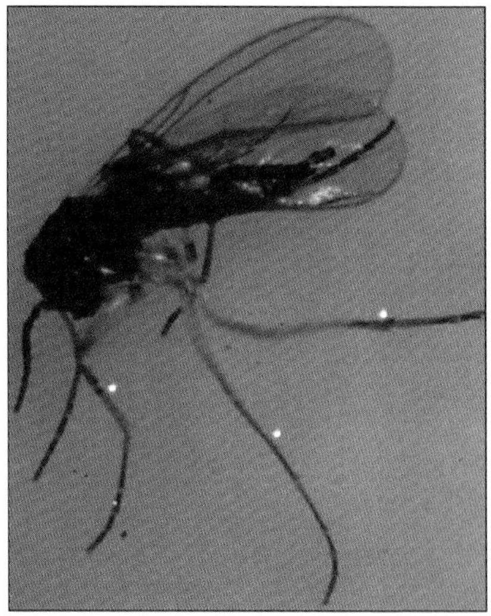

Fig. 4.11 The adult fungus gnat on yellow card displays the distinct Y shape on the wings and the enlarged thoracic region. *Photo: Stanton Gill*

Fig. 4.10 This adult female fungus gnat is in the process of laying eggs. *Photo: John Sanderson*

Fig. 4.12 The black head capsule of fungus gnat is characteristic of this pest. *Photo: Stanton Gill*

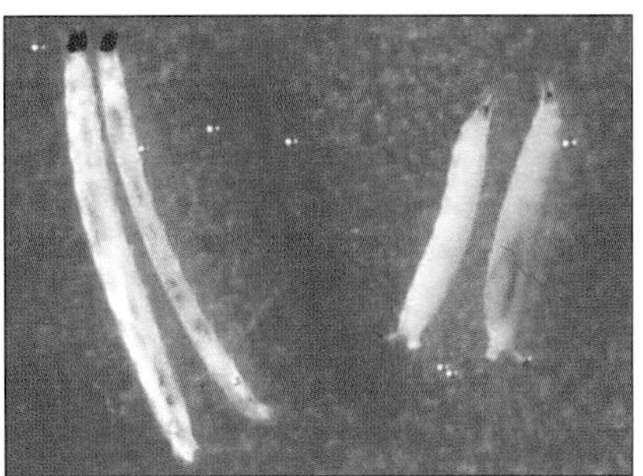

Fig. 4.13 Comparison of fungus gnat (*left*) and shore fly larvae (*right*). Shore fly larvae are wedge shaped and do not have the black head capsule. *Photo: John Sanderson*

to capture on yellow sticky cards. Use only freshly captured adults for field identification.

Fungus gnats, families Sciaridae, Phoridae, and Mycetophilidae. Fungus gnats are dark-bodied, slender, long-legged, mosquito-like insects in the order Diptera. *Fungus gnat* is a general term identifying flies in three families, Sciaridae (fig. 4.8), Phoridae, and Mycetophilidae (fig. 4.9). In production greenhouses most fungus gnats found damaging plant material are in the family Sciaridae.

Adult sciarid fungus gnats are 4 to 5 mm (.157 to .196 inches) long and dark brown to black (fig. 4.10). The antennae are long and beaded (see fig. 4.8). As members of the order Diptera, fungus gnats have only one pair of wings. A distinctive characteristic to look for on the wings is a Y-pattern in the tip third of the wing (fig. 4.11). Adults run rapidly on media surfaces, but are weak fliers. Females lay 100 to 300 eggs on media surfaces over a seven- to 10-day life cycle.

The slender larva has a black head capsule and transparent body (fig. 4.12). With mandibles for gnawing and tunneling in plants, the larva feeds on decaying plant material and soil fungi. It can also feed on fine roots and root hairs, as well as on stems, generally at the soil line. The larvae develop through four larval instars (fig. 4.13). Fungus gnats pupate in the soil. The adults mate soon after emergence, and a female can begin depositing eggs within two days after emergence. Generations can be continuous and overlapping in the greenhouse (see table 4.1). This has made most control strategies difficult.

Table 4.1 Sciarid fungus gnat generational development

Stage	Days[a]
Egg	4–6
Larvae	10–15
Pupae	4–5
Adult emergence to egg deposition	2–3
Total, laid to laying	20–29

[a]At 22 to 24C (70 to 75F)

Biological control of fungus gnats

Bacillus thuringiensis. A highly effective, spore-forming bacterium, *Bacillus thuringiensis* var. *israelensis* (Bti) produces a toxin protein crystal that acts as a larvicide for a number of larvae in the order Diptera. Bti is produced by fermentation, similar to the manufacture of natural antibiotics. This naturally occurring organism is commonly found in nature.

Bti formulations for greenhouses, sold under the trade name Gnatrol, are applied as soil drenches. Treatment should be made to soil surfaces of pots, market packs, and soil under the bench. There is no danger to greenhouse workers, and there is no reentry restriction time.

Entomopathogenic nematodes. Entomopathogenic nematodes are microscopic, multicellular worms. Three species of entomopathogenic nematodes, *Steinernema carpocapsae, Steinernema feltiae,* and *Heterorhabditis bacteriospora*, have been used in controlling the larvae of fungus gnats. Several suppliers are now marketing nematodes for the greenhouse and nursery, and the cost of nematode application is now competitive with those of many conventional insecticides.

The entomopathogenic nematodes are well suited to the moist environment of greenhouse soilless media. The nematodes are applied as a drench to the plants on the greenhouse bench and to the soil below the bench. The nematodes produced commercially contain an infective juvenile form, called "J3" or "dauer" stage. Once applied to the soilless media, the nematodes search for soil-inhabiting insects.

Upon locating an insect, the nematodes enter through the mouth, anus, and spiracles (breathing openings). Once inside the host, nematodes empty their gut bacteria into the insect's bloodstream, then feed on these bacteria. The insect dies of bacterial septicemia (fig. 4.14). In the warm, moist environment of greenhouse soilless media, the nematodes complete their life cycle within the infected host. Infective juveniles molt to form adults, which in turn mate and produce infective dauer juveniles that migrate out, searching for new insect hosts.

Entomopathogenic nematodes and their associated bacteria have been tested extensively for toxicity to nontarget organisms. They have been found to be safe both for the human applicator and the greenhouse plants, causing no known phytotoxicity.

***Hypoaspis miles*, family Laelapidae.** *Hypoaspis* (= *Geolaelaps*) *miles* is a predator native to the United States that commonly inhabits the upper layers of soils. The species is light brown and only 0.5 mm (.019 inches) long (fig. 4.15). *H. miles* feeds upon a variety of soil-inhabiting insects and mites. It is well adapted to moist conditions and will survive in greenhouses on a variety of growing media. Short days of winter (under 10 hours of light per day) do not appear to restrict the activity of this mite.

In greenhouses *H. miles* has been used primarily to control fungus gnat larvae. The mite is also reported to contribute to control of thrips, feeding primarily on the thrips pupating in the soil. Like most biological control options, *H. miles* should be applied when the fun-

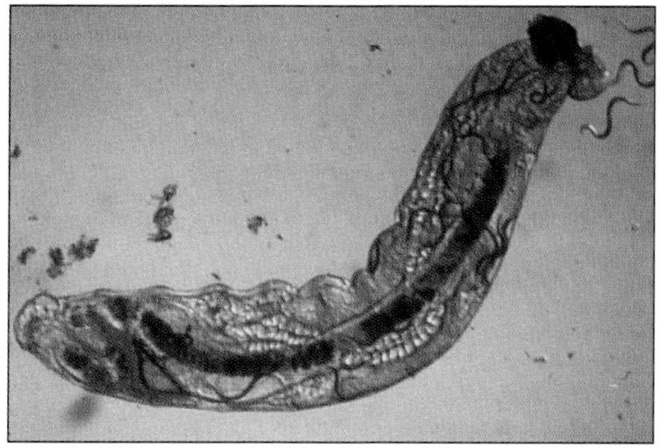

Fig. 4.14 Fungus gnat larva with the entomopathogenic nematode, *Steinernema feltiae*, inside. This nematode is an excellent biological control organism for fungus gnat larvae. *Photo: George Poiner*

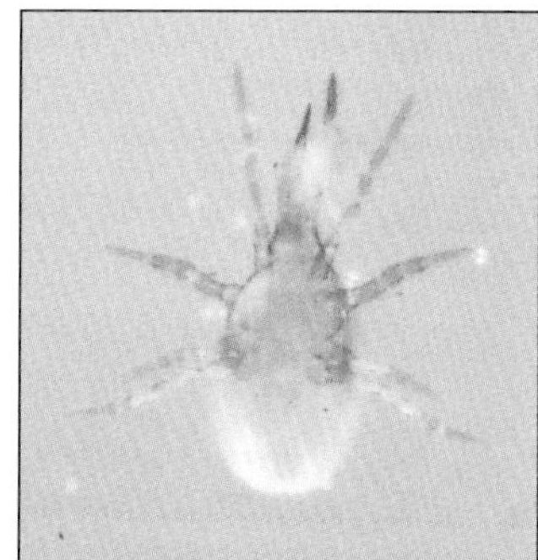

Fig. 4.15 The soil dwelling adult *Hypoaspis miles* mite feeds on fungus gnat larvae and other soil insects. *Photo: Stanton Gill*

gus gnat population is low. It is best to apply the mites to the soil within the first few weeks after planting.

H. miles populations include both sexes, but males are much smaller and rarely seen. Using a 10 to 15× hand lens, you should be able to see nymphs and adults, which move rapidly across soil surfaces. This mite reproduces in the greenhouse environment, going from egg to adult in seven to 11 days. Barring an application of a soil drench insecticide, it may not need to be reintroduced into the crop after the initial release. The female mites lay their eggs in the soil, and they hatch in two to three days. *H. miles* is compatible with releases of beneficial nematodes or use of *Bacillus thuringiensis* var. *israelensis.*

Synacra pauperi. *Synacra pauperi* is a common parasitoid of fungus gnats and is primarily found in unsprayed greenhouses. The wasps are about the same size as a fungus gnat (see figs. 1.7, 1.8). They have a long and a short pair of wings with reduced wing veins on the large forewing and no veins on the short rear wings. There is a noticeable constriction between the head and the thorax, and the thorax and the abdomen, and the abdomen tapers to a sharp tip. Females are brown to reddish brown, with black eyes. Their antennae are elbowed, and near the antennal tips the segments are darker and swollen. There are no noticeable antennal hairs. The males are black with long antennae that are nearly the length of the body. The antennal segments are similar in size and shape, and each has several hairs.

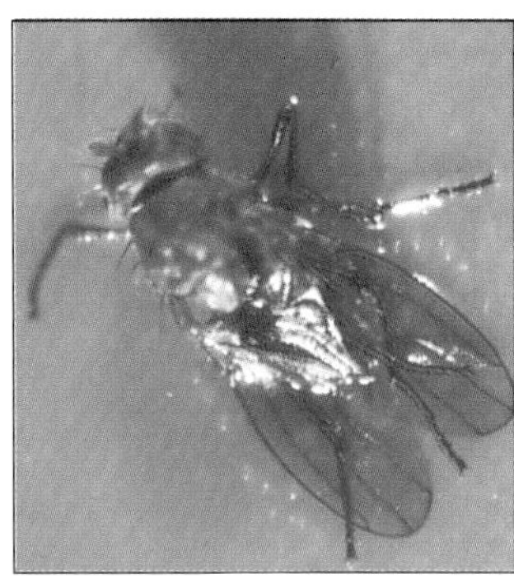

Fig. 4.16 Adult shore fly showing wings and antennae shapes. *Photo: Stanton Gill*

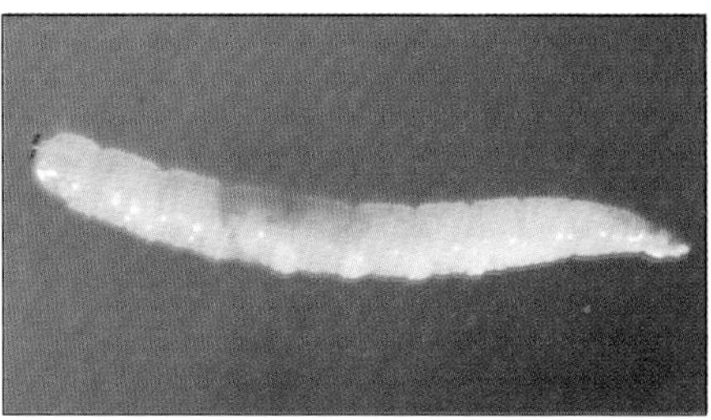

Fig. 4.17 The shore fly larva is white and wedge shaped. *Photo: John Davidson*

Females insert their eggs into fungus gnat larvae, and adult wasps emerge from fungus gnat pupae. They are commonly discovered on yellow sticky cards, though with careful observation, they may be noticed as they walk on the surface of the growing medium, searching for fungus gnat larvae. Their impact on fungus gnat infestations is unknown.

Shore flies, humpbacked flies, moth flies

Shore fly, *Scatella stagnalis* (Fallen), family Ephydridae. The insect most often misidentified as a fungus gnat is the shore fly. Shore flies have larger, more robust bodies and larger, protruding heads, compared to humpbacked flies.The antennae of shore flies are short and knoblike, not long and beaded like adult fungus gnats (fig. 4.16). Adults have white spots on gray wings.

Shore fly larvae are algae eaters and do not feed on plant roots or stems. Shore flies do not have visible mandibles but have mouthhooks. The larvae of shore flies are white, maggotlike, and wedge shaped, and they have no obvious black head capsule (fig. 4.17).

Female shore flies lay eggs on moist soil in pots and flats. Often as plant material becomes crowded in a greenhouse and foliage shades the surface of the pot or flat, algae will grow on the surface of moist soil media. Females will lay eggs in such an ideal location (fig. 4.18). Females will also lay eggs in the soil media between rocks or cracks in concrete that is under benches. The larvae hatch in two to four days and feed on algae, bacteria, and yeasts for four to six days (fig. 4.19).

Hexacola hexatoma is a parasitoid of shore flies and is commonly found in unsprayed greenhouses. The wasps are shiny black (fig. 4.20) and about half the size of a shore fly (see fig. 1.11). They have long antennae, about three-fourths the length of the body, made up of many tiny beads. There is a constriction between the thorax and the abdomen. The veins in the first pair of wings are very reduced and consist mainly of dark veins near the leading edge of the wing. The hind wing is also reduced and without veins. In side view, the thorax and abdomen have a very circular profile.

They are most often discovered on yellow sticky traps. If they are abundant, careful observation may reveal them walking on growing media or other substrates where shore fly larvae may be found. They will fly if disturbed.

Fig. 4.18 Eggs of shore fly are white and are usually laid on surfaces where algae is growing. *Photo: John Davidson*

Fig. 4.19 Pupae of shore flies are generally found in the area where the larvae were feeding. Note the forked spiracles at the end of the puparium. *Photo: Dan Gilrein.*

Fig. 4.20 Adult *Hexacola hexatoma* shore fly larvae parasitoid. *Photo: John Sanderson*

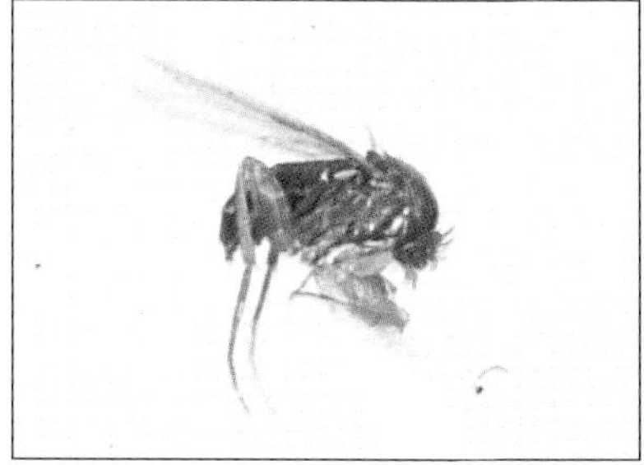

Fig. 4.21 The humpbacked fly has membranous wings and a humped thorax behind its head. *Photo: Stanton Gill*

Fig. 4.22 This moth fly adult on a blue sticky card shows the characteristic hairs on the wings. *Photo: Stanton Gill*

Fig. 4.23 The moth fly has long, 13-segmented antennae and hairs that appear fringed on the edges of its wings. *Photo: Richard Lindquist*

Humpbacked flies, family Phoridae. Humpbacked flies are so called because the body segment (thorax) behind the head is humped (fig. 4.21). The wings of humpbacked flies are membraneous. The larvae of humpbacked flies are white, maggotlike, and wedge shaped, without an obvious black head. Adult humpbacked flies normally scavenge on decaying plant material and animal matter. Adult females lay eggs on surfaces where decaying plant material is present. Of the other gnats and flies found in the greenhouse, humpbacked flies are the strongest fliers. Adults are often found on yellow sticky cards and misidentified as shore flies.

Moth flies or drain flies, family Psychodidae. Moth flies or drain flies are light tan brown. *Psychoda* species are the most common examples found in greenhouses. The distinct characteristic of body and wide wings densely covered with long hairs gives these flies a mothlike appearance, hence the common name *moth fly*. Another common name for *Psychoda* spp. is *drain fly* since the larval stage of the insect is often found feeding in drain systems.

The wings and body of *Psychoda* are tan brown. The antennae have 13 segments, each having a bulbous swelling with a whorl of long hairs (figs. 4.22, 4.23). Adult *Psychoda* are often attracted to sticky cards used for insect monitoring.

The larvae of moth flies feed on sediment, decaying vegetation, and microscopic plants and animals (fig. 4.25). The insect causes no injury to the plants in the greenhouse. Since larvae often feed within drainage tubes, regular cleaning with a stiff brush and drain cleaner should remove the gelatinous lining and sediment that the larvae feed on.

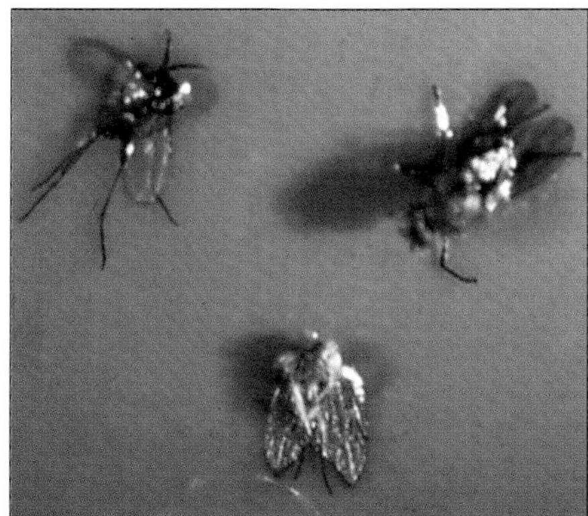

Fig. 4.24 A comparison of fungus gnat (*left*), moth fly (*right*), and shore fly (*center*) adults. *Photo: Stanton Gill*

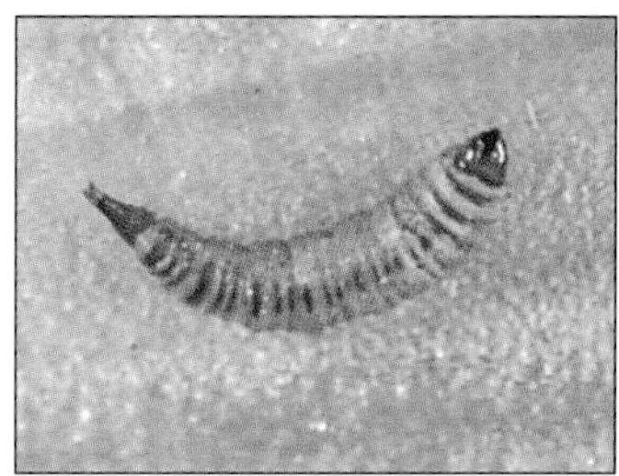

Fig. 4.25 Moth fly larvae feed on decaying vegetation. *Photo: Richard Lindquist*

CHAPTER 5

Leafminers

Numerous insects live and feed as immatures within leaves, including certain wasp, fly, moth, and beetle species, collectively called leafminers. The most common leafminer pests of greenhouse crops are tiny flies in the insect family Agromyzidae, which can cause serious crop losses, especially on chrysanthemum, gerbera, gypsophila, cineraria and many bedding plant species (fig. 5.1). Much information is now known about these pests as a result of the serious problems they caused in the 1980s in America and Europe.

Several species of leafminers are greenhouse pests elsewhere in the world but not currently in the United States (e.g., *Liriomyza bryoniae* and *L. strigata* are pests of vegetables in European greenhouses); these will not be discussed here in detail. The other insect species that create mines within leaves of ornamental crops generally occur outdoors in landscape settings and will not be discussed here.

General description

Damage

Leafminers primarily cause aesthetic damage to floral crops, although heavy infestations can reduce rates of photosynthesis. Damage is caused in two ways. First, small leaf punctures are made by egg-laying adult females, who feed from these punctures and sometimes lay an egg within them. Each puncture leaves a white speck, which, when numerous, are unsightly (fig. 5.2).

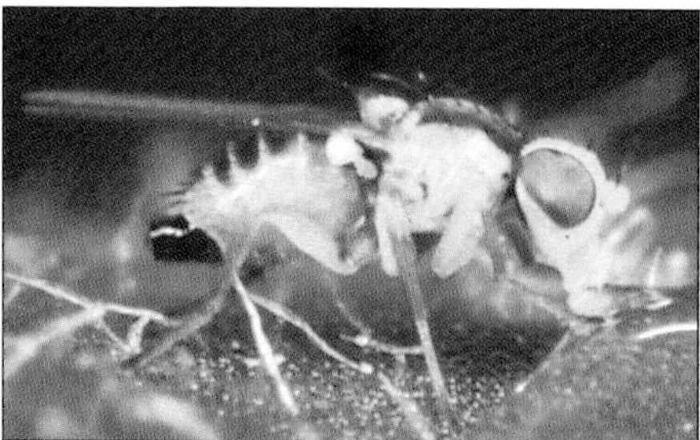

Fig. 5.1 *Liriomyza trifolii* leafminer adult with a bright yellow body and black patterns on thorax and abdomen. Note prominent, cannon-shaped ovipositor at the end of the abdomen. *Photo: Michael Parrella*

Fig. 5.2 Leafminer egg-laying punctures on mum foliage. *Photo: Michael Parrella*

Fig. 5.3 Serpentine leaf mines caused by *Liriomyza* larvae. *Photo: John Sanderson*

Fig. 5.4 Heavy leaf mine damage to mum. *Photo: Michael Parrella*

Fig. 5.5 Adult leafminers on leaf. Note small size and black and yellow coloration. *Photo: John Sanderson*

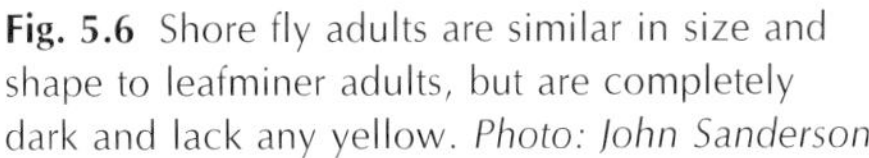

Fig. 5.6 Shore fly adults are similar in size and shape to leafminer adults, but are completely dark and lack any yellow. *Photo: John Sanderson*

Fig. 5.7 Leaf punctures and mines from leafminer on mum. *Photo: John Sanderson*

The larva (maggot) that emerges from the egg feeds within the leaf. As it tunnels through the leaf, it produces the unsightly, typically meandering mines that gives the pest its collective name *serpentine leafminers* (fig. 5.3). The mine becomes wider each time the maggot molts to the next instar (twice) (fig. 5.4).

Agriculture inspectors often look for leaf punctures as well as mines because these may contain living insects.

Group characteristics

Adult serpentine leafminers that are greenhouse pests are small (2.5 to 3.5 mm, .098 to .137 inches), yellowish black flies about the same size and shape of a shore fly adult, although shore flies have no yellow color (fig. 5.5, 5.6). The leaf mines begin from a leaf puncture and become wider as they randomly snake over the leaf surface. Most species mine only the top of the leaf, others mine the bottom, and some mine both (figs. 5.7, 5.8). The mines of some species are confined along main leaf veins.

The insects pupate within the last larval skin (called a puparium), which is brownish tan and shaped similar to a tiny gelatin capsule (fig. 5.9). Because pupation generally occurs in the soil, pupae are not usually noticed. If found, they are usually under the surface of the soil or under a pot. On some plants, such as gerbera, the insects may be unable to reach the soil, so pupae may be found on the leaf.

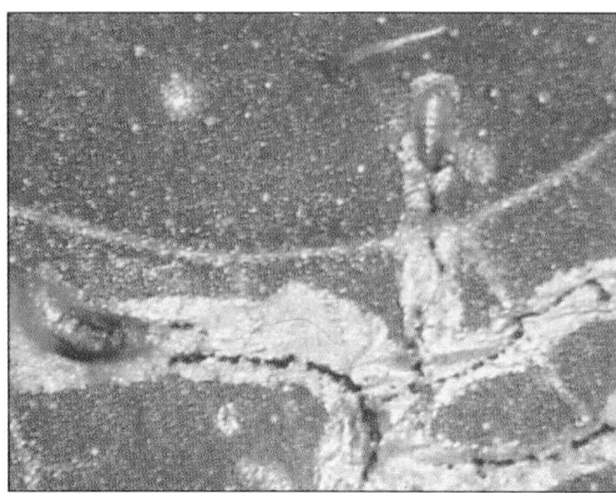

Fig. 5.8 Leaf mine up close, showing leafminer larvae within. *Photo: Michael Parrella*

Fig. 5.9 Leafminer puparia (pupal stage) are brown and capsule shaped. They usually pupate on the substrate below a plant. *Liriomyza huidobrensis* puparium (*bottom*) is larger than the *L. trifolii* (*top*). *Photo: Michael Parrella*

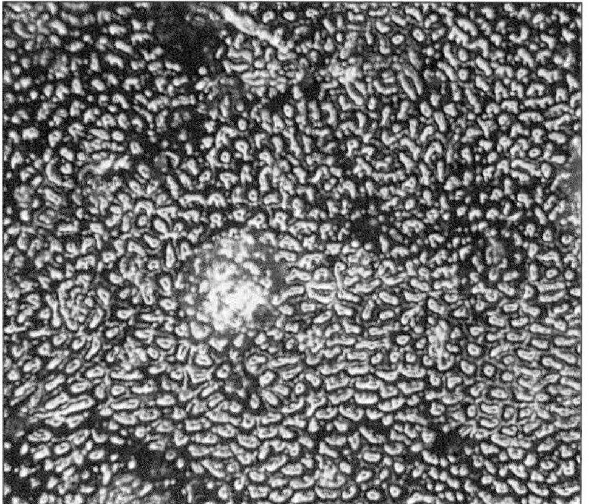

Fig. 5.10 Leaf punctures caused by a female *Liriomyza* ovipositor. *Photo: Michael Parrella*

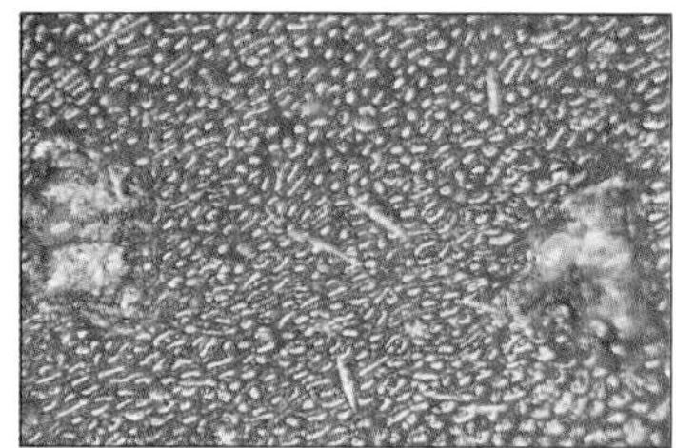

Fig. 5.11 Dissection of leaf punctures reveals whitish, oblong leafminer eggs. *Photo: Michael Parrella*

Biology

Eggs are generally deposited singly in the leaf in a puncture wound made by the adult female leafminer (figs. 5.10, 5.11). The larva hatches and begins mining within the leaf, passing through three instars (fig. 5.12). The last larval instar cuts a semicircular slit in the leaf and either falls to the ground to pupate or, in some species, pupates in the leaf (fig. 5.13). It seeks a dark place to pupate.

Adults emerge, mate, and live for three to four weeks. At approximately 26.7C (80F), the eggs hatch in three days, larval development takes five days, and the pupal stage lasts 10 days.

PEST IDENTIFICATION

Monitoring

Growers should ask suppliers or note which plant species and cultivars are susceptible to leafminer attack, then monitor these plants very closely. A scout or grower should become familiar with the characteristic leaf punctures and early leafmining damage to help in early detection. In some cases, early detection may enable some growers simply to remove infested leaves, preventing a more serious problem.

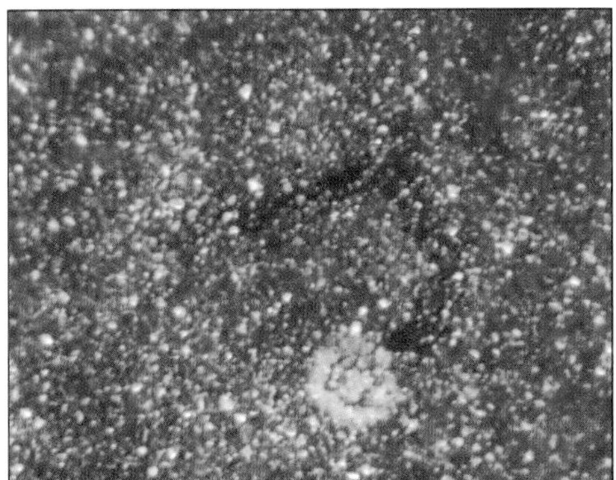

Fig. 5.12 After hatching from an egg laid in a whitish oviposition puncture, the larva begins to make a serpentine mine. *Photo: Michael Parrella*

Fig. 5.13 Yellow last instar leafminer larva and the hole it chewed from its mine to drop from the leaf to pupate. *Photo: Michael Parrella*

Fig. 5.14 *Liriomyza* leafminer adult captured on a yellow sticky card. Note black and yellow body and prominent cannon-shaped ovipositor. *Photo: John Sanderson*

Fig. 5.15 *Liriomyza trifolii* adult. Note that the black top of the thorax is dull rather than shiny. *Photo: Michael Parrella*

Yellow sticky cards attract adult leafminers and can be used to monitor adult activity. Place cards vertically just above the crop canopy, spaced about every 50 feet. If adults are detected on cards, the foliage of susceptible plants species located near the cards should be examined.

Research in California has led to statistically accurate procedures for sampling *L. trifolii* on chrysanthemum, including monitoring adult flies with yellow sticky cards and larvae with leaf samples (fig. 5.14). This information is used to time control tactics.

Species identification

Accurate identification of leafminers can be tricky. Some morphological and leafmining characteristics that distinguish between leafminer species are subtle and require a careful, trained eye. The following descriptions will be useful in most cases, but an expert should be consulted when definitive identification is required.

***Liriomyza trifolii* (Burgess)**. This most serious leafminer pest has no official common name (fig. 5.15). It infests many floral and vegetable crops, particularly species within the Compositae. It can often be confused with the vegetable leafminer, *Liriomyza sativae* (fig. 5.16). These two pests attack many of the same crops, but *L. sativae* does not infest chrysanthemum, which is a major plant host of *L. trifolii. Liriomyza sativae* is primarily a pest of vegetables.

Liriomyza trifolii appears generally paler in color, and the top of the thorax is grayish, rather than shiny black, as in *L. sativae*. Also, *L. trifolii* has a large area of yellow behind the eye, with two stout bristles both arising from this yellow area, while one of the two bristles of *L. sativae* arises from a small black area, and the other arises from a yellow area.

Pea leafminer, *Liriomyza huidobrensis* (Blanchard). Within the U.S., the pea leafminer is currently found in California and is a quarantined pest in many other states (fig. 5.17). Among floral crops, this leafminer attacks field-grown gypsophila and bedding plants such as primula and dianthus. Eggs are generally deposited near the base of the leaf petiole, and the mines often follow along the side of major leaf veins (fig. 5.18). The larvae usually mine the lower leaf surface, so some mines can be difficult to see from the upper leaf surface (figs. 5.19, 5.20).

Fig. 5.16 The vegetable leafminer, *Liriomyza sativae*. Note that the black top of the thorax is shiny. *Photo: Michael Parrella*

Fig. 5.17 The pea leafminer, *Liriomyza huidobrensis*, is larger and darker than *L. trifolii* and has more of an off-white than a yellow color. *Photo: Michael Parrella*

Fig. 5.18 Pea leafminer eggs are often laid near the leaf petiole, and mines follow along the sides of leaf veins. *Photo: Michael Parrella*

Fig. 5.20 Leaf mines of the pea leafminer as seen after turning over a leaf to look at the lower surface. *Photo: Michael Parrella*

Fig. 5.19 Mines of the pea leafminer are often not seen from the top of the leaf, because the larva mines the lower leaf surface. *Photo: Michael Parrella*

The pea leafminer can be distinguished from *L. trifolii* by both its appearance and its habits. The adult is generally larger and darker than *L. trifolii* and has more of an off-white than a yellow color. Pea leafminer larvae are often a mixture of yellow and white, while *L. trifolii* larvae are typically yellow (fig. 5.21). Finally, pea leafminer pupae are larger than *L. trifolii* pupae and have six to nine pores in the posterior spiracles, rather than three pores (see fig. 5.9).

Chrysanthemum leafminer, *Chromatomyia syngenesiae* Hardy. Although this species is the most common leafminer pest of chrysanthemums in England, it is rarely found on mums in the U.S. In California it is reported found on Marguerite daisy, cineraria, and many weed species.

It is easy to distinguish from the *Liriomyza* species. Adults are a dull gray, with many stout, black bristles over the body, and they have no yellow or off-white areas (fig. 5.22). Pupation occurs within the mine, not in the soil, and the spiracles of the pupa protrude from the mine (fig. 5.23).

Biological control

***Diglyphus* spp. *(D. isaea, D. intermedius,* and *D. begini),* family Eulophidae.** This commercially available wasp parasitizes late second- and third-instar leafminer larvae. The female wasp paralyzes the larva, then lays an egg near it. The hatching parasitoid is an ectoparasite, attaching itself to the larva host and feeding on it

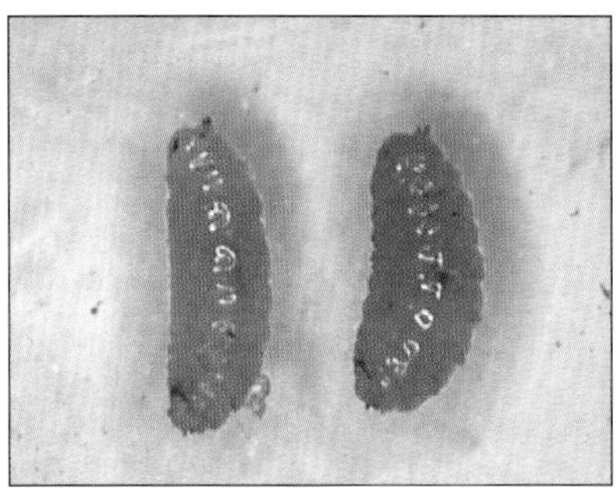

Fig. 5.21 Pea leafminer larvae (*left*) are often a mixture of yellow and white, while *L. trifolii* (*right*) are typically yellow. *Photo: Michael Parrella*

Fig. 5.22 The chrysanthemum leafminer is dull gray and has many stout, black bristles on the body. *Photo: Michael Parrella*

from outside the host's body. As it develops, it turns from being colorless and transparent to yellow to blue-green.

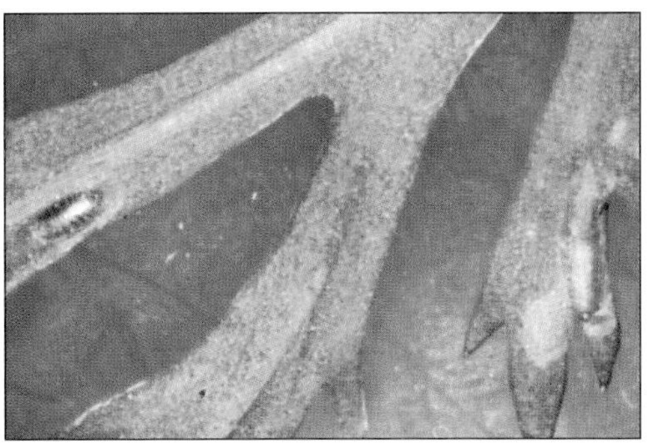

Fig. 5.23 Unlike the other leafminer pests of greenhouse crops, chrysanthemum leafminers pupate within the leaf mine. *Photo: Michael Parrella*

Pupation takes place in the mine a short distance from the host. The pupa is first green with red eyes, turning to black with red eyes, and it soon takes the shape of an adult wasp. The adult emerges by chewing a round hole in the upper surface of the leaf. This round hole demonstrates that a parasitoid emerged from the mine rather than a leafminer, which chews a semicircular slit in a leaf prior to dropping out of the leaf to pupate. The adult wasp is dark, with antennae that are just a little longer than the head, and the forewings have only a single vein, which runs along the leading edge of the wing.

***Dacnusa sibirica* (Hymenoptera), family Braconidae.** This is another commercially available leafminer parasitoid. It is an endoparasite; the female wasp lays an egg inside the first or second instar of the host. It is difficult to tell whether leafminer larvae are parasitized with *D. sibirica* unless they are dissected to reveal the parasitoid inside. The adult wasp is dark brown to black, has thread-like antennae about as long as the body, and has wing veins on the front half of the forewing.

CHAPTER 6

Mites

Mites have worldwide distribution and rival insects in the environmental diversity to which they have adapted. Fortunately, not all mites are destructive to plants. Some species are used for biological control, being predators of insects and other mites.

General description

Plant damage

A number of viruses transmitted by mites in several families have been reported for grain crops, vegetable crops, and fruit crops. The two-spotted spider mite may carry and excrete viruses, but it does not inject the causative agent during feeding. Several plant-pathogenic viruses have been suspected of being transmitted by mites, including rose rosette, a witches'-broom effect on infected plants, transmitted by eriophyid mite species.

Mites, like other organisms that move from plant to plant, can be agents in spreading fungal spores or other plant diseases. Because mites lack wings, unlike many insects, their involvement in the spread of disease is usually of minor importance. However, there are a few exceptions. Stewart's bud rot of carnations, caused by *Fusarium poae,* is spread by the eriophyid mite *Siteroptes cerealium.* It has been reported in the literature that the acarid *Rhizoglyphus echinopus,* the bulb mite, spreads bulb rot fungi, including *Fusarium, Pythium,* and *Rhizoctonia,* in lily, tuberose, flowering onion, and gladiolus.

Group characteristics

Mites are in the class Arachnida, which also includes scorpions, spiders, harvestmen, and other eight-legged arthropods. Mites are in the subclass Acari, differing from other arachnids by the lack of body segmentation.

Mites have two obvious body regions, the gnathosoma (mouthparts) and the idiosoma, the fused remainder of the body, bearing legs and reproductive structures. Mites that damage plant material in greenhouses and interiorscapes generally fall into one of five families: Acaridae (acarid mites), Eriophyidae (eriophyid mites), Tarsonemidae (tarsonemid mites), Tenuipalpidae (false spider mites), and Tetranychidae (spider mites).

Mites can be distinguished from insect pests by several external characteristics (fig. 6.1). Mites completely lack antennae and wings. Plant-feeding mites have forceplike or needlelike mouthparts, called *chelicerae.* These are pushed into plant tissue to obtain sap and cellular contents. While insects have six legs, the majority of adult mites have eight legs. Young, newly hatched mites, called larvae, have only three pairs of legs. After the larvae molt into nymphs and adults, they have eight legs.

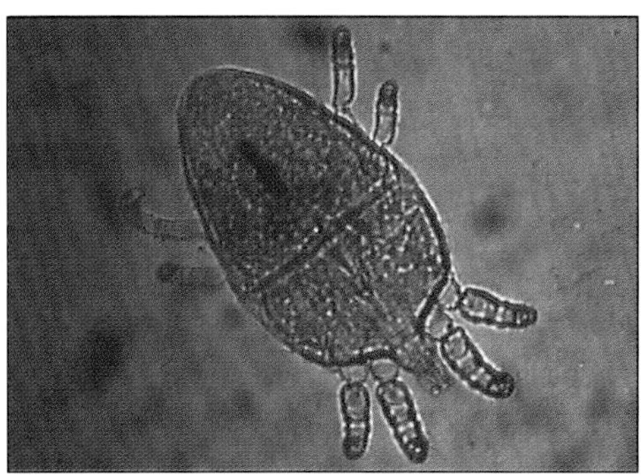

Fig. 6.1 A microscopic view (40x) of the false spider mite shows the short, thick legs and egglike body shape. *Photo: Gay Williams*

Biology

Mites can be carried on wind currents, arrive on infested plant material, carried on infested plant material relocated on a bench or in a bed, or carried on workers' clothing when workers contact mite-infested plants. When two-spotted mite (*Tetranychus urticae)* population levels are very high, gravid (pregnant) females migrate to the plant tips in an effort to disperse.

Monitoring

Yellow sticky cards are ineffective in monitoring for mites. Plants need to be sampled and foliage and stems examined closely using magnification such as a 10× hand lens. Tetranychid mites can be monitored by placing a sheet of white paper under foliage suspected to have mites feeding. The foliage is tapped sharply, and dislodged mites will be obvious on the sampling paper.

SPECIES IDENTIFICATION

Spider mites, family Tetranychidae

The tetranychidae mites are small in size, ranging from 0.2 mm to 0.4 mm (.007 to .015 inches) in length. Tetranychid mites develop through egg, larva, protonymph, deutonymph, and adult stages. Many spider mites thrive in hot, dry conditions and have short generation intervals, with the ability to continuously reproduce in the greenhouse and interiorscape environment. Tetranychid species inhabiting temperate regions usually enter a diapause (resting) stage during the winter months when temperatures and photoperiod decline. Diapause may take place either as fertilized females or as overwintering eggs.

The color of adult spider mite females generally varies between hibernating forms and actively feeding adults. In northern species the females are usually shades of green, while the southern species are shades of red. Hibernating *T. urticae* females are bright orange, sometimes confused with *P. persimilis,* unless examined carefully. Male tetranychids often appear similar to the nymphal stages, being smaller, slender, and shades of yellow.

The two-spotted spider mite, *Tetranychus urticae* Koch, is known by several common names in the greenhouse industry, including *red spider, greenhouse spider mite,* and *red spider mite.* These unofficial common names have often referred to a complex of web spinning mites that, besides *T. urticae,* also includes *Eotetranychus lewisi, E. cucurbitacearum, T. multisetus,* and *T. cinnabarinus.* Mites have been recorded on more than 150 host plant species, including many greenhouse crops.

We will describe the life cycles of three major tetranychid mites: *Tetranychus urticae* Koch, (two-spotted spider mite), *Tetranychus cinnabarinus* (Boisduval) (carmine spider mite), and *Eotetranychus lewisi* McGregor (Lewis mite).

Two-spotted spider mite, *Tetranychus urticae* Koch. The two-spotted spider mite is one of the most important arthropod pests of food and ornamental crops. It is by far the most common spider mite pest of greenhouse crops. It not only feeds on a wide variety of foliage and flowering greenhouse and interiorscape plants but also feeds on weeds, such as chickweed, wild mustard, oxalis, and henbit, that are found growing under greenhouse benches or in areas close to the greenhouse.

The mite pierces the epidermis of the host plant with its stylet-like mouthparts. Depending on the thickness of the leaf, the spongy mesophyll cells, and sometimes most cells in the lowest palisade layers are damaged. When the chloroplasts are sucked out, a

Fig. 6.2 Examination with a 10∞ hand lens reveals spider mite stippling very clearly. *Photo: Stanton Gill*

Fig. 6.3 Plants with nutrient deficiencies may, at first, appear to have mite injury. Here a poinsettia with magnesium deficiency shows damage that could be mistaken for mite injury. *Photo: Stanton Gill*

Fig. 6.4 As mite populations build to high levels, webbing will be formed over foliage, stems, and flowers. *Photo: Richard Lindquist*

Fig. 6.5 The webbing of mites is noticeable as sunlight highlights the silk between the leaves of this pittosporum. *Photo: John Sanderson*

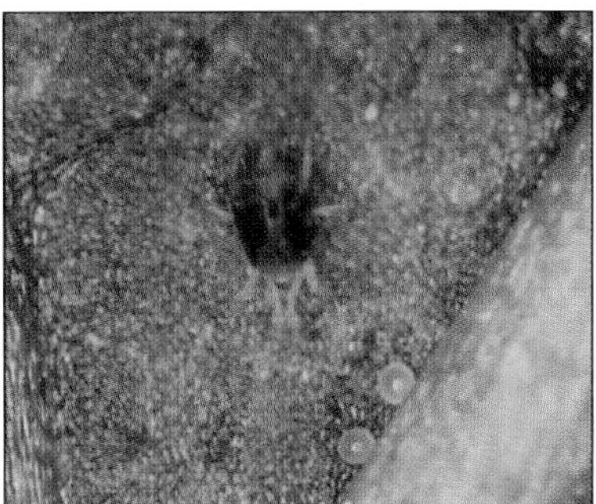

Fig. 6.6 Adult two-spotted spider mite—the large dark spots on either side make this mite easy to distinguish. *Photo: John Sanderson*

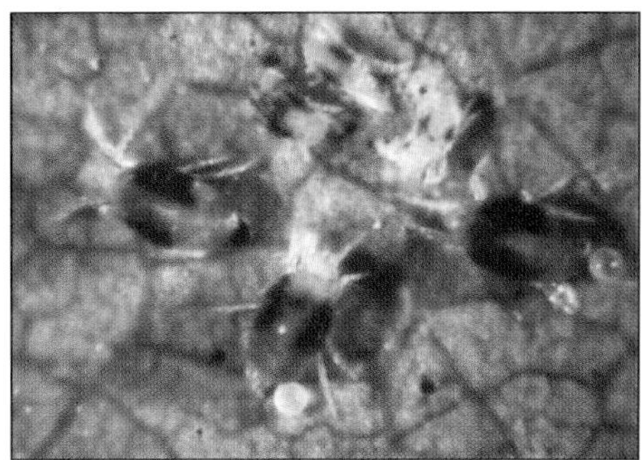

Fig. 6.7 Adult two-spotted spider mites have oval-shaped bodies with distinct black spots on the side. *Photo: Marilyn Steiner*

chlorotic spot (called a *stipple*) forms at each feeding site. Feeding usually causes a stippled effect to the foliage (fig. 6.2). Leaf browning may occur on susceptible plants when damage to mesophyll cells is extensive. A heavy infestation causes leaves to yellow and drop. Webs of the mites, in heavy infestations, may cover foliage and flowers (figs. 6.4, 6.5).

The name *two-spotted spider mite* is based on the one or two large, black spots seen on each side of the dorsal (top) surface (figs. 6.6, 6.7). Two-spotted spider mites usually colonize the lower leaf surface on most plants, but on some plant species, they may prefer to feed on the upper surface. When populations are high, two-spotted spider mites can be found on all leaf surfaces and stems. They prefer nitrogen-rich, young leaves, but in well established colonies older leaves become heavily infested. As the population develops, the mites usually spin sufficient webbing to cover the entire plant.

The optimum temperature for development is 30 to 32C (85 to 90F). At this temperature a complete life cycle, egg to adult, can be completed in eight to 12 days. The average life span of adult females is approximately 30 days, during which the average number of eggs laid by a female is 90 to 200. The spherical eggs are transparent when first laid and mature to straw yellow before hatching. The mite larvae have six legs and are pale green to light yellow. They develop into eight-legged protonymphs, then finally deutonymphs, which are pale green to brownish green. The large, black spots may be evident on some deutonymphs. The latter molt into adults.

In outdoor environments and occasionally in greenhouses, two-spotted spider mite populations have an overwintering diapause that cannot be broken without a certain period of time having elapsed. This resting diapause stage is initiated by shortened periods of light, decreased temperatures, and unfavorable food supplies. These overwintering females turn yellowish orange, stop feeding and egg laying, leave the host plants, and hibernate on the ground under leaf litter, in cracks and crevices, or in other protected locations.

Carmine spider mite, *Tetranychus cinnabarinus* (Boisduval). In semitropical areas the carmine spider mite is a pest of low-growing plants. This mite is well adapted to greenhouse and interiorscape environments, where it will continue activity throughout the winter without a diapause (resting stage).

The carmine spider mite is very closely related to the two-spotted spider mite but was separated from it in 1968 because of differences in morphology, habits, host preferences, and crossbreeding results. The immature stages of carmine spider mite and two-spotted spider mite cannot be distinguished. During the summer, though, the adult stage of the carmine spider mite is more brick red or carmine in color than the two-spotted spider mite, but the color varies with the host plant the mites are feeding on.

The damage caused by the carmine spider mite is distinctly different from that caused by the two-spotted spider mite. Infested leaves turn chlorotic, with small, transparent lesions. Bright yellow patches develop, eventually turning dark, with heavily infested leaves dropping.

Carmine spider mite eggs are deposited singly, directly on the undersides of leaves. The number of eggs laid and duration of life stages is similar to those of the two-spotted spider mite. Because the carmine spider mite reproduces throughout the year in greenhouses, there may be 20 generations per year. The optimum temperature for development is 31 to 32C (88 to 90F). Control methods for carmine spider mite are similar to those for two-spotted spider mite.

Lewis mite, *Eotetranychus lewisi* (McGregor). Most species of *Eotetranychus* inhabit trees, shrubs, and citrus trees. The Lewis mite has been reported feeding on greenhouse poinsettias in the southwestern United States, Michigan, Ohio, Massachusetts, California, and Washington State. In central America and Mexico, it has been found damaging papaya and citrus. The damage from this pest looks very much like two-spotted spider mite damage, with stippling of foliage, webbing, and yellowing of foliage in severe infestations (figs. 6.8, 6.9). The Lewis mite's webbing is not as extensive as that of the two-spotted spider mite.

The Lewis mite looks similar to the two-spotted spider mite (fig. 6.10). The distinguishing external characteristics can be seen only on slide-mounted specimens with the aid of a compound microscope. The Lewis mite is a tiny, slender, straw-colored or somewhat greenish mite with several small spots along each side of the body (fig. 6.11).

The mite egg is pearl colored, globular in shape, and with a short stalk on top. The life cycle from egg to adult in greenhouses averages 12 to 14 days. Females oviposit two or three eggs per day during an approximately 30-day life span.

Fig. 6.8 Seen from a distance, spider mite injury to foliage appears similar to a nitrogen deficiency. *Photo: Stanton Gill*

Fig. 6.9 Examining the foliage up close will show the typical stippling injury of spider mite. *Photo: Stanton Gill*

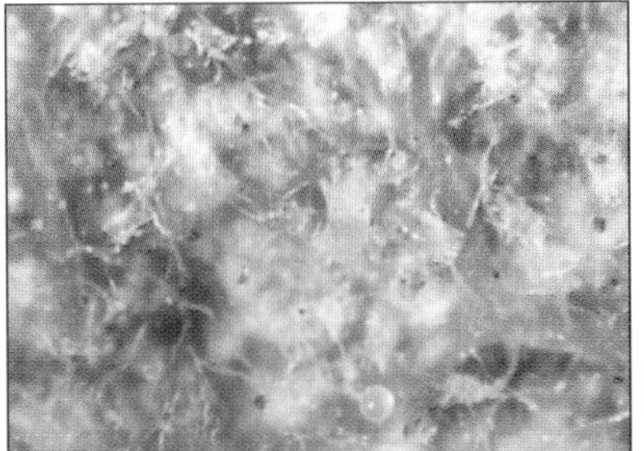

Fig. 6.10 The Lewis mite is straw colored and similar in body shape to the two-spotted spider mite. Eggs are round. *Photo: Stanton Gill*

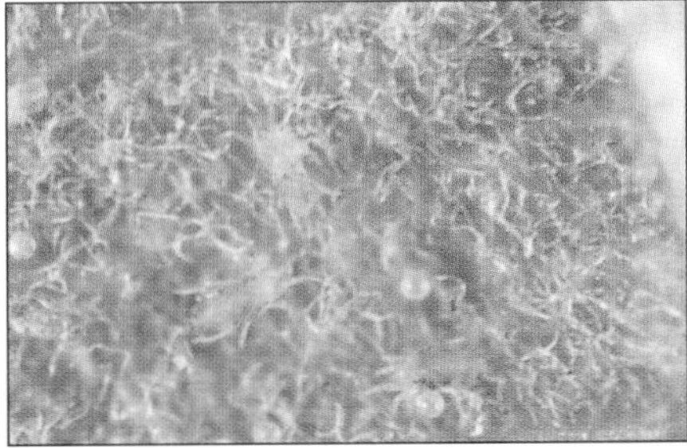

Fig. 6.11 Adult Lewis mites have eight legs, and larvae have six legs. *Photo: Stanton Gill*

Tarosonemid mites, family Tarsonemidae

Mites in the family Tarsonemidae are minute (smaller than 0.2 mm, .007 inches). A greenhouse manager will notice damage caused by these mites before actually seeing them. A pocket magnifier microscope with at least 30× is needed to see the mites.

Most species damaging plants are colorless, and they are often translucent. The outer cuticle is hard and shiny, and there are relatively few setae (hairs) on the body, compared to other plant-damaging mites. Not only are male tarsonemid mites smaller than females of the same species, but their general body contours are often markedly different. The females are generally ovoid in shape, while the males are more elongate oval. Both males and females are flattened in profile, a body configuration that makes these mites quite able to feed in confined spaces, such as in bulb sheaths, between surfaces of unexpanded leaves, or near leaf buds.

Adult females move about on three pairs of legs, with the fourth pair being reduced to very thin segments. Males rarely use their hind legs for walking. They often carry their hind legs in a semierect position above and behind the body, where they transport females that are transforming into adults.

Females that are unfertilized lay eggs that hatch only into males. Eggs are laid singly by gravid (egg-bearing) females. The eggs tend to be large compared to the size of the adult. Some eggs, such as from the cyclamen mite, *Phytonemus pallidus,* are white, ovoid, and smooth. Other eggs, such as from broad mite, *Polyphagotarsonemus latus,* have the egg surface covered by numerous white tubercles.

The optimum environment for tarsonemid mites is a combination of high humidity, warm temperatures, and low light intensities. Some species inject a toxin during feeding, causing leaf or stem tissue to deform into twisted or gnarled growth. Dispersion of tarsonemid mites in the greenhouse may occur when infested plants are used for propagation. Bulb scale mites spread onto new bulbs while still in storage.

In nature most tarsonemid species feed on fungi or algae and do not feed on higher plants. The two species known to feed on greenhouse and interiorscape plants are *Phytonemus pallidus* and *Polyphagotarsonemus latus.*

Cyclamen mite, *Phytonemus pallidus* (Banks). The cyclamen mite, *Phytonemus pallidus,* causes injury to cyclamen, gerbera, begonia, African violet, ivy, snapdragon, chrysanthemum, larkspur, fuschia, geranium, petunia, daisy, watercress, and strawberry. This mite is widely distributed, being reported in North America, Hawaii, Europe, and Asia. The feeding damage is exhibited in buds and flowers that are distorted and often stunted (fig. 6.12). Leaf buds of badly infested plants are sometimes completely destroyed. On gerbera the cyclamen mite causes bronzed patches along the midrib and slight curling of the foliage. Flowers of gerbera are attacked in the bud, causing the flower rays to become deformed. On cyclamen and African violet, where it is commonly found, the mite causes rosettes of stunted, distorted leaves at the crown of the plant.

Adults and larvae of cyclamen mite both occur in hidden areas on plants. They appear to avoid direct light, and they require humidity levels near saturation, which is found between tightly packed, young leaves or around flower buds.

Female cyclamen mites lay eggs in clusters of two to three eggs, usually between young leaves of the bud or at the crown of the plant (fig. 6.13). Each female lays 10 to 40 eggs over a 12- to 16-day life cycle. Eggs are white, ovoid, and smooth (fig. 6.14) and hatch in three to seven days at average greenhouse temperature. The larva is white in color and has six legs, with microscopic claws and suction cups. There is a quiescent stage for about two to seven days, when it looks like a swollen, immobile larva. Adult females are yellowish. The legs are often colorless to yellowish brown. With

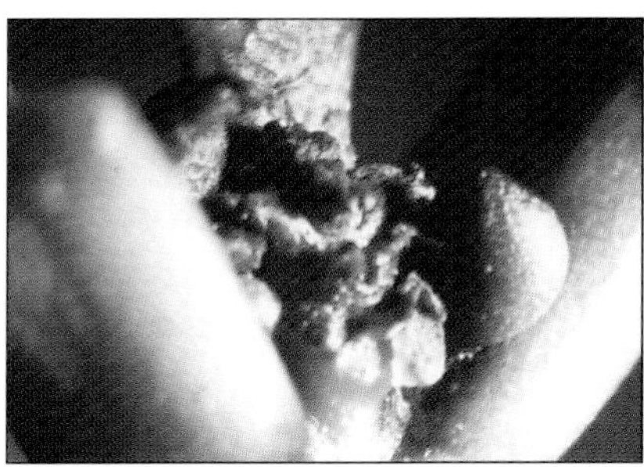

Fig. 6.12 Cyclamen mite injury shows on tip growth of kalanchoe plant. *Photo: Stanton Gill*

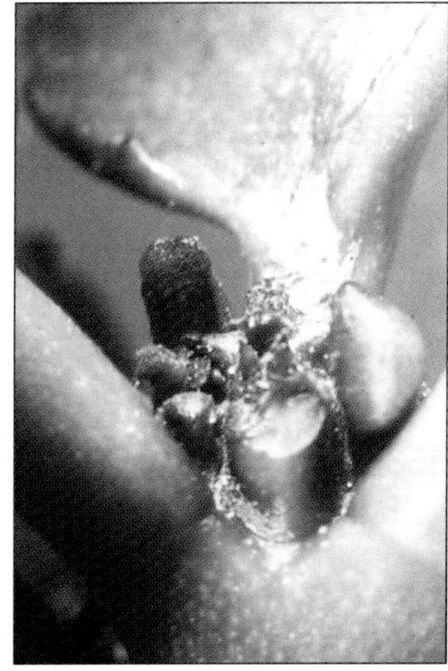

Fig. 6.13 Cyclamen mites hide in small, cryptic areas of plant parts causing feeding injury that results in distorted growth. *Photo: Stanton Gill*

their semierect hind legs, males often pick up and transport females that are transforming into adults. Female cyclamen mites can reproduce without mating (parthenogenetically).

The cyclamen mite is very difficult to control since its habitat is in tight, confined parts on the plant. Early detection of damage symptoms and subsequent destruction of infested plants is the best course of action that a greenhouse manager can take. Damage to the plant is already done when the symptoms are observed, and the mites may be gone at this point. See the "Biological control" section about predatory mites for information on natural enemies of cyclamen mites, particularly *Neoseiulus cucumeris.*

Broad mite, *Polyphagotarsonemus latus* (Banks). The broad mite is distributed throughout the tropical regions of the world and is also known as the yellow tea mite, yellow jute mite, broad rust mite, and tropical mite. In interiorscapes the broad mite injures mango, schefflera and papaya. In greenhouses broad mite has been reported injuring gerbera, African violet, cyclamen, zinnia, snapdragon, begonia, dahlia, azalea, impatiens, lantana, marigold, peperomia, and verbena. When feeding on gerbera and impatiens, the mite feeds almost entirely on the lower leaf surface, causing the leaf to become rigid and rolled under at the leaf edge. As the leaf ages, it may split or crack open. On some plants, the foliage appears crinkled, followed by blister patches. Severely infested plants stunt and die. The curling and twisted growth is caused by toxins in the salivary secretions from the mite. The injury persists after the mite is gone.

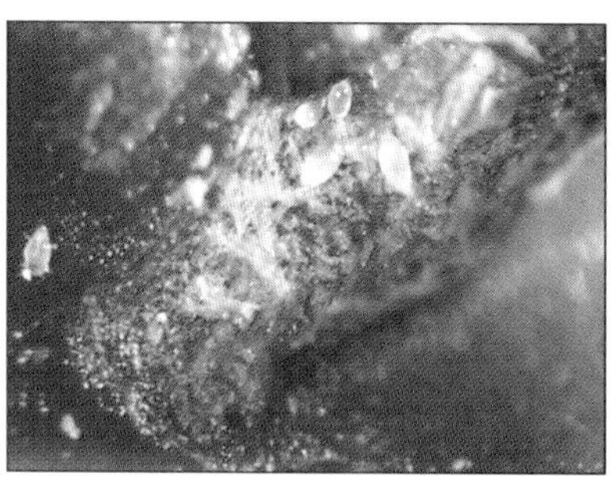

Fig. 6.14 Cyclamen mite eggs are white, ovoid, and smooth. *Photo: Stanton Gill*

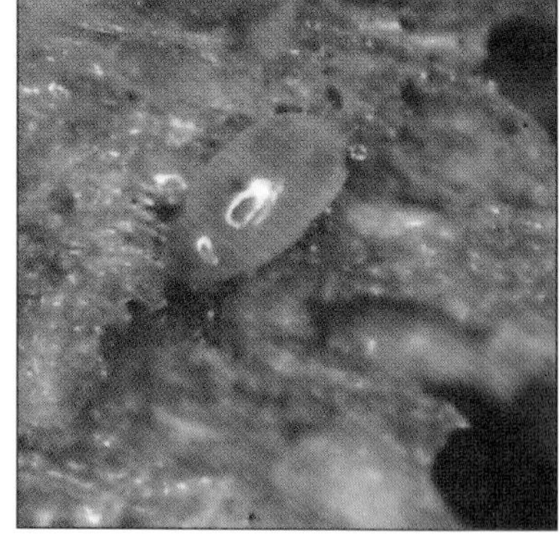

Fig. 6.15 Bulb mite adults appear smooth and creamy white to translucent color. *Photo: Mark Ascerno*

Like the cyclamen mite, the male broad mite has modified, semierect rear legs that it uses to pick up and carry maturing females. Males often carry females to new leaves or plants. Females lay 30 to 70 eggs over an eight- to 14-day period. The egg is usually oval, and about 0.8 mm (.031 inches) long, with the surface covered with tubercles (bumps). The egg hatches in two to four days, and a six-legged larva emerges. It moves very slowly and in two to five days becomes quiescent (resting). Adult males pick up quiescent females and carry them until they become sexually mature.

Control of this mite is difficult. Like with cyclamen mite, infested plants should be identified quickly and destroyed before the mites disperse themselves throughout the greenhouse or interiorscape.

Acarid mites, family Acaridae

Bulb mites, *Rhizoglyphus echinopus* (Fumouze and Robin). *Rhizoglyphus echinopus* adults are 0.5 to 1.0 mm (.019 to .039 inches) in length and have eight legs. The body of the adult bulb mite is shiny white to almost translucent (fig. 6.15). The short legs of the bulb mite are reddish brown (fig. 6.16).

Females lay 100 to 150 white, elliptical eggs on the bulb surface or near injured bulb or rhizome tissue. The larval stage that hatches from the egg is oval and white with six legs. Bulb mites then go through three eight-legged stages which are called protonymph, deutonymph, and tritonymph before reaching the adult stage. A complete life cycle from egg to adult takes 10 to 14 days.

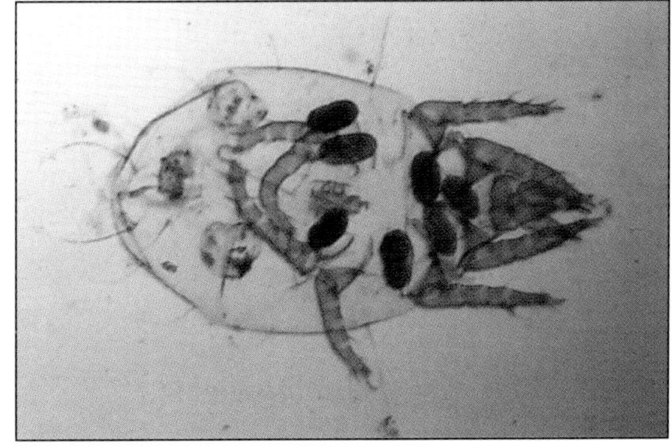

Fig. 6.16 Bulb mite (100x) adults have short legs and relatively few short hairs on the body. *Photo: John Davidson*

Rhizoglyphus echinopus has been recorded feeding on tuberose, lily, hyacinth, tulip, gladiolus, freesia, Dutch iris, narcissus, and orchid. The mite has been found in bulb crops throughout North America, Canada, Japan, and Europe. Bulb mites are easily transported on shipments of bulbs and tubers. The mite may spread among bulbs in storage.

Low populations of the mite cause stunting or off-color growth. Severely infested bulbs will fail to produce new growth. Bulb mite feeding often provides a wound entry site for pathogenic fungi, such as *Rhizoctonia, Pythium,* and *Fusarium. R. echinopus* may penetrate lily stems, causing the stems to become brittle (figs. 6.17, 6.18).

See the "Biological control" section about natural predators of bulb mites, especially *Hypoaspis miles.*

False spider mites, family Tenuipalpidae

False spider mites are very tiny, red-brown, and slow moving. Most species usually feed on plant leaves near the midribs or veins. Some species feed on the bark of plants, some in the flowers, and some are specialized, causing plant galls.

***Brevipalpus* spp.** Several species of *Brevipalpus* mites attack greenhouse crops, including *B. californicus, B. obovatus, B. chilensis, B. lewsii, B. lilium, B. oncidii,* and *B. phoenicis.* Individual mites of *Brevipalpus* spp. tend to lie flat on leaf surfaces and move slowly, making them difficult to detect. The body's red color is detectable against green foliage, though, and cast skins are usually evident. The eggs are elliptical, bright red, and stuck to the leaf during oviposition.

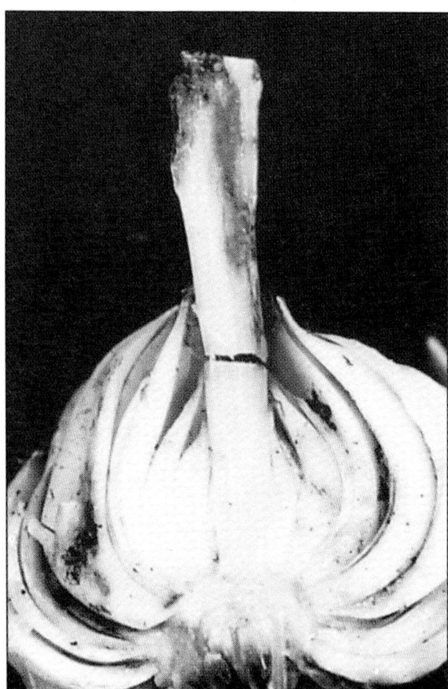

Fig. 6.17 Bulb mite injury to lily bulb. *Photo: Mark Ascerno*

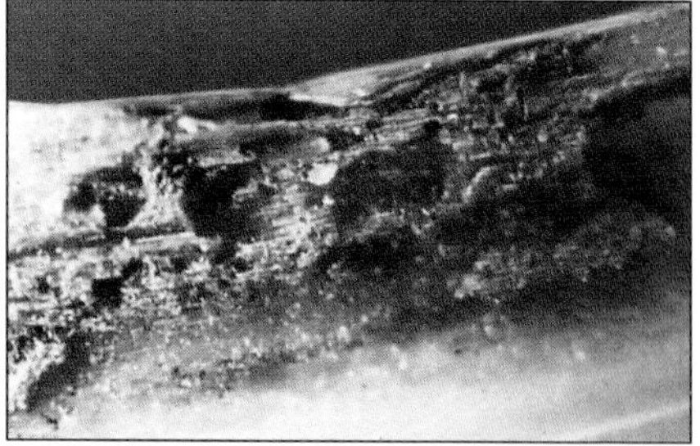

Fig. 6.18 Bulb mite feeding causes necrotic tissue on a bulb stem near the soil line. *Photo: Mark Ascerno*

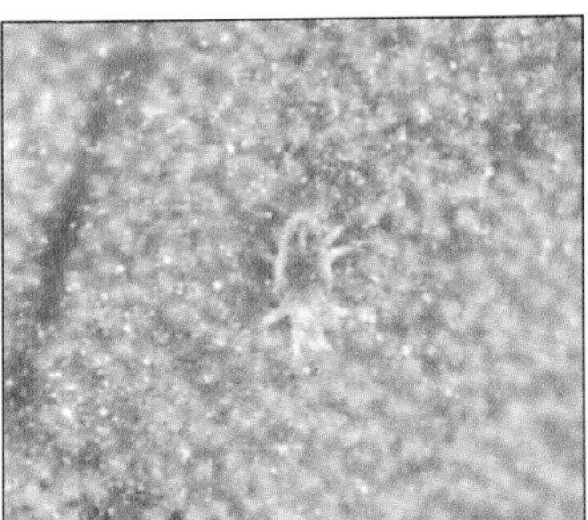

Fig. 6.19 False spider mite adult body is a red-brown color. *Photo: Stanton Gill*

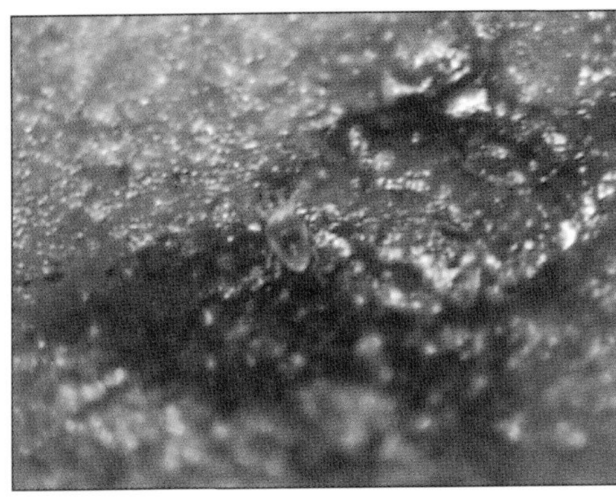

Fig. 6.20 False spider mite with feeding injury on a leaf. *Photo: Gay Williams*

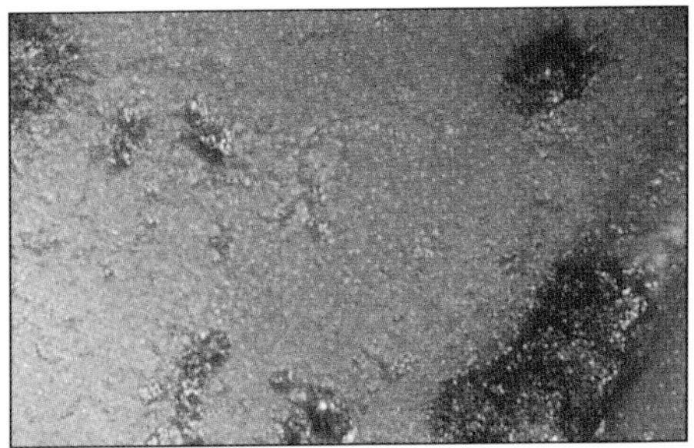

Fig. 6.21 False spider mite injury may appear as raised blistering of necrotic tissue. *Photo: Gay Williams*

The larvae are dull red, but after feeding a characteristic black pattern usually forms. The adult female resembles the larva in color, but the male does not have a black pattern (fig. 6.19).

Brevipalpus mite feeding causes leaf patches of silvery color, which frequently become sunken and brown (figs. 6.20, 6.21). A wide variety of ornamental plants, including citrus, are damaged by the feeding activity of this mite. The mite feeds on all parts of the orchid.

Privet mite, *Brevipalpus obovatus* Doonadieu. *Brevipalpus obovatus* feeds on over 50 species of ornamental plants, including citrus and privet. The egg of *B. obovatus* is elliptical and bright orange to red. Just before hatching, the egg's outer layer assumes an opaque, white appearance. The larvae and nymphs are orange to red. The adult females vary in color, ranging from orange to dark red, with various patterns of pigmentation. Females of this mite produce female offspring parthenogenetically and males are rarely found. The mites reproduce throughout the year in greenhouses.

Eriophyid mites, family Eriophyidae

Eriophyid mites are known as gall, rust, bud, and blister mites, based on the type of injury they cause to plants. Eriophyids, among the tiniest known arthropods, are almost invisible to the unaided eye. They are one of the most specialized groups of exclusively plant-feeding mites. The various species have a narrow range of acceptable plant hosts species, feeding on only a few closely related species or genera of plants. Several species of eriophyid mites, such as *Eriophyes tulipae, E. hibisci, E. dianthi, E. georghioui, E. paradianthi,* attack greenhouse crops, including carnation, tulip bulbs, hibiscus, chrysanthemum, star cactus, and some aloe.

They are unique among mites because they have only two pairs of legs; no other mite has just two pairs of legs at any stage of its development. These mites are wormlike or spindle shaped, with two body sections, the gnathosoma (mouthparts) and the idiosoma (remainder of the body) (fig. 6.22).

Fig. 6.22 Eriophyid mites are sausage shaped with only four legs. They are exceptionally tiny; these mites are viewed under high magnification of a dissection microscope. *Photo: Richard Lindquist*

***Eriophyes aloinis* Keifer.** *Eriophyes aloinis* is a slender, purple, wormlike mite. This mite lives in small crevices on the host plant. Mite-affected plants have a proliferation of irregular outgrowths clustered densely together, often clustered in leaf axils. The bases of leaf axils develop wartlike growths that appear lumpy and rough looking. The mites can attack the flower and cause galled blooms. This eriophyid mite attacks goldentooth aloe, spider aloe, and star cactus or wart plant. There are no known natural enemies for this mite.

Biological control

Predatory mites

Common in soil, moss, animal waste products and plant foliage, predaceous mites feed on small arthropods, such as mite pests, or

Fig. 6.23 The two-spotted spider mite predator, *Phytoseiulus persimilis*, is orange to reddish in color with long legs. *Photo: Stanton Gill*

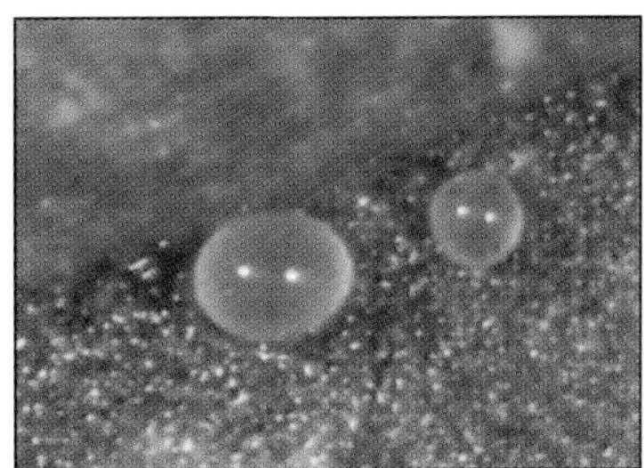

Fig. 6.24 The eggs of *Phytoseiulus persimilis* differ from two-spotted spider mite eggs. *P. persimilis* eggs are oblong, slightly orange, and almost twice as large as two-spotted spider mite eggs, which are spherical. *Photo: John Sanderson*

their eggs. Ground forms are commonly long-legged, fast-moving mites equipped with long, narrow chelicerae.

Family Phytoseiidae. This mite family contains some of the most important natural enemies of spider mites (family Tetranychmidae). These predators are long legged and fast and prey on plant-feeding mites and their eggs generally. They are usually tan colored, except for *Phytoseiulus* species, which are orange.

Phytoseiulus persimilis Athias-Henriot is specialized to feed exclusively on tetranychid mites (figs. 6.23, 6.24). This beneficial predatory mite, readily available from commercial insectories, has successfully controlled two-spotted spider mite in greenhouses, interiorscapes, and nursery situations.

P. longipes and *P. macropilis,* almost morphologically (physically) identical to *P. persimilis,* are more tolerant of high temperatures, so they are often released in warm greenhouses. The predaceous *P. macrophilis* sometimes moves into unsprayed greenhouses from outside in its native Florida.

***Amblyseius (=Neoseiulus)* spp.** This genus of generalist predaceous mites is known to feed on various mite pests as well as thrips and pollen. *Neoseiulus californicus* is a straw-colored mite that feeds on Tetranychidae (spider) mites. *Amblyseius (=N.) cucumeris* and *Iphiseius (=A.) degenerans* also feed on spider mites, but their use in the greenhouse needs further investigation. *A. cucumeris* Oudemans is commercially available mainly to control first- and second-instar thrips, but it has successfully controlled cyclamen mite on strawberries. Again, additional field research needs to be conducted to determine its best greenhouse applications.

***Hypoapsis miles* Berlese.** This general-feeder predator of arthropods is a fairly common inhabitant of North American soil (see fig. 1.28). Both the immature and adult mites prefer to feed on larval bulb mites, consuming up to 30 of these pests a day. *H. miles* is available commercially, but data are still needed on such factors as release rates for effective control.

Metaseiulus occidentalis. This predator has also been employed for spider mite control.

Predatory insects

Several general predators used for greenhouse arthropod control will feed on spider mites, in particular. The diet of minute pirate bugs, *Orius* spp., consists of thrips, aphids, and spider mites. Lacewing larvae also feed on spider mites, but they probably are not the most efficient predators for this purpose.

CHAPTER 7

Scale Insects and Mealybugs

Scale insects often go undetected because their small size, sessile lifestyle, and protective coloration enable them to blend in with bark or appear as naturally occurring parts of foliage and stems. Several scale species commonly infest greenhouse and conservatory plant material. Many turn up on plants imported directly from tropical areas. Though most scale insects are found on woody foliage plants, a few species are found infesting herbaceous plants, such as ferns and coleus.

There are presently approximately 6,000 described species of scale insects in the world, representing 20 families. About three-quarters of these species produce a protective waxy covering, which can vary from soft, fluffy, white wax to a hard, shell-like covering. The majority of scale pests that attack greenhouse and conservatory plants are found in the armored scale (Diaspididae), soft scale (Coccidae), mealybug (Pseudococcidae), and Magarodid scale (Magarodidae) families. In some cases cover detail and host plant species may be used to identify the genus or species of scale insect. In most cases, however, the scale insect must be chemically treated and mounted on a microscope slide for identification by a specialist.

Scale insects can be distinguished by the presence of one claw on each leg, instead of two, as are found on all other insects. Scales of all families have three life stages: egg, nymph, and adult. All scale species have an active crawler (first-instar nymph) stage, but over half the species spend the majority of their nymphal instars and adult life stages as sessile, or permanently attached, plant parasites. Some species of mealybugs, soft scales, and scales in the family

Margarodidae (cottony cushion scale) are mobile in nymphal and adult stages.

All female scale insects are wingless. In the armored scale family, the female is sedentary and protected by a hard wax cover (sometimes called a shield or test) when mature. Female scales feed throughout their development. There are three instars in female armored scales, three or four instars in female soft scales, and four instars in female mealybugs. Adult females live from weeks to months, depending on the number of generations per year for each species. Under greenhouse conditions reproduction is continuous and dependent on temperature.

Adult male scale insects, when present, are very delicate, gnatlike insects with two wings that live only 24 to 48 hours. All male scales have five instars, but they feed in only the first two instars and generally do less damage than the female.

GENERAL DESCRIPTION

Plant damage

Scale insects feed on plants through a long stylet (strawlike mouthpart), which is inserted into the plant. Armored scales damage plants by piercing plant tissue and sucking up cell contents from stems or leaves, depending on the species. Armored scales do not produce honeydew. Soft scales and mealybugs feed on phloem sap and therefore produce honeydew. Early damage symptoms of armored scale feeding are chlorosis of the foliage immediately surrounding the feeding site of each scale. If many scales are present, this may be followed by browning and defoliation. Plants severely infested with scale species feeding through bark may show slow dieback, leaf shedding, and general unthriftiness. Honeydew deposits are usually the first signs of feeding by soft scale and mealybugs. Environmental stress from excess or lack of water, or cultural factors such as high temperature or light may intensify scale feeding injury. Research on landscape plants indicates that fertilization with high rates of nitrogen fertilizer increases the number of eggs female scales lay and the survivability of their offspring. Scale-infested trees may continue to survive for several months, even years, looking less attractive each year, until they die.

Group characteristics

The only certain way to identify a scale insect correctly is to send it to a specialist. However, with practice, it is possible to identify some of the most common species without making microscopic slide mounts. The shape and color of the scale insect (and cover, if present), the host plant, and the scale's location on the plant are probably the most useful factors in identifying a species of scale in the greenhouse. Some scale species are known to prefer certain plant genera or families of plants, which usually makes identification easier.

Identifications are primarily made from female scale insects; males are rarely used for identification. The best time to identify female soft scales is when they are fully enlarged and laying eggs. Many scale species, especially soft scales, exhibit characteristic color patterns at this stage. Colors and patterns of soft scales fade after eggs are laid. Soon after, the female soft scales die and their bodies become a hardened cover protecting the eggs that lie under them.

Armored scales can be distinguished from other scales by the presence of a wax cover, which can be removed from the female's body using a probing needle. The armored scale cover may remain on the host, even after the male or female insect dies, and its shape and color may be diagnostic. In some genera the male cover is different in shape and color from the female armored scale cover. Adult female armored scales are legless.

The most distinguishing characteristic of Magarodid scales, such as the cottony cushion scale, is the large, elongated, cottony white egg sac that protrudes from the posterior end of the female. Another characteristic is that all nymphs and adults are mobile.

Mealybugs and soft scales retain their legs throughout life. The bodies of mealybugs are always soft. The most diagnostic characteristic is that the body is covered with white, granular or cottonlike wax. The shape and number of marginal wax filaments are sometimes used as visual clues for identifying species of mealybug. Another helpful feature of many mealybugs is that eggs are usually laid in white, cottony material under the female. Mealybugs can sometimes be identified by their host plants and the number and length of marginal white wax projections. Location on the plant may also be helpful in the identification process. Root mealybugs have no marginal wax projections and are found feeding on the roots of plants.

If there is no separate cover or powdery white wax attached to the body of the scale insect, the chances are that it is a soft scale. Soft scale females must be alive and mature to show characteristic color patterns.

SPECIES IDENTIFICATION

Identification of the scale species is absolutely necessary to determine its life cycle if the plant material is growing outdoors. This information is also used to determine whether biological control is an option. If you choose to use chemical control, life cycle information will enable you to determine which pesticide to select and the optimum time to apply it. Life cycle information becomes less important in greenhouses and interiorscapes, where plants are kept at even temperatures over a year or longer time period. Over long periods indoors, scale generations often overlap, and all stages will be present at the same time.

Monitoring

Early detection, identification, and elimination of scale insects is the best management approach. Since many scale insects have covers that enable them to blend in with plant parts, detection may require close inspection using a 10× hand lens. If new plants are being moved into the greenhouse or interiorscape, they should be closely inspected prior to coming into contact with clean plants. Examine a small number of plants thoroughly on their upper and lower leaf surfaces, leaf axils, buds, and stems. If scales are found, expand the sample to exclude all infested plants for treatment before placing them with uninfested plants.

The presence of honeydew and sooty mold is a good indication of the presence of soft scales and mealybugs. Ants and wasps will feed on honeydew, and their presence on plants can be a good indicator of soft scale or mealybug infestation.

Armored scale insects are generally more difficult to detect, with many species having coverings that blend in with the plant tissue. Plant parts, such as woody lenticels, or disease structures can be mistaken for armored scale insects. If the plant is suspected to be infested with an armored scale, use a small needle probe and see if you can pop off the cover, revealing a yellow-, pink-, or orange-bodied scale. If the scale is dead, the body may be brown or black in color and appear shriveled and dry.

Soft scales, family Coccidae

In the greenhouse some female soft scales reproduce parthenogenetically, without males (asexually). Females produce 50 to 1,000 eggs or live young, depending on the species. The crawlers (first instar) that hatch are mobile for 12 to 24 hours. The crawlers have antennae and legs. At this stage they can move to new parts of the plant or be dispersed by wind currents.

When the soft scale is feeding on leaves, its cover tends to be wide and almost round. When feeding on slender twigs, the cover tends to be narrower and more elliptical.

All soft scale insects excrete a sugary, sticky honeydew, which adheres to the foliage and stems of plants. A black, sooty mold often grows on the honeydew.

Many parasites and predators attack soft scale, but only a few have been investigated for use in greenhouses and are readily available from commercial insectories. For example, the wasp *Metaphycus alberti* has been very effective in controlling brown soft scale and long brown scale, and the mealybug destroyer feeds on soft scale if it can't find mealybugs.

Black scale, *Saissetia oleae* (Olivier). Like many of the soft scale insects, the shape of the adult black scale is quite variable, depending on the plant species it is feeding on. The adult female is brown to deep black, usually elongate oval. The scale is 3 to 5 mm (.118 to .196 inches) long. Mature females of *Saissetia oleae* and two closely related species, *S. miranda* (Mexican black scale) and *S. neglecta* (Caribbean black scale), have raised ridges present in the form of the letter H on the back (fig. 7.1). This is one of the good field characteristics to narrow a scale down to these three species.

This soft scale is found on many greenhouse and interiorscape woody plants such as *Fatsia japonica, Nerium oleander, Pittosporum, Citrus,* and *Hibiscus.*

Barnacle scale, *Ceroplastes cirripediformis* Comstock. The barnacle scale is a member of a soft scale genus whose members are known as wax scales, being characterized by a thick, gummy wax

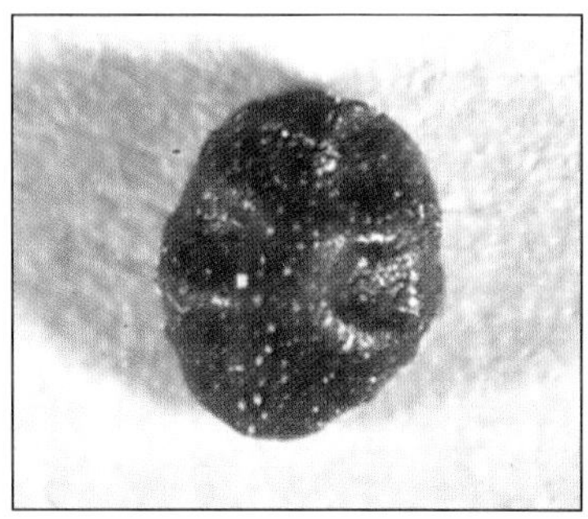

Fig. 7.1 Black scale, *Saissetia oleae*, has a raised H design on the backs of mature females. *Photo: Stanton Gill*

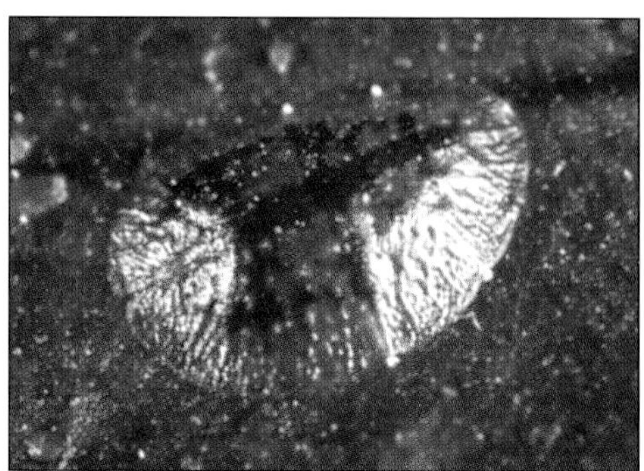

Fig. 7.2 Brown soft scale, which has brown to black mottling, prefers ferns and camillias as hosts. *Photo: John Davidson*

that completely covers the body of the circular adult female. The large size, light color, and lateral wax plates with dark centers make detection and identification easy. The male wax scale is small and elongate in shape.

In most areas of the U.S., the barnacle scale has only one generation per year outdoors, but in greenhouses in Maryland it has been reported to have one-and-a-half to two generations per year. Females lay several hundred eggs beneath their bodies. Males may be present in small numbers, but parthenogenesis seems to be the primary method of reproduction. Crawlers usually settle on stems and remain there for the duration of their lives. There are four instars in the female and five in the male. This scale insect secretes honeydew, but not as copiously as other wax scale species.

Barnacle scale attacks several genera of plants, including *Dizygotheca* (false aralia), *Amaranthus, Gardenia,* and *Citrus.*

Brown soft scale, *Coccus hesperidum* Linnaeus. Brown soft scale is the most frequently encountered soft scale on interiorscape plants. Brown soft scale may be found on many species of evergreen foliage trees, shrubs, and perennial plants. Populations often become encrusted on stems and leaves of plants, and large amounts of honeydew are produced.

Adult females of the brown soft scale, 2 to 3 mm (.078 to .118 inches) long, are pale yellow when young. They darken to brown with black mottling as they mature on preferred hosts (e.g., camellia or fern) (fig. 7.2). On nonpreferred hosts (e.g., fatsia) they are much smaller and do not develop black mottling (fig. 7.3).

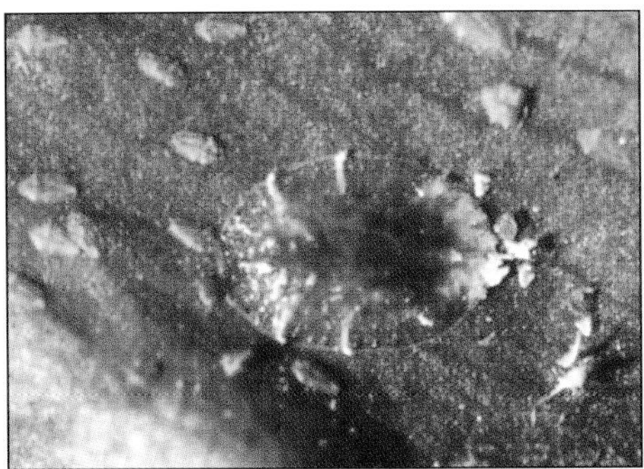

Fig. 7.3 Brown soft scale on nonpreferred host such as fatsia are smaller in size and do not develop the black mottling. *Photo: John Davidson*

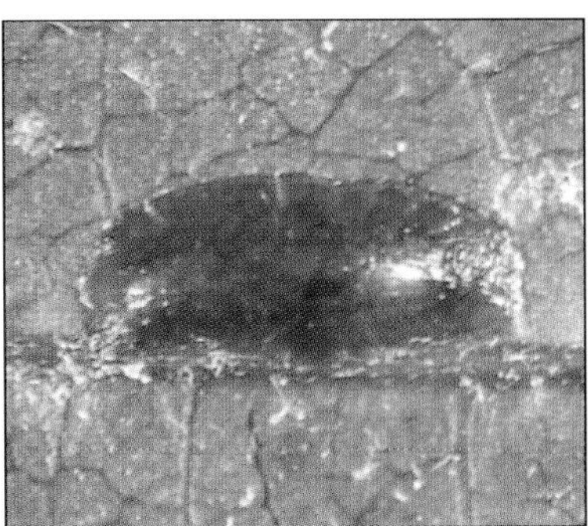

Fig. 7.4 Long brown soft scale is light to dark brown and looks like an elongated version of brown soft scale. *Photo: Stanton Gill*

Fig. 7.5 Hemispherical scale viewed from above appears round in shape. *Photo: John Davidson*

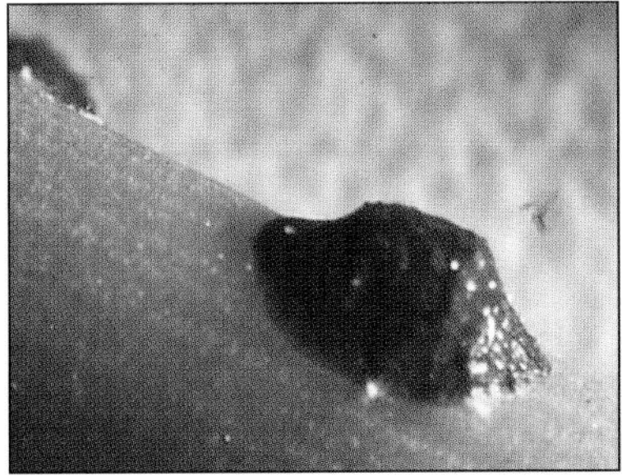

Fig. 7.6 Hemispherical scale viewed from the side appears hemispherical in shape. *Photo: Stanton Gill*

Males are absent. All stages of the scale can be present throughout the year in greenhouses and interiorscapes. It takes 50 to 60 days to complete a generation, with three to seven generations per year in greenhouses, depending on temperatures. Unlike most adult female soft scales, those of this species do not swell up to lay eggs. A female may produce two to three quickly hatching eggs per day for 30 to 60 days.

Long brown scale, *Coccus longulus* (Douglas). The cover of this soft scale is light brown to dark brown. It looks very similar to *C. hesperidum,* the brown soft scale, but the cover is more elongated and somewhat elevated (fig. 7.4). An adult female cover is 4 to 6 mm (.236 inches) in length. It can be found feeding on plants similar to *C. hesperidum.*

Hemispherical scale, *Saissetia coffeae* (Walker). Viewing this soft scale from above, the cover appears round (fig. 7.5). Viewed from the side, it appears hemispherical in shape (figs. 7.6, 7.7). The young female is light brown. Mature females may be shiny dark brown. A female often reproduces asexually, lays 600 to 700 eggs under its cover (fig. 7.8), then dies. This scale attacks a wide range of plants, including *Ficus* sp., gardenia, lantana, croton, citrus, myrtle, oleander, ferns, and palms. This scale is found on leaves and stems of the plant. Large amounts of honeydew are produced.

Tessellated scale, *Eucalymnatus tessellatus* (Signoret). Adult females reach 4 to 5 mm (.157 to .196 inches) in length. The adult females are flat, reddish to dark brown, and easily identified by the variously shaped polygonal plates (tessellations) formed by the hardened dorsal body surface (fig. 7.9). The body is usually somewhat oval in outline. Males are unknown. There are probably sev-

Fig. 7.7 Hemispherical scale viewed from the side, clustered on a branch. *Photo: John Davidson*

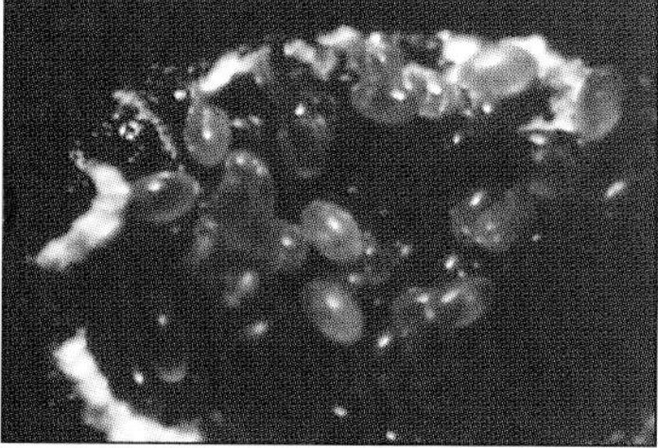

Fig. 7.8 Hemispherical scale flipped over to expose a cluster of eggs. *Photo: Stanton Gill*

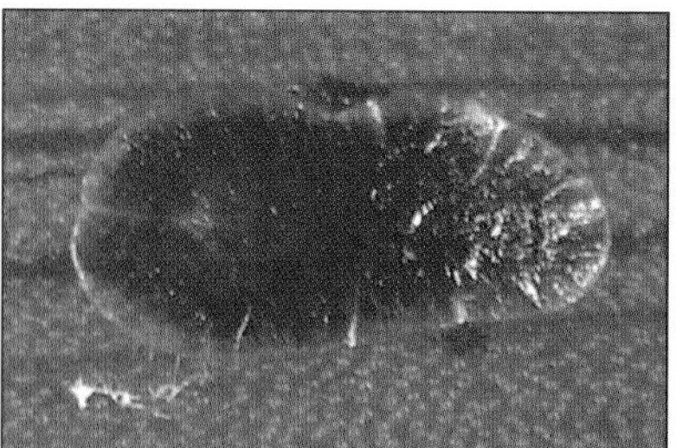

Fig. 7.9 Tessellated scale is flat, reddish to dark brown, and has variously shaped polygonal plates (tessellations) formed by the hardened dorsal body surface. *Photo: John Davidson*

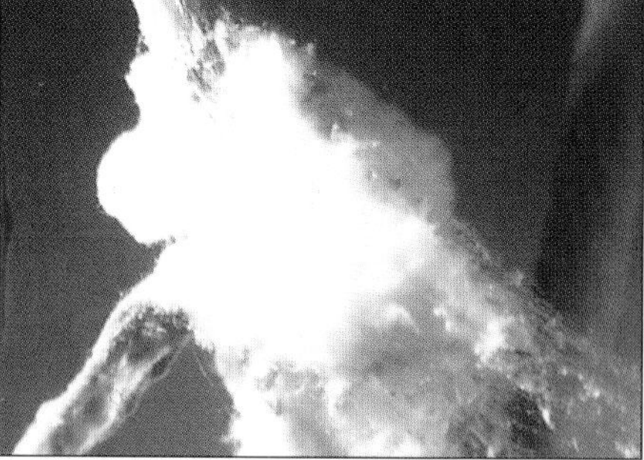

Fig. 7.10 Mealybugs produce a large mass of white wax. *Photo: Stanton Gill*

eral generations a year in the greenhouse, but the life cycle is poorly understood. This pest feeds on many plant genera but prefers palms.

Mealybugs, family Pseudococcidae

Mealybugs derive their name from the white, powdery, or mealy appearing wax secretions that cover their bodies. Although mealybugs belong to the scale insect group of families, they do not develop a hard body like mature soft scales, or hard coverings like armored scales. Females are soft, oval, flattened, with distinct segmentation, which is visible in the wax. Mealybugs are found feeding on all parts of the plant including stems, crown, flowers, fruits, and in the case of root mealybugs, on the root system. The most common species belong to the genera *Planococcus, Pseudococcus, and Rhizoecus.*

Female mealybugs have legs and in many species are mobile throughout their lives. The citrus mealybug produces a mass of fluffy, white, waxy threads that protects the yellow eggs (up to 600). The longtail mealybug does not lay eggs but produces live young. Young mealybugs search for suitable plant parts to settle on and feed. Female mealybugs have four instars, and males have five instars.

The male develops an elongated, white, waxy cocoon, from which it emerges as a two-winged adult with posterior white, waxy filaments. Males find adult females through a sex pheromone produced by virgin females. Males mate repeatedly, then die within 24 to 48 hours. Inseminated females lay eggs or produce live young over one to two weeks, then die. Some mealybug species common in greenhouses may undergo five to six generations per year.

The best citrus mealybug biological control has been reported using combinations of predator beetles and parasitic wasps. Field trial results have been quite variable, depending on what plant species the mealybug population is established on, the greenhouse temperature, and the size of the greenhouse. See the "Biological control" discussions of the mealybug destroyer, a ladybug, and the wasp *Leptomastix dactylopii*, in particular.

Citrus mealybug, *Planococcus citri* (Risso). The citrus mealybug injects toxins into plants, causing distortion in some plant species. The female produces a ventral cottonlike egg sac made of white wax (fig. 7.10). The eggs are yellow. The first instar nymph does not have wax covering, is yellow bodied, and is 0.5 to 0.7 mm (.196 to .275 inches) long. The second instar is a little darker in color and less active than the first instar. After the second instar, the male forms a dark brown prepupal and pupal stage. The adult male is yellow-orange bodied, with one pair of wings (fig. 7.11). A female in the fourth instar is relatively immobile once egg sac production begins. The female is oval in shape and covered with powdery white wax.

The citrus mealybug can be distinguished from longtailed and root mealybugs by the faint gray stripe down its back. Another sign on citrus mealybug is the presence of 18 pairs of short wax filaments on the margin of its body, gradually lengthening posteriorly and ending with one pair of equal-length wax filaments on the scale's posterior end, which are longer than the other wax filaments (fig. 7.12).

Fig. 7.11 Adult male mealybugs have delicate yellow-orange bodies and one pair of wings. *Photo: John Davidson*

Fig. 7.12 Citrus mealybug has a faint gray stripe running down its back and 18 pairs of short wax filaments on the margin of its body. *Photo: Stanton Gill*

Fig. 7.13 Longtailed mealybug does not lay eggs but gives live birth. The fourth instar females have two long posterior wax filaments. *Photo: Stanton Gill*

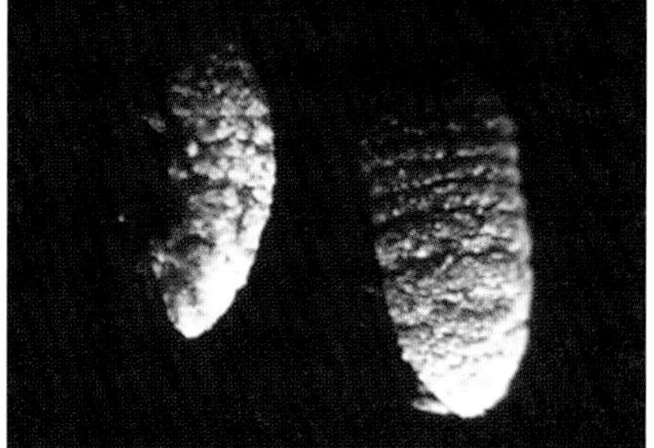

Fig. 7.14 Root mealybugs generally cluster together on roots of plants. *Photo: Douglass Miller*

Fig. 7.15 Root mealybug is oval shaped and has short wax filaments covering the body, which make it look like it was rolled in flour. *Photo: Douglass Miller*

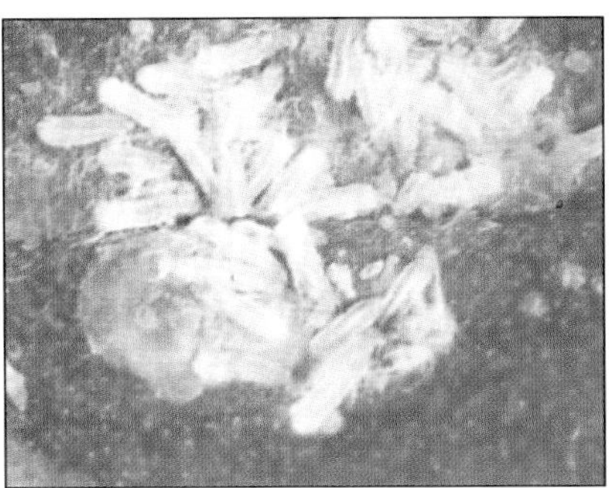

Fig. 7.16 The cover of Herculeana scale, *Clarvaspis rapax,* is circular, white to light yellow, and semitransparent. Male covers are elongate. *Photo: John Davidson*

Citrus mealybug is tropical in origin and the most common mealybug in greenhouses. It has been reported feeding on over 25 families of plants and is common on gardenia, croton, cactus, citrus, and coleus.

Longtailed mealybug, *Pseudococcus longispinus* (Targioni-Tozzetti). The longtailed mealybug is much less commonly found than the citrus mealybug in greenhouses. This mealybug is often found in sheltered places on the plant. Females do not lay eggs but produce live young. The life cycle of the longtailed mealybug is otherwise similar to that of the citrus mealybug. The first instar nymphs are yellow bodied and fairly active, seeking out new sites on plants on which to feed. It is easy to recognize the fourth instar female by the presence of two posterior, long, white, waxy filaments that are two to three times the length of its body (fig. 7.13). Longtailed mealybug is commonly found feeding on a wide range of tropical foliage trees and shrubs.

Root mealybug, *Rhizoecus falcifer* Künckel d'Herculais. The root mealybug is one of the most difficult of the mealybugs to detect damaging plants, since its life cycle is spent in the root zone of the plant. Indication of an infestation may be wilting of the plant. Examination of the root zone will reveal the white, oval-shaped mealybugs (fig. 7.14). Root mealybug has short, white, wax filaments covering its body (fig. 7.15), which appears as if it was rolled in baker's flour.

Root mealybug is found feeding on a wide range of plant material.

Armored scale, family Diaspididae

A hard, waxy covering caps the armored scale feeding beneath. The scale covering of the female can be removed from the body by a probing device. Armored scales tend to be more host-plant-specific than mealybugs and soft scale insects. Armored scales found in greenhouses and interiorscapes primarily infest leaves and stems, but some species also feed on fruit or bark of trunks. Armored scales do not produce honeydew like soft scales and mealybugs.

Female armored scale covers vary among genera, and male covers are usually shaped differently from female covers. Cover shapes range from elongated to circular (fig. 7.16). Male covers, as a general rule, are more elongated and narrower than females covers.

Most armored scale females produce eggs under their covers, but a few produce live young. The crawler stage actively searches out places to feed on the plant. Crawlers can be carried on air currents in

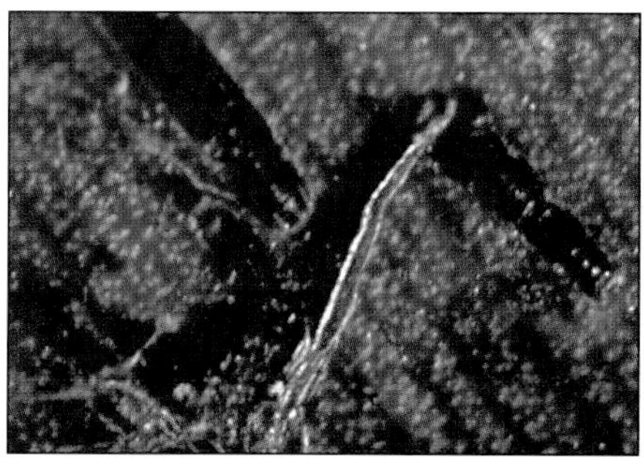

Fig. 7.17 Black thread scale, *Ischnaspis longirostris*, is black, thin, and threadlike. *Photo: John Davidson*

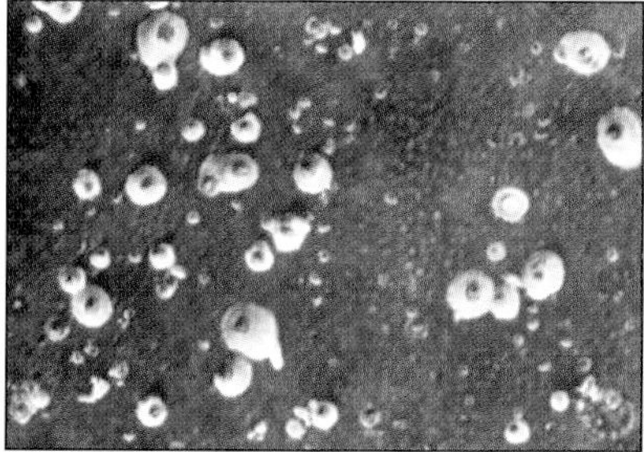

Fig. 7.18 Cactus scale, *Diaspis echinocacti*, which is white and circular, has a crawler cast skin that is pale brown. *Photo: John Davidson*

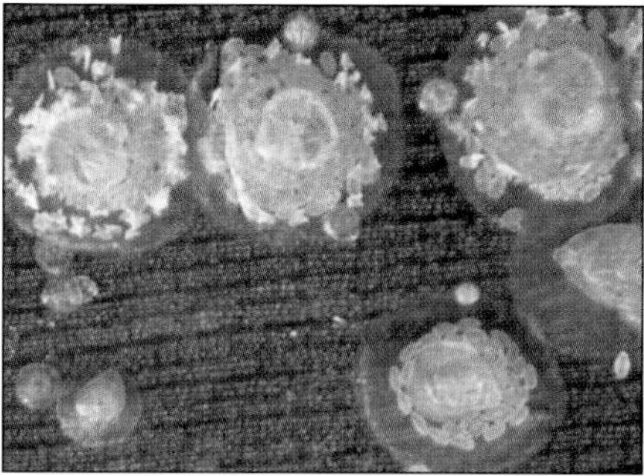

Fig. 7.19 Coconut scale, *Aspidiotus destructor*, females are circular, semitransparent, and light yellow. *Photo: John Davidson*

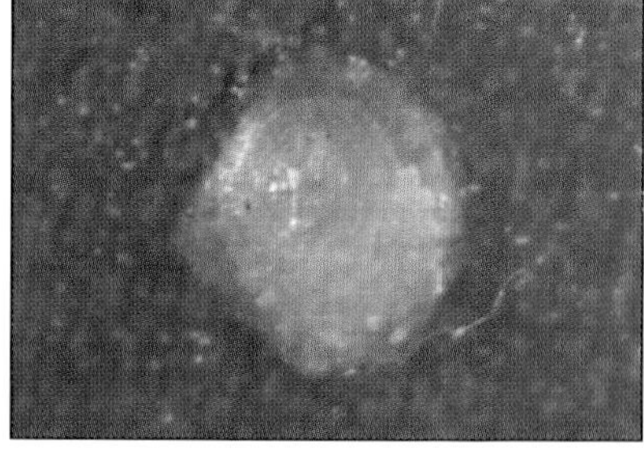

Fig. 7.20 Cyanophyllum scale, *Abgrallaspis cyanophylli*, female is circular or oval, white to light yellow, and semitransparent. *Photo: John Davidson*

the greenhouse to new plants. Plants with overlapping foliage provide a natural bridge for crawlers to migrate to new plants. Crawlers are mobile for 12 to 24 hours, after which they settle and excrete a waxy, protective covering.

The shed skins are incorporated into the cover of the scale as it goes through subsequent instars. The scale remains sessile through three instars for females, and five for males. The female feeds through all life stages, while the male feeds in only the first two instars. Adult male armored scales, with one pair of wings, mate with several females over a 24- to 48-hour period, then die.

In outdoor landscapes, armored scale insects may have only one to four generations per year. In a greenhouse or interiorscape, armored scale insects may have overlapping generations, with all life stages simultaneously present.

Biological control strategies for armored scales have been inhibited by the lack of commercially grown natural enemies for the diverse number of species of armored scale insects found on tropical plant material in greenhouses and interiorscapes. Further research is needed to identify suitable parasites and predators and make them commercially available. For example, *Aphytis melinus* is a known parasite of armored scales outdoors and Korean two-stabbed lady beetle, a predator, but neither has been well studied for greenhouse situations (see “Biological control”).

Black thread scale, *Ischnaspis longirostris* (Signoret). The cover of the adult female is black, thin, threadlike, and 2 to 3 mm (.078 to .118 inches) long (fig. 7.17). The crawler's cast skin that is incorporated into the adult cover is pale brown. Black thread scale attacks a wide range of tropical plants and is commonly reported on several species of palms.

Cactus scale, *Diaspis echinocacti* (Bouché). The cover of the adult female is circular and white. A crawler cast skin is pale brown (fig. 7.18). Mature females are about 1 mm (.039 inches) long. This scale is limited to several genera of cacti.

Coconut scale, *Aspidiotus destructor* Signoret. Covers of adult females are circular, semitransparent, and light yellow (fig. 7.19). They are 1.5 to 2 mm (.059 to .078 inches) in diameter. In Florida this scale pest has been reported on coconut and screw pine (*Pandanus* sp.). In greenhouses it is found on a wide range of tropical trees and foliage plants.

Cyanophyllum scale, *Abgrallaspis cyanophylli* Signoret. The mature female cover is circular or oval, white to light yellow, and semitransparent (fig. 7.20). This scale, a general feeder, is commonly found on *Herculeona* and cacti.

Flyspeck scale, *Gymnaspis aechmeae* Newstead and Pineapple scale, *Diaspis bromeliae* (Kerner). The female cover of flyspeck scale is round, dark black colored, and 0.5 mm (.019 inches) in diameter. This insect is primarily found on bromeliads and occasionally on orchids. Pineapple scale occurs primarily on bromeliads, cacti, and orchids. The cover of the adult female is white with a crawler cast skin that is pale brown (fig. 7.21).

Florida red scale, *Chrysomphalus aonidum (*Linnaeus). The adult female cover is flat, circular, and somewhat variable in color but usually quite dark, with a crawler cast skin that is pale brown to white (fig. 7.22). The size of cover is 1.0 to 1.5 mm (.039 to .059 inches).

Fern scale, *Pinnaspis aspidistrae* (Signoret). Fern scale mainly infests true ferns and liriope. Infected ferns are disfigured by the presence of male second-stage armor, which is conspicuous against the dark green foliage. The adult female is oyster shell or pear shaped and 1.5 to 2.5 mm (.059 to .098 inches) long. The male is white, felted, three-ridged, and the crawler cast skin is beige to yellowish brown (figs. 7.23, 7.24).

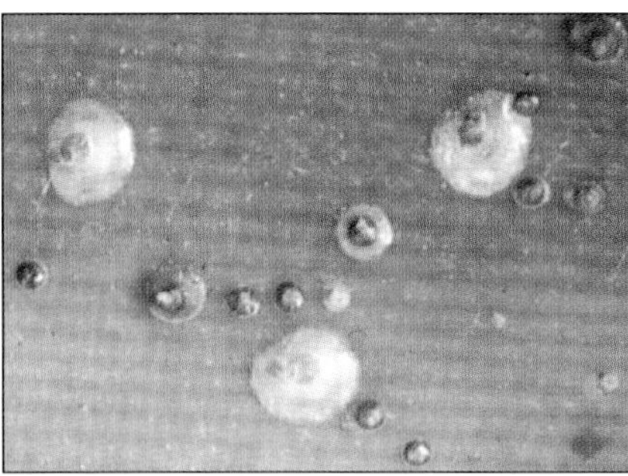

Fig. 7.21 Pineapple scale, *Diaspis bromeliae,* female cover is white with a crawler cast skin that is pale brown. Black fly speck scale is round, dark colored, and relatively small (.5 mm). *Photo: John Davidson*

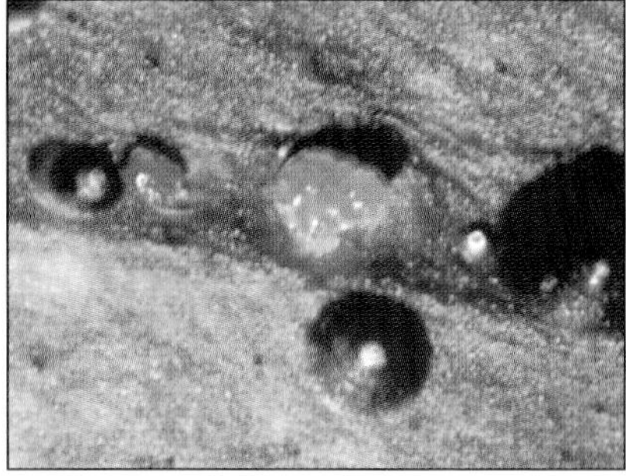

Fig. 7.22 Florida red scale, *Chrysomphalus aonidum,* adult females are flat, circular, and dark colored. *Photo: John Davidson*

Fig. 7.23 Fern scale, *Pinnaspis aspidistrae*, adult female cover is oyster-shell shaped. Male covers are white, felted, and three-ridged. The crawler skin is beige to yellowish brown. *Photo: Stanton Gill*

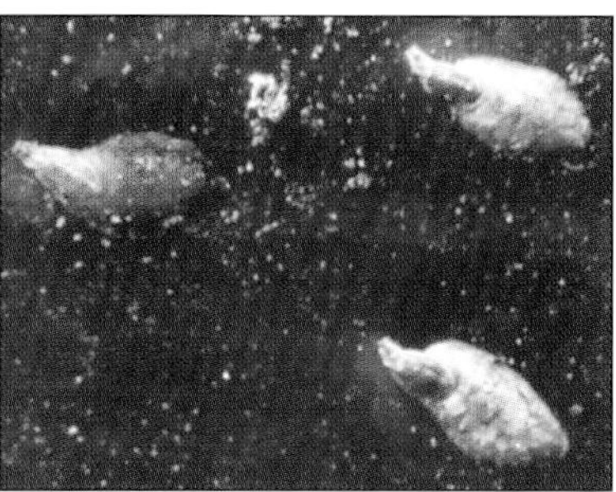

Fig. 7.24. Fern scale, *Pinnaspis aspidistrae*, female has a piercing mouthpart that is used to extract plant juices. *Photo: John Davidson*

Fig. 7.25. The oval female covers are gray for the Greedy scale, *Hemiberlesia rapax*, seen here feeding on ponytail palm. *Photo: Stanton Gill*

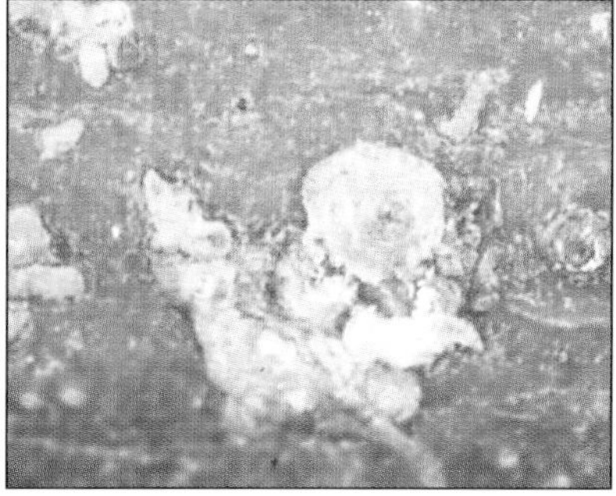

Fig. 7.26. Herculeana scale, *Clarvaspis herculeana*, female covers are circular, white to light yellow, and semitransparent. The male cover is elongated and snow white. *Photo: John Davidson*

Greedy scale, *Hemiberlesia rapax* (Comstock). Adult female covers are oval, grayish, highly convex, with a brown cast skin in the center and .9 to 1.0 mm long (.035 to .039 inches) (fig. 7.25).

Herculeana scale, *Clarvaspis herculeana* (Doane & Hadden). The cover of the adult female is circular, white to light yellow, and semitransparent. The male cover is elongated, about 1 mm (.039 inches) in length, and snow white (fig. 7.26). This scale has been reported infesting several genera of tropical shrubs and trees. The scale appears to prefer royal poinciana, soursop (*Annona muricata*), and sugar apple (*Annona squamosa*).

Fig. 7.27. The female cottony cushion scale, *Icerya purchasi. Photo: Stanton Gill*

Fig. 7.28. Cottony cushion scale, *Icerya purchasi*, female produces a large, elongated, cottony white and fluted egg sac. *Photo: USDA*

Magarodid Scale, family Margarodidae

Cottony cushion scale, *Icerya purchasi* Maskell. The most distinguishing characteristic of this scale is the large, elongated, cottony, white and fluted egg sac that protrudes from the posterior end of mature females (figs. 7.27, 7.28). The white, fluted ovisac becomes two to two-and-a-half times as long as the body, 10 to 15 mm (.393 to .590 inches) long. Inside the sac are 600 to 1,000 bright red eggs.

This scale retains its long legs and its ability to move until egg laying begins. The legs are generally black to dark brown in color. The newly hatched crawlers are red bodied with dark legs. Crawlers feed on leaves and small twigs. In later instars the insects migrate to larger stems.

Cottony cushion scale is found on many tropical trees, shrubs, and herbaceous plants.

Biological control

Predators

***Rodolia cardinalis* (Mulsant).** The predacious Vedalia beetle (*Rodolia cardinalis*), is very effective in controlling cottony cushion scale. Adult beetles feed on scales, and female beetles lay eggs underneath the scale or attach eggs to the scale egg sacs. The larvae feed on all scale stages.

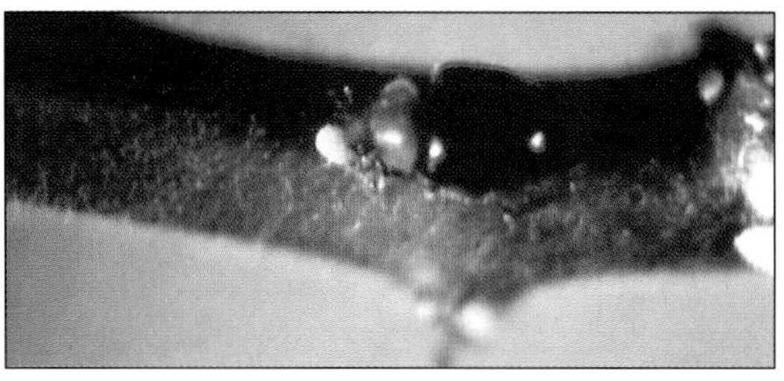

Fig. 7.29. Six adult *Cryptolaemus* ladybugs. These ladybugs feed in the adult and larval stage on mealybugs. *Photo: Stanton Gill*

Mealybug destroyer, *Cryptolaemus montrouzieri* Mulsant. *Cryptolaemus montrouzieri* is a member of the family Coccinellidae, ladybird beetles (fig. 7.29). Both larval and adult beetles feed on mealybug eggs, nymphs, and adults, completely devouring the insects. Four larval instars and adults all feed on immature scale insects, and the mealybug destroyer also feeds on aphids.

This predator has been used on several mealybug species throughout the world. Native to Australia, the mealybug destroyer was introduced into the United States at the beginning of the twentieth century to control citrus mealybug in orchards. The beetle is most effective when mealybug populations are relatively high. Plants grown together in large numbers or with dense, bushy growth are best suited to mealybug control with *C. montrouzieri*. If mealybugs are not present in the greenhouse, the mealybug destroyer will feed on soft scales.

Adult beetles are winged and will fly off to new areas, however, if not enough prey are found. Therefore, mealybug destroyer releases in the greenhouse work best with microscreening, preventing adult migration. The beetle's favored temperature range is 21 to 25C (70 to 77F), with a humidity level of 60 to 80 percent. Do not apply broad-spectrum insecticides within four weeks before a mealybug destroyer release. However, insecticidal soaps, horticultural oils, and several of the insect growth regulators (IGRs) when applied just before a beetle release seem to have minimal impact on these beetles.

Release rates have ranged from two to five beetles per square meter of infested growing area. Releasing the parasitic wasp *Leptomastix dactylopii* in combination with the mealybug destroyer has proven extremely effective.

C. montrouzieri will mate in a greenhouse environment. The female lays 200 to 700 eggs on mealybug egg sacs, such as of citrus mealybug. Since the longtailed mealybug gives live birth, however, oviposition is not possible, so there is little beetle egg laying around an infestation of that species.

During its 12- to 20-day larval stage, the mealybug destroyer feeds on 250 to 1,000 mealybug eggs, nymphs, and adults. The larva actually resembles a mealybug somewhat, with long, white, waxy filaments covering its elongated body. Larvae pupate in sheltered areas.

Besides eating mealybugs whole, the adult mealybug destroyer has been observed to pierce them with its mandibles and leave them to bleed to death. The adult beetle, about 4 mm (.157 inches) long, has an orange head, thorax, and abdomen. The rest of the beetle is mostly dark brown, but the male can be distinguished from the females by the color of the front legs. The male's leg is yellow, whereas the female's is dark gray.

Green lacewing, *Chrysoperla (=Chrysopa) carnea*. The larvae of green lacewing are voracious predators of a wide variety of insects, including immature soft scales. Since they do feed on a wide variety of insects, they are not recommended for use when other natural enemies are being used. A more complete description of green lacewings is given under the whitefly biological control section.

Korean twicestabbed lady beetle, *Chilocorus kuwanae* (Silvestri). This ladybird beetle, native to China, Korea, and Japan, has been used extensively in the United States for control of the outdoor armored scale *Unaspis euonymi*, the euonymus scale. This predator has been found feeding on 23 species of armored scales, in fact. It has potential, but has not been thoroughly investigated for controlling armored scales in interiorscapes or greenhouses.

The beetle larva and adult feed on all stages of scale by chewing holes in the scale cover or by going under the scale cover. The adult beetle, black with one red spot on each wing cover, is active when temperatures are between 50 and 90F (10 to 32C).

Parasites

***Metaphycus alberti* (Howard).** This small wasp in the family Encyrtidae attacks young nymphal stages of several species of soft scale after their crawler stage. *Metaphycus alberti* has been very effective in controlling brown soft scale and long brown scale.

Adults are yellow and about 1 mm (.039 inches) long. Each female lays eggs under the bodies of settled scales and destroys them by feeding on them. The wasp emerges by cutting a small hole in the scale. Females also kill scale insects that they pierce with their ovipositor and feed on the body fluids of the scale.

Metaphycus helvolus **(Compere).** This wasp, closely related to *M. alberti,* attacks several species of soft scale, including black and hemispherical scales, soft brown scale, and nigra scale. *M. alberti* has been more effective in controlling brown soft scale.

The female wasp is orange-yellow and about 1 mm (.039 inches) long; the male is dark brown. The female kills scales either by ovipositing into the scale or by piercing the scale with her ovipositor and feeding on the fluids. The female will lay up to 400 eggs. The wasp larvae develop singly inside the scale bodies.

Leptomastix dactylopii **(Howard).** This parasitic wasp in the order Hymenoptera is native to South America and is readily available from biological insectories. It is an endoparasite, laying its eggs inside of host mealybugs. Release rates have been tried at four to five wasps per square meter of infested plant material. Great success against mealybug has been achieved by complementing this wasp with the predatory mealybug destroyer.

The adult wasp is yellow brown and about 2.5 to 3 mm (.098 to .118 inches) in length. It is a good flier and has excellent searching abilities, finding mealybugs even in relatively low infestations. The long antennae probe areas for mealybugs. The adult male has bent, hairy antennae. The female oviposits 60 to 100 eggs in third instar or adult mealybugs over a 10- to 14-day period. Female mealybugs that have had wasp eggs laid in them turn hard and dark brown. Unfertilized female wasps, incidentally, lay eggs that hatch into males.

Aphytis melinus **(DeBach).** This parasitic wasp, native to Pakistan and India, attacks armored scales, including oleander scale and California red scale. This wasp has been used in outdoor situations for control of armored scale, but has not been thoroughly tested in greenhouse environments.

The female wasp lays eggs on third instar female scales, inserting eggs through the scale cover onto the soft body of the scale. The larva of the wasp feeds externally on the scale insect. When larval development is complete, the wasp pupates, then cuts a round hole through the scale cover and emerges as an adult.

CHAPTER 8

Thrips

The word *thrips,* like the word *deer,* is both singular and plural in usage. Thrips are recognized as one of the most difficult groups of insect pests to control in greenhouses. They feed on a wide range of plant material, have relatively rapid reproduction, and have cryptic life stages, making effective control with pesticides difficult. In addition, thrips rapidly develop resistance to pesticide applications, and several species vector viruses which render plants unsalable.

Many thrips species have dispersed from their original environments, commonly spread by human transportation or by wind currents to new environments, such as greenhouses and nursery fields, where they reproduce rapidly and cause major loss to growers. Thrips occur throughout the world, and several species have adapted to the greenhouse environment, often becoming year-round pests.

General Description

Feeding damage

Most thrips are plant feeders, with the larvae and adults feeding on flowers, leaves, or buds. Thrips feed by piercing plant cells with a single mandible and sucking out the cellular contents with the strawlike stylets (maxillae). The damage to plant cells caused by thrips feeding can result in deformed flowers, leaves, and shoots. Some thrips species, such as the Cuban laurel thrips, cause a curling, twisting, and matting of apical foliage. There is often a silvery streaking and flecking on expanded leaves (fig. 8.1). Flower petals are often scarred, and flower buds may abort in heavy infestations. Thrips often deposit tiny, greenish black fecal specks in areas where they feed (fig. 8.2).

Fig. 8.1 Impatiens with thrips injury to leaves. *Photo: Stanton Gill*

Virus transmission

At least three thrips species have been identified as transmitting two plant-damaging tospoviruses, impatiens necrotic leaf spot virus (INSV) and tomato spotted-wilt virus (TSWV). The thrips species that can transmit INSV and TSWV are *Frankliniella occidentalis* (western flower thrips), *F. fusca* (tobacco thrips), and *Thrips tabaci*

Fig. 8.3 Fava bean plant is an excellent indicator plant that is used in greenhouses for early detection of INSV. Keep the blooms removed from the fava bean plant so thrips will feed on the foliage which will rapidly show symptoms of the disease. *Photo: Stanton Gill*

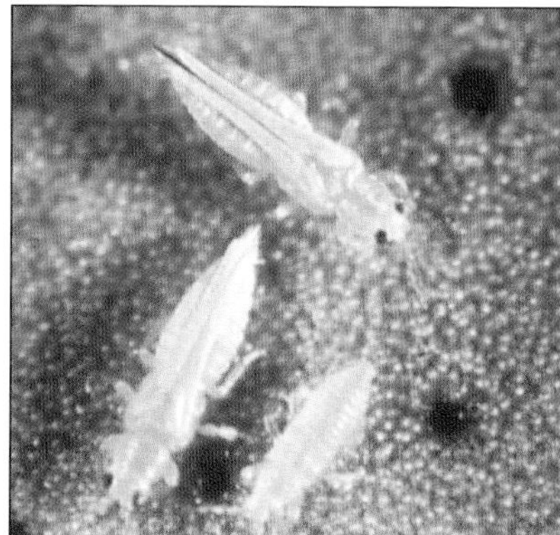

Fig. 8.2 Thrips often deposit tiny, greenish black fecal specks in the area in which they feed. *Photo: Stanton Gill*

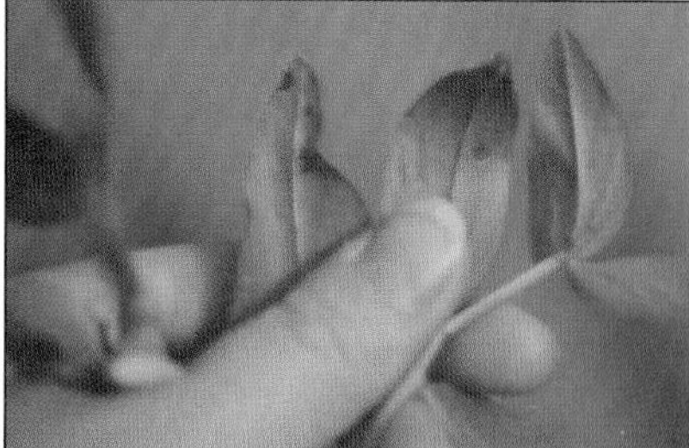

Fig. 8.4 Fava bean leaf with INSV symptoms. *Photo: Stanton Gill*

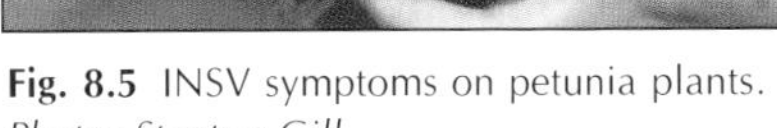

Fig. 8.5 INSV symptoms on petunia plants. *Photo: Stanton Gill*

Fig. 8.6 INSV on snapdragon leaf. *Photo: Ethel Dutky*

(onion thrips). Western flower thrips is currently the most prevalent species of thrips attacking horticultural crops throughout the United States. The thrips can become infected with the tospovirus only if it feeds on an infected plant while in the larval stage. Once it is infected with the INSV or TSWV virus, it can transmit the virus in both the larval and adult stages when feeding on another plant.

INSV and TSWV are extremely detrimental to herbaceous plants. Most of the tospovirus found in greenhouses is INSV. Early detection and destruction of infested plants is extremely important if any of the aforementioned thrips species are present. Indicator plants, plants that rapidly show symptoms of tospovirus infestation, should be placed on the greenhouse bench and checked on a regular basis. A positive identification of tospovirus symptoms on the indicator plant indicates that tolerance levels of thrips drops to very low levels. Good tospovirus indicator plants include fava bean (figs. 8.3, 8.4), and petunias (fig. 8.5).

Due to the wide host range, symptoms are variable and may resemble those caused by fungi. Symptoms may include irregular, necrotic (dead) spots on leaves, discolored veins, black and purple stem streaks, falling of leaves or buds, stunting, irregular leaf shapes, black leaf spots, necrotic young leaves, and colored spots or stripes on petals. Black, brown, reddish, concentric rings, although not always present, are virtually certain symptoms of virus infection.

Antirrhinum (snapdragons). The most distinctive symptom of INSV in snapdragons is a brown ooze that occurs on the stems of the plant. Infected plants often are stunted, and they eventually die (figs. 8.6, 8.7).

Cyclamen. Distinctive ring patterns to yellow ring spots on the leaves are evident on plants infested with INSV (fig. 8.8). Brown

Fig. 8.7 INSV on snapdragon stem. *Photo: Ethel Dutky*

Fig. 8.8 INSV symptoms on cyclamen. *Photo: Ethel Dutky*

Fig. 8.9 INSV on gloxinia. *Photo: Stanton Gill*

Fig. 8.10 INSV symptoms on hanging basket impatiens. *Photo: Stanton Gill*

streaks, in addition to rings, may be present on petioles. Flowers are often malformed. Corms may be constricted into elongated shapes, and, when cut, the vascular corm tissues appear as brown streaks. Plants stop growing, brown spots appear on leaves and leaf edges, and eventually the plant wilts and dies. The roots usually look fine until the plant is near death. It may take three months or longer from the time the plants were infected for symptoms to appear.

Gloxinia. Symptoms include stunting of new leaves or browning of the central or basal portion of the plant, followed by collapse and plant death. Older plants that become infected may show brown or yellowish ring spots, large circular areas of brown, dying tissue, and browning of the midrib (fig. 8.9).

Impatiens. Small, dark purple ring spots often occur on leaves; flowers many also display ring spots, but the rings are usually white. Dark

Fig. 8.11 INSV symptoms on New Guinea impatiens. *Photo: Ethel Dutky*

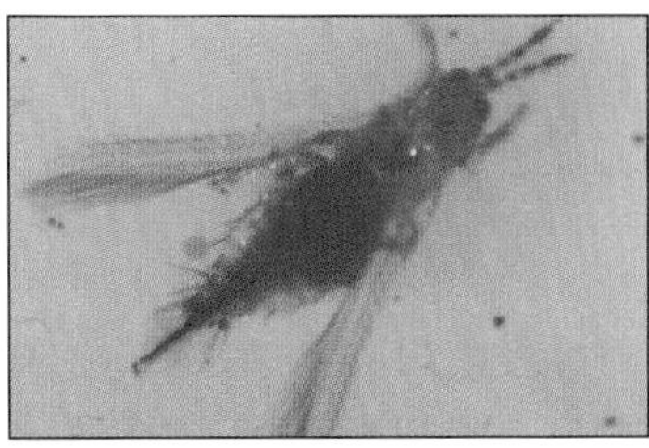

Fig. 8.12 Thrips, which have narrow, pointed wings with no veins, are monitored by using sticky cards placed just above the plant canopy. *Photo: Stanton Gill*

streaks on stems or leaves, especially involving the midrib, leaf yellowing, leaf malformation, and stunting may occur (figs. 8.10, 8.11).

Group characteristics

Adult thrips found in greenhouses are small in size, generally 1 to 2 mm (.039 to .078 inches) in length. The bodies of adults are tubular. They have narrow, pointed wings with no veins but fringed with long setae (hairs) (fig. 8.12). The wings are folded flat over the back and are difficult to see when the thrips is at rest. The adult female thrips has a sawlike ovipositor, which pierces plant tissue and deposits eggs in protected locations on the plant.

Thrips can reproduce sexually (male and female mate) or asexually (the female is self-fertile). Females are the most common sex. The number of eggs laid by females varies from 30 to 300 according to which species of thrips and is dependent on the amount and quality of the plant food source. For most species, the eggs are inserted into the leaf tissue and are difficult to detect without magnification (fig. 8.13).

Thrips go through five stages, including egg, two larval instars, prepupal, pupal, and adult stages. The total development time depends on the temperature. At lower temperatures, say of 59F (15C), it may take 34 days from egg to adult stage. At 86F (30C) this can be as short as 14 days. Thrips metamorphosis is intermediate between simple and complete.

As soon as thrips emerge, the larvae start to feed on plant tissue. The two larval instars feed on all aerial parts of the plant and can be extremely active, crawling and jumping. Plants infested with thrips

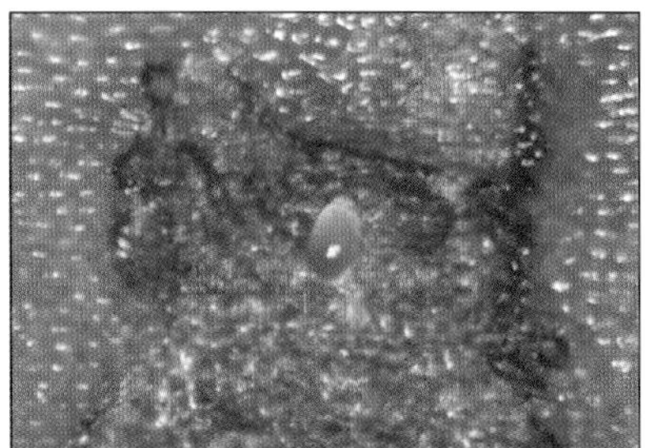

Fig. 8.13 Thrips eggs are usually not seen in the field. These thrips eggs were dug out of the mesophyll of a leaf. *Photo: Michael Parrella*

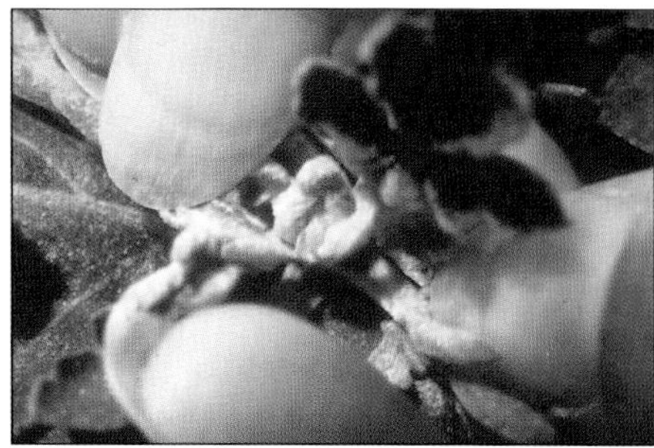

Fig. 8.14 Thrips like to hide in tight, cryptic spots. *Photo: Karen Robb*

(several species) often have black fecal material deposited in spots on leaf surfaces.

Two nonfeeding, inactive stages, called the prepupal and pupal stages, occur. In flower-feeding thrips species, the prepupal and pupal stages usually occur in the soil or leaf litter. Leaf-feeding forms of thrips, such as the Cuban laurel thrips, have prepupae and pupae on leaves.

Microscreening can be very effective if installed properly over intake vents, infested plants are not moved in, and workers are informed of the necessity of keeping doors closed. Controlling the weeds under the bench is essential. Weeds serve as a reservoir for thrips colonies or can be infected with INSV and TSWV tospoviruses.

Pest Detection

Monitoring

A thrips infestation can start on a few plants and spread throughout the greenhouse. Thrips infestations can start when insects are brought into a greenhouse on plant material. When weather is warm outdoors, thrips will migrate from outside into the greenhouse. The migrant thrips enter through vents and doorways and will often infest plants near these entryways.

Many thrips species tend to be found in tight, hidden places on plants (fig. 8.14), while other species are found on leaf surfaces. Adults congregate in open flowers and can be easily tapped out of flowers into catch containers. Plants should be constantly monitored to detect the first appearance of thrips. They should then be identified.

Several individuals should be collected and placed in vials of 70% isopropyl alcohol. Samples can be sent to the cooperative extension service in your state.

Sticky cards. Adult thrips can be monitored by sticky cards clipped vertically to florist stakes and placed just above the plant canopy. As the crop increases in height, move the sticky cards up, so they remain just above the canopy. Yellow sticky cards will capture thrips, but blue sticky cards are particularly attractive to thrips.

INSV indicator plants. Certain plant species can be used as indicators of early infestation of tospovirus in a greenhouse. Fava bean plants and petunias are good virus indicator plants and should be planted in four to six pots and grown on the bench among INSV- and TSWV-susceptible plants. These indicator plants should be examined at least once a week. If a tospovirus is present, the white to brown necrotic spots caused by thrips feeding will be surrounded by darkened brown tissue (see figs. 8.4, 8.5). Placement of INSV and TSWV indicator plants among the crop, combined with regular monitoring of these plants, can help growers identify virus problems early and take action to destroy infested plants and control thrips populations.

Species identification

Cuban laurel thrips, *Gynaikothrips ficorum* (Marchal). Cuban laurel thrips is found anywhere *Ficus* species are growing. Host plants include Indian laurel, weeping fig, India rubber plant, figs, and several herbs. Cuban laurel thrips feeds on new tip growth of plants (figs. 8.15, 8.16, 8.17). Sunken, reddish spots form along the midrib vein. Heavily infested leaves turn leatherlike and often drop.

Fig. 8.15 Cuban laurel thrips damage to tip growth of this ficus tree. *Photo: Stanton Gill*

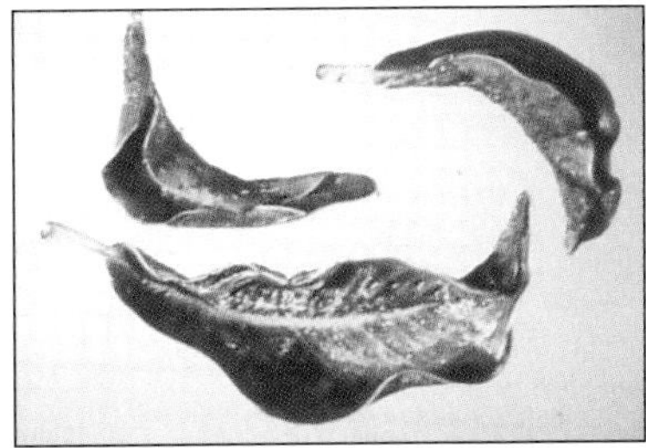

Fig. 8.16 The leaf damage from Cuban laurel thrips is caused by feeding of larvae and adults. *Photo: Stanton Gill*

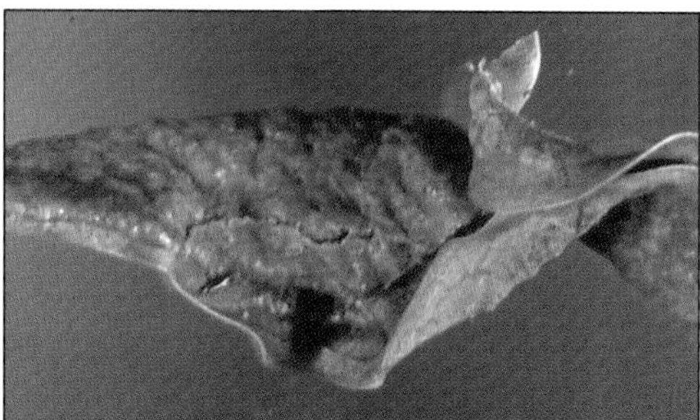

Fig. 8.17 Cuban laurel thrips cause a curling and twisting damage to foliage. *Photo: Stanton Gill*

Fig. 8.18 Cuban laurel thrips, *Gynaikothrips ficorum*, nymphs and eggs are found in curled, distorted tip foliage. *Photo: John Davidson*

Fig. 8.19 Adult Cuban laurel thrips are large, dark-colored thrips while the larvae are light colored. *Photo: John Davidson*

Fig. 8.20 Adult *Echinothrips* is dark brown. With magnification, you can see the two basal antennal segments are dark brown while the tip of the antennae is light brown. *Photo: Ron Oetting*

All stages are found at any one time inside the curled tip leaves (fig. 8.18). Adult Cuban laurel thrips are black and are active fliers (fig. 8.19). They lay eggs inside the surface of curled leaves. Immature thrips cause a pocket gall to form in which they can develop in a protected environment.

Echinothrips americanus **Morgan.** *Echinothrips americanus* has been reported feeding on poinsettia, impatiens, and chrysanthemums. This thrips is a greenhouse pest mainly in the eastern United States.

The body color of the adult *Echinothrips americanus* is dark brown (fig. 8.20). Use magnification to detect the two antennal segments closest to the head, which are dark brown, while the antennal tips are light brown. Adults are 1.3 to 1.6 mm (.051 to .062 inches) in length. This thrips can be found feeding on upper and lower leaf surfaces but is most commonly found on the undersides of leaves. Adult females lay eggs in slits made with the ovipositor into leaf tissue. All life stages may be present throughout the year in a greenhouse.

Flower thrips, *Frankliniella tritici* (Fitch). *Frankliniella tritici* is commonly found in the greenhouse and on outdoor plants. This thrips species is reported throughout the United States. Both males and females are present, with the male being slightly smaller and lighter in color than the female. Adults are yellow to dark brown and 1 to 1.25 mm (.039 to .047 inches) long. Females lay eggs into slits made in the leaf tissue or flowers. There are two larval instars, which are lemon yellow.

The small size of *F. tritici* enables the thrips to be carried by winds to new areas. Flower thrips often migrate from outdoors into greenhouses during spring and summer months. Microscreening can help exclude them.

Gladiolus thrips, *Thrips simplex* (Morrison). *Thrips simplex* is a pest of field- and greenhouse-grown gladiolus. The thrips overwinters in any stage on gladiolus corms or on greenhouse plants. The thrips is native to Africa and cannot survive extended, outdoor winter temperatures below 10C (50F). Despite these limitations, this thrips species has become widespread due to the ease with which gladiolus corms, a favorite feeding site, are transported.

Female thrips generally predominate, but reproduction can be sexual or asexual. A female lays 100 to 200 kidney-shaped eggs in leaves or corms. The first- and second-instar larvae have red eyes and yellow bodies. The prepupal and pupal stages are orange. Adults are 0.8 to 1 mm (.031 to .039 inches) in length.

Gladiolus infested with this thrips have a stipled, bleached appearance. Flowers that are severely damaged fail to open. Feeding can cause stunting of the plant (figs. 8.21, 8.22).

Greenhouse thrips, *Heliothrips haemorrhoidalis* (Bouché). This thrips is found throughout the world but is probably native to Central and South America. Greenhouse thrips has been recorded feeding on azalea, begonia, croton, cyclamen, fern, fuschia, orchid, palm, and rose (fig. 8.23).

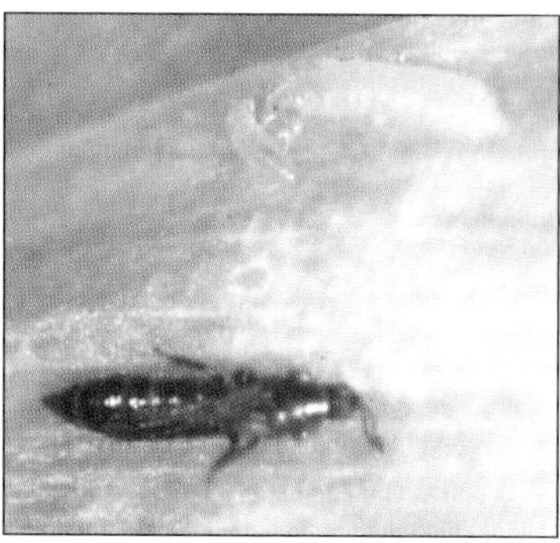

Fig. 8.21 Adult gladiolus thrips and first and second instar. *Photo: Stanton Gill*

Fig. 8.22 Adult gladiolus thrips are found with larvae in the close confines of the foliage. *Photo: Stanton Gill*

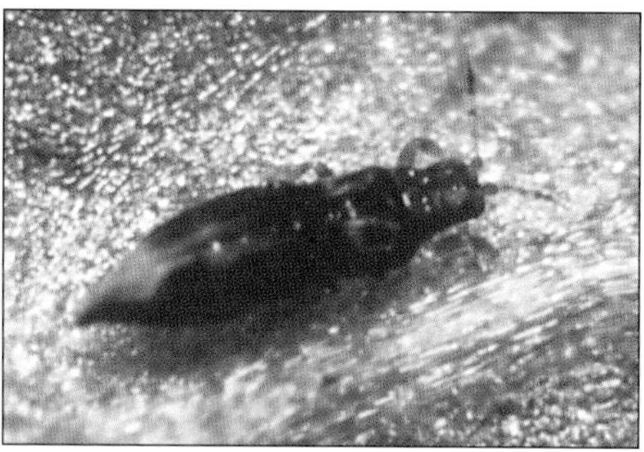

Fig. 8.23 Adult greenhouse thrips are slow moving and usually fly only when disturbed. *Photo: Marilyn Steiner*

Fig. 8.24 The color of the adult *Thrips tabaci* varies from gray to yellow to brown. *Photo: Michael Hoffmann*

Adult greenhouse thrips are slow moving and rarely fly. The thrips prefers cool, shady, and fairly moist conditions. Males are rarely found, and reproduction is mainly parthenogenetic. Females lay 20 to 50 eggs into leaf tissue. The two larval stages feed on leaves, flowers, and stems of plants.

Onion thrips, *Thrips tabaci* Lindeman. Commonly called the onion thrips, *Thrips tabaci* was once the major thrips species found damaging greenhouse crops. Though still active in the greenhouse, the onion thrips appears to have been displaced by populations of western flower thrips. The onion thrips, like the western flower thrips and the tobacco thrips, can be a vector of tospovirus. Outdoors this thrips infests tobacco, onions, and cotton. In greenhouses it can infest tomatoes, melons, sweet peppers, and several herbaceous plant species.

A first-instar larva is light in color, with a relatively large head and bright red eyes. A second-instar larva is light yellow to yellowish green. The color of the adult depends on the food source, varying from gray to yellow to brown (fig. 8.24).

Males are rather rare, and reproduction is mostly asexual by female thrips. Adults are 0.8 to 1 mm (.031 to .039 inches) in length and tubular in shape. A female inserts 70 to 100 eggs into leaves during its adult stage. The onion thrips can be found on all parts of the plant, but tends to be found primarily on leaves. A microscope slide mount should be made of adult females to distinguish between onion thrips and all *Frankliniella* thrips.

Tobacco thrips, *Frankliniella fusca* (Hinds). This thrips species is of major economic importance since it can vector INSV and TSWV. *F. fusca* is found attacking flowering greenhouse crops and field-grown flowers. The adult thrips looks very similar to the gladiolus thrips. The difference is that tobacco thrips is slightly larger with lighter colored antennae. Also, tobacco thrips do not aggregate together like gladiolus thrips under bracts of flowers.

Adult thrips live three to five weeks, and both male and female are usually present, though females can reproduce without males (asexually). An adult female will lay 55 to 60 eggs, inserting them into leaves. Adults can occur as short- or long-winged forms. The long-winged forms generally form outdoors to aid the thrips in migration.

***Thrips palmi* (Karny).** The body color of *Thrips palmi* is clear yellow, with thick, black body setae. Both male and females are found, and reproduction can be asexual or sexual. Adult females lay eggs singly into slits made in leaf tissue. The first- and second-instar larvae are usually found feeding on older leaves. The prepupal and pupal stages are in the ground.

Adults are most commonly found on new leaves and feeding on flowers or fruit. The piercing feeding of the thrips concentrates along the leaf midrib and the veins. Stems near the growing tips may be injured from feeding. Heavy infestations cause a silver to bronze color of the leaves, and continued feeding results in plant death. Populations increase rapidly, often causing severe injury.

Thrips palmi has a wide host range of herbaceous plants, vegetables, and some fruits. Distribution of this pest includes southeast Asia, Pacific islands, and the Caribbean. Biological control may be

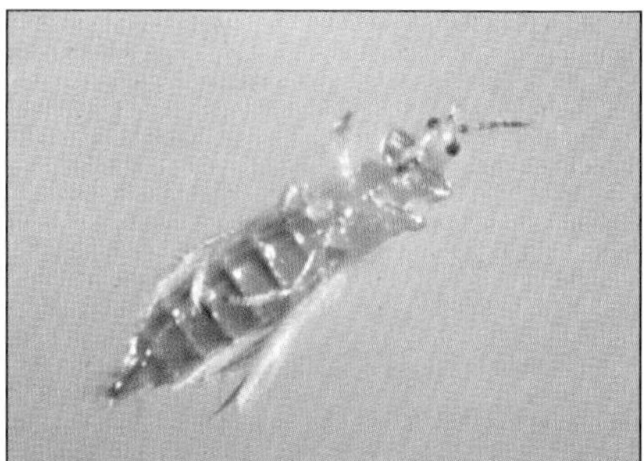

Fig. 8.25 The western flower thrips, *Frankliniella occidentalis*, (ventral view), has a modified left mandible that it uses to pierce plant tissue. *Photo: Stanton Gill*

Fig. 8.26 First instar western flower thrips is yellowish to translucent and wingless. *Photo: Michael Parrella*

possible using species of predacious phytoseid mites. The minute pirate bug, *Orius* spp., will feed on all life stages of *T. palmi.*

Western flower thrips, *Frankliniella occidentalis* (Pergande). This polyphagous (general feeding) thrips has been found on just about every species of bedding and pot crop. Originally, the western flower thrips was found primarily in the United States and Canada, but it has become entrenched in greenhouses throughout the world. Western flower thrips is very common outdoors in fields from spring to early summer. Western flower thrips favors certain crops and is commonly found on impatiens, fuchsia, chrysanthemum, carnation, ivy and zonal geranium, marigold, hibiscus, verbena, rose, and petunia.

Flowers and foliage are damaged by the piercing mouthpart (a single mandible) (fig. 8.25). The feeding injury to flowers and foliage reduces the value of a greenhouse crop. This species of thrips can have a strong impact on a crop if it becomes infected with the tospoviruses INSV and TSWV, which render plants totally unsalable.

F. occidentalis larvae are yellow to orange in color (figs. 8.26, 8.27, 8.28). The adult western flower thrips looks similar to the tobacco thrips (*T. tabaci*), but is often slightly larger and slightly lighter in color (fig. 8.29). A microscope is necessary to see the clearest difference, the number of antennal segments. The western flower thrips has eight antennal segments, and the tobacco thrips has seven.

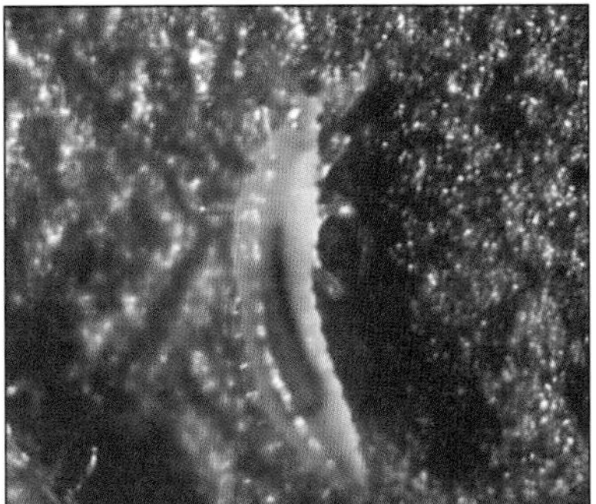

Fig. 8.27 Second instar western flower thrips will often use its abdomen to "whip" its body if disturbed. *Photo: John Sanderson*

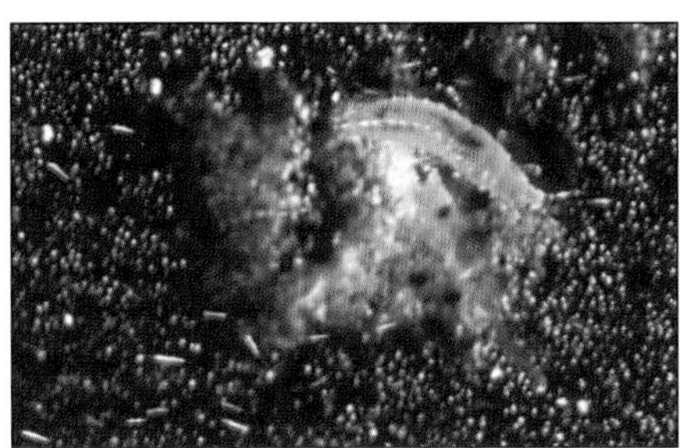

Fig. 8.28 Second instar western flower thrips with damage to leaf. When thrips feed on new growth, the growth does not expand, causing distorted leaves. Feeding on mature growth produces a silvery appearance. *Photo: John Sanderson*

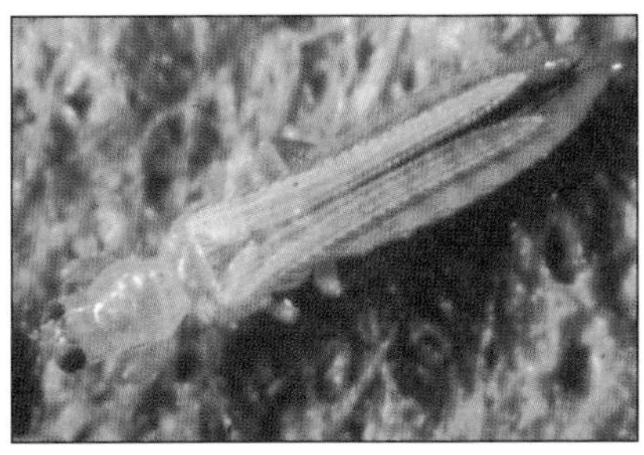

Fig. 8.29 Adult western flower thrips: This species can only be determined using a microscope. *Photo: Michael Parrella*

Fig. 8.30 Pseudo-pupae of western flower thrips are often found in soil. *Photo: Michael Parrella*

F. occidentalis tends to hide in growing points, flower buds, and flowers and is often found on the upper portion of the plant. Cupping your hands over flowers and blowing warm breath into the flower center often makes thrips more active and also drives them into the open.

The life stages consist of egg, two larval instars, and two pseudo-pupal stages. Like most thrips, the western flower thrips usually pupates in the soil, but it has been observed pupating on leaves, in flowers or in other sheltered places (fig. 8.30). It takes approximately 12 to 44 days, depending on temperature, to complete the life cycle.

Biological control

Predators

***Amblyseius* (= *Neoseiulus*) *cucumeris* and *Iphiseius* (= *Amblyseius*) *degenerans*.** These predatory phytoseid mites appear to be well suited to immature thrips control on greenhouse crops. Like thrips, they prefer small niches, where contact between predator and prey is likely even without specific searching. These predators are pollenphagous (pollen feeding) when thrips populations are low.

A lot of questions remain to be answered on the best timing, frequency of releases, and usefulness of these predators on various crops and on various thrips species. These mites must be introduced before a thrips population has built up to damaging levels.

The mites establish themselves on leaves, usually on the undersides, and are most effective in attacking young (first-instar) larvae of thrips. They use their chelicerae to pierce the thrips and suck out the cellular fluids. The predaceous mites will establish themselves on crops that produce pollen, mate, and can reproduce in the greenhouse. The limitation is that these mites are susceptible to many insecticide sprays, and the grower must use biological control for other pests or be selective in pesticides used, also selecting insect growth regulators or biorational chemicals that have minimal impact on predators.

The predatory mites can be supplied in shaker bottles. The grower shakes the mites and a grain carrier onto the crop. The predatory mites can also be applied in paper sachets, which are hung on plants or on marker stakes (fig. 8.31).

Adult *N. cucumeris* feeds on one thrips per day for its 30-day life. An adult *I. degenerans,* on the other hand, feeds on four to five thrips per day for its 30-day life. Another difference is that *I. degenerans* does not go into a winter resting stage (diapause) like *N. cucumeris* will. This will be important if you live in northern or southern latitudes and are making releases in late fall through the winter. For releases made during the short days of winter, the best choice would be to release *I. degenerans.* If using supplemental light to extend days during the winter, this can prevent diapause in *N. cucumeris.*

If using predaceous mites for controlling western flower thrips, it is essential that this tactic is combined with INSV-monitoring plants or on-site INSV serological testing kits.

***Orius* spp.** There are about 70 species of predatory true bugs in the genus *Orius* (family Anthocoridae), minute pirate bugs. They predominately feed on thrips, aphids, and mites. Three species are generally available from commercial insectories for release in greenhouses including *O. insidiosus* (insidious flower bug), *O. tristicolor* (minute pirate bug), and *O. albidipennis*.

Orius embed eggs into leaf tissue, usually in a vein or a stem. Red eyes are evident in all nymphal instars. Young nymphs (first instars) are yellow. In second- and third-instar nymphs, the body is yellow-orange or brown. The head is triangular with a strawlike stylet mouthpart. The adult *Orius* is brown to black, with wings that are tan brown. Adults are 2 to 3 mm (.078 to .118 inches) in length (see fig. 1.19).

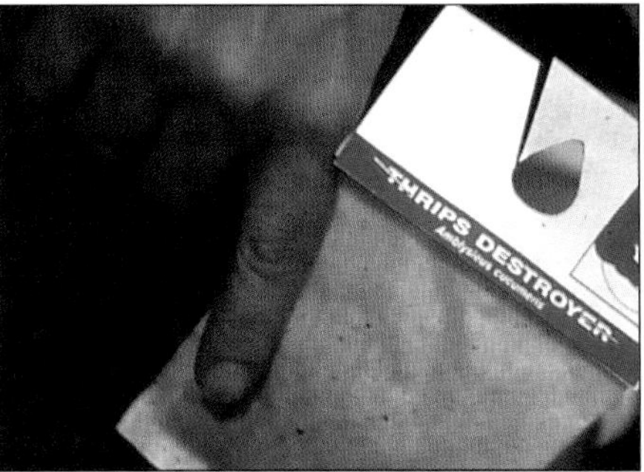

Fig. 8.31 The predacious mite, *Neoseiulus cucumeris*, can be released into a greenhouse crop through a breeding sachet. *Photo: Stanton Gill*

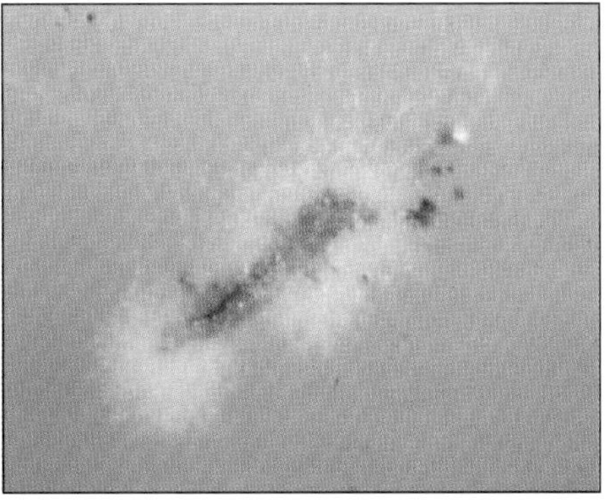

Fig. 8.32 Western flower thrips that has been treated with an entomopathogenic fungi, *Beauveria bassiana*. Note hyphal bodies growing out of insect. *Photo: Stanton Gill*

Pathogens

Pathogens have been found occurring naturally among thrips populations. Several of these are fungi that are being investigated for potential thrips control in commercial greenhouses, fitting into an IPM approach.

Beauveria bassiana. The fungus *Beauveria bassiana,* applied as a fine mist spray directly onto thrips, has potential to reduce populations in greenhouse environments where humidity levels are maintained above 35% (fig. 8.32).

Metarhizium anisopliae. The fungus *Metarhizium anisopliae* is probably one of the more promising entomopathogenic fungi for thrips control. When spores land on a thrips, they break through to the inside using enzymes and mechanical force. The insect dies within a few days.

Paecilomyces fumosoroseus. This fungus was found in Florida greenhouses and is presently being formulated for greenhouse control of whitefly and, potentially, thrips. This fungus requires humidity levels of 90% for infection and must be repeatedly applied.

Verticillium lecanii. In Europe *Verticillium lecanii* has been used to reduce thrips populations in greenhouses with high humidity levels and temperatures of 18 to 25C (64 to 77 F). It is being researched for potential control of onion thrips and western flower thrips. *Verticillium lecanii* has also been used in Europe for control of whiteflies and certain aphid species. It has been reported to have little effect on beneficial predatory insects.

CHAPTER 9

Beetles and Weevils

Scarab beetles and weevils are two beetle families (order Coleoptera) with several species that feed on a wide number of ornamental plants. Adults of this large insect order are characterized by two *elytra* (forewings) that form a hard covering over the hind wings when at rest (fig. 9.1), meeting in a straight line over the back. The adults and larvae have chewing mouthparts. The larvae of scarab beetles and leaf-notching weevils, commonly called grubs, are white and are found in soil.

Plant damage

Adult scarab beetles that are pests feed on the foliage of plants. Female scarab beetles lay eggs in soil, and the grubs that hatch from these eggs feed on root systems (fig. 9.2). Greenhouse growers shipping crops out of state may have sales restricted because of grub-infested plant material. Most scarab beetle adults enter a greenhouse during the summer months. Placing large-mesh screening (screen door mesh screening is sufficient) over the doorways and vent intakes during adult flight activity periods is the easiest way to prevent adults from feeding on plants and laying eggs in potting soil.

Adults of notching weevils feed on leaf margins, often giving a notched appearance to the foliage (fig. 9.3). Some weevil larvae feed either on the root system or at the base of the plant, causing a girdling of the plant. Weevils often overwinter as larvae or adults in soil or in leaf litter. Since they are flightless, they can reach only the plants they can crawl up onto. Greenhouse crops grown on the floor

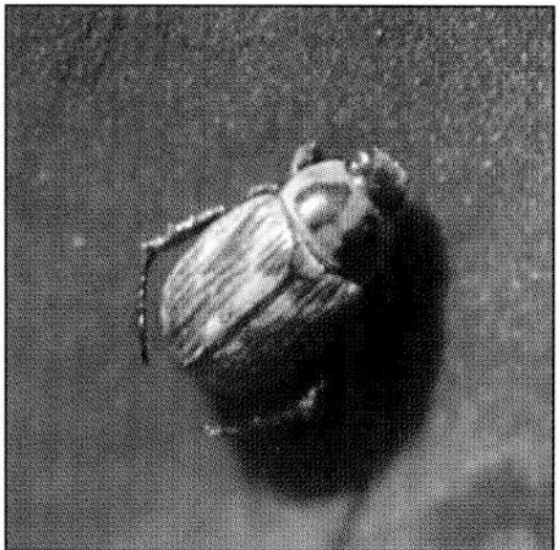

Fig. 9.1 Oriental beetle adult showing elytra (forewings). *Photo: Stanton Gill*

Fig. 9.2 Root injury to container plant is from oriental beetle larvae feeding. *Photo: Stanton Gill*

Fig. 9.3 Notching of leaves is a characteristic feeding injury from adult notching weevil. *Photo: Stanton Gill*

Fig. 9.4 Adult Japanese beetles have metallic brown and green markings. *Photo: John Sanderson*

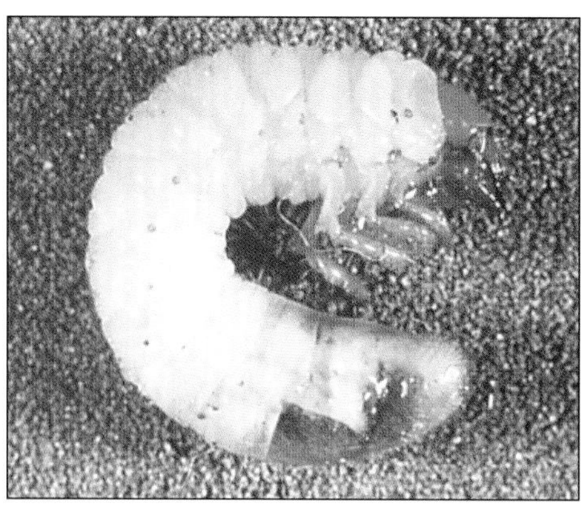

Fig. 9.5 White grubs are C-shaped with long legs. *Photo: Lee Hellman*

will thus be most prone to weevil injury. Placing crops on benches and putting a barrier band around the legs of the bench during adult activity time will keep adults from feeding on foliage and laying eggs into soil substrate.

Species Identification and Control

Scarab beetles, family Scarabaeidae

Japanese beetle, *Popillia japonica* Newman. The Japanese beetle, *Popillia japonica,* feeds on over 300 species of ornamental plants. Both the adult beetle and the larva seriously injure plants. Adult beetles may be attracted into greenhouses, where they will feed on susceptible species of plants as skeletonizers, devouring the tissue between veins.

Adult beetles are 9 to 11 mm (.354 to .433 inches) in length and metallic greenish brown in color (fig. 9.4). Ornamental grasses and rosaceous species of ornamental plants may attract female adults to lay eggs into the soil. Females burrow into soil substrate and oviposit eggs. A female can lay 40 to 60 eggs. Larvae will feed on roots of plants as they go through three instars (fig. 9.5). Grub injury may be unnoticed until the plants are badly damaged. Outdoors the Japanese beetle overwinters as partially grown grubs in the soil below the frost line. In the spring the larvae resume feeding, and adults emerge in early summer in the mid-Atlantic area. Adults are active for 30 to 40 days during the summer.

Oriental beetle, *Exomala orientalis* Waterhouse. The oriental beetle, *Exomala orientalis* Waterhouse, is native to the Philippine Islands. It reached mainland America in 1920. The oriental beetle (see fig. 9.1) is very similar in size to the Japanese beetle. Adult oriental beetles are rarely seen and feed very little compared to Japanese beetle adults. Adults have been seen feeding on roses, phlox, dahlias, and petunias.

In central North America eggs are laid during the summer months. Females lay eggs into soil, and the larvae can cause extensive damage to root systems of plants. Larvae are typical C-shaped, white grubs characteristic of the family Scarabaeidae. They are identical in size and shape to Japanese beetle larvae and can be distinguished from them only by the palidia, two parallel rows of 10 to 16 hairs (setae) pointing toward the median line of what is called the raster pattern. First-instar larvae range from 4 to 8 mm (.157 to .314 inches) long. Third instar larvae are 20 to 25 mm (.878 to .984 inches).

Biological control. Entomopathogenic nematodes can be applied as soil drench to control the grub stages of scarab beetles. Several species of entomopathogenic nematodes have been reported to be effective, including *Steinernema carpocapsae, S. glaseri,* and *Heterorhabditis bacteriospora (= heliothidis).* The insect disease-causing bacterium, *Bacillus thuringiensis* 'Buibui' strain appears to present a good biological control of the white grub stage of scarab beetles.

Weevils, family Curculionidae

Black vine weevil, *Otiorhynchus sulcatus* (Fabricius). The black vine weevil is a major pest of landscape plants and several greenhouse crops, such as rose, gloxinia, geranium, hosta, sedum, fern, and several herbaceous perennial crops. This weevil is parthenogenetic (does not require males to reproduce). Adults cannot fly because the elytra (hardened forewings) are fused together. The adults are 7 to 9 mm (.275 to .354 inches) long, dark black weevils (fig. 9.6).

Females lay eggs on the soil surface. The larvae hatch in approximately two weeks and feed on roots. The larvae, legless

Fig. 9.6 Black vine weevil female adult reproduces without mating. *Photo: Marilyn Steiner*

Fig. 9.7 Pupae of black vine weevil are usually found in soil surrounding the plants that adults were feeding on. *Photo: Stanton Gill*

grubs that are white and wrinkled, go through six instars. Pupation occurs in the soil and lasts three weeks to several months, depending on temperature (fig. 9.7). Adults remain in the pupal cell as the body hardens and darkens before emerging. Outdoors the black vine weevil has one generation per year. In a greenhouse environment the life cycle depends on temperature rather than time of year, and there may not be a clear-cut generation.

Biological control. Entomopathogenic nematodes can be applied as a soil drench to control larval stages of black vine weevils. Several species of entomopathogenic nematodes have been reported to be effective, including *Steinernema carpocapsae, S. glaseri,* and *Heterorhabditis bacteriospora (= heliothidis).* Soil temperatures must be above 10C (50F) and the soil must be kept moist, for nematode survival. The nematodes will reproduce inside the infested larvae, and the infective larvae will migrate out into the soil and look for other larvae to infect. Several of these entomopathogenic nematodes are available through commercial distributors.

The entomopathogenic fungus *Metarhizium aniospliae* has been reported to control larvae of black vine weevil. The fungus is applied as a soil drench before the eggs hatch on the soil surface. Commercial formulations are not yet registered in the United States on greenhouse crops.

Monitor for adults by placing horizontal sticky cards on benches. Adults will often hide during the day under harborage and be trapped at night. Place corrugated cardboard or pitfall traps among the susceptible crops, and check them on a regular basis to determine whether adults are present.

Cucumber beetles, family Chrysomelidae

Striped cucumber beetle, *Acalymma vittatum* (Fabricius), spotted cucumber beetle, *Diabrotica undecimpunctata undecimpunctata* Mannerheim and western striped cucumber beetle, *Acalymma trivittatum* (Mannerheim). Several species of cucumber beetles are found throughout the continental United States, Canada, and Mexico. All cucumber beetle species damage cucumbers, related plants, and several ornamental plants, causing the same type of damage. The larvae feed on young seedling plants. Adults of all three species cause more serious damage, feeding on

Fig. 9.8 Spotted cucumber beetle has a yellowish green color with black spots. *Photo: Michael Hoffmann*

Fig. 9.9 Striped cucumber beetle has alternating yellow and black stripes. *Photo: Michael Hoffmann*

leaves, stems, and flowers of several ornamental plants. In addition, the beetles are vectors of organisms causing bacterial wilt and mosaic in several vine crops. Excluding cucumber beetle adults from the greenhouse through microscreening is the most effective control measure.

The adult beetle has a black head and is about 6.3 mm (.248 inches) long. The spotted cucumber beetle adult has greenish yellow elytra and black spots on its back. Western and striped cucumber beetles are yellowish orange with black stripes on the elytra (figs. 9.8, 9.9).

Flea beetles, family Chrysomelidae

Several species of flea beetles attack the leaves of greenhouse vegetables, herbs, and bedding plants. All flea beetles are small jumping beetles with well-developed, enlarged hind legs with springlike muscles that enable them to hop or leap when disturbed (fig. 9.10). Flea beetle adults chew numerous holes in leaves, reducing the market value of greenhouse plants.

Adult beetles overwinter, becoming active in spring and remaining active through the summer. Females lay eggs around the bases of plants, and the larvae primarily feed on the roots. Pupation occurs in the soil. Flea beetle adults are highly mobile and disperse readily. Adults invade areas en masse and can cause damage to plants very rapidly.

Among the most common flea beetles in the U.S. is the striped flea beetle, *Phyllotreta striolata* (Fabricius), which is black or brown, with two crooked, yellow stripes down the back. The crucifer or cabbage flea beetle, *Phyllotreta albionica* (LeConte), which attacks ornamental cabbage and kale, is black with a blue or green luster. The palestriped flea beetle, *Systena blanda* (Melsheimer), common on peppers and eggplant, is about 6 mm (.236 inches) in length and has a black stripe running down the middle of the back.

Fig. 9.10 Flea beetle adults often will quickly leap away if disturbed. *Photo: Stanton Gill*

CHAPTER 10

Whiteflies

Whiteflies can infest several major floral crops, including chrysanthemum, fuchsia, gerbera, geranium, hibiscus, rose, to name just a few, and many foliage crops. They are the major insect pest of poinsettias. Whiteflies can be very damaging greenhouse pests because of their broad host range, resistance to insecticides, and potential ability to vector a variety of plant virus diseases. *Bemesia argentifolia* has been found to vector tomato yellow leaf curl virus (TYLCV) in greenhouse-grown vegetable transplants.

The two most common whitefly species, which cause the majority of problems to greenhouse crops, are the silverleaf whitefly, *Bemisia argentifolii* (formerly known as strain B of the sweetpotato whitefly, *B. tabaci*), and the greenhouse whitefly, *Trialeurodes vaporariorum.* One reason these whiteflies are serious pests is that they attack a wide range of floral crops. It is not uncommon to find both whitefly species in the same greenhouse, even on the same leaf. The bandedwinged whitefly, *Trialeurodes abutilonea,* is occasionally found in some areas of the U.S., especially as adults from outdoors captured on yellow sticky cards. Nymphs have also been found on the foliage of poinsettia and some bedding plants. The cloudywinged whitefly, *Dialeurodes citrifolii* (Morgan), can infest citrus, gardenia, and *Ficus nitida.* The citrus whitefly, *Dialeurodes citri,* can occur on citrus and gardenia. The iris whitefly, *Aleyrodes spiraeoides,* can occur on iris or gladiolus, and the azalea whitefly, *Pealius azaleae* (Baker & Moles), can be found on azaleas. Other species that may be found in greenhouses, at least captured on sticky traps, include the mulberry whitefly *Trialeurodes mori* (Quaintance), and the ash whitefly, *Siphoninus phillyreae* (Halliday).

General description

Plant damage

Whiteflies are considered pests of floral crops primarily because their presence detracts from the crops' aesthetic value. Their feeding can sometimes cause plants to become chlorotic. Honeydew excretions cause leaves to become sticky and shiny and serve as a substrate for the growth of grayish black sooty fungus, which interferes with photosynthesis, as well as detracts from the plant's appearance (fig.10.1). Furthermore, the silverleaf whitefly can cause tomato fruit to become mottled (uneven ripening), leaves of squash to turn silver green (hence the common name), hibiscus foliage to have yellow speckles, and in severe infestations, stems and bracts of red poinsettia cultivars to turn whitish yellow (figs. 10.2, 10.3). Several whitefly species are capable of transmitting plant viruses.

Group characteristics

All whitefly life stages are almost always found on the lower surfaces of leaves. The adult is a small (1 to 2 mm, .039 to .078 inches), white, flylike insect, which is where the pest gets its name. The white appearance of the adults comes from wax secreted from the abdomen, with which they cover their bodies.

Whitefly eggs are very tiny and spindle-shaped. They usually stand vertically on the leaf surface, attached to the leaf by a tiny *pedicel,* or stalk, at the base of the egg (fig. 10.4). For many species, eggs are white when first laid, turning dark gray (greenhouse whitefly) (fig. 10.5) or amber brown (silverleaf whitefly) (fig. 10.6) with time.

The crawler and other nymphal stages of the most common species are oval, greatly flattened, and somewhat translucent, with a white, light green, or light yellow cast. The four nymphal stages are identified by their relative sizes. Length and width increase with each successive molt (fig. 10.7).

Fig. 10.1 Honeydew and sooty mold on poinsettia leaf is produced by immature whiteflies feeding on the plant. *Photo: John Sanderson*

Fig. 10.2 Poinsettia white stem caused by silverleaf whitefly. *Photo: John Sanderson*

Fig. 10.3 Yellowed bracts of poinsettia caused by feeding of silverleaf whitefly. *Photo: John Sanderson*

Fig. 10.4 Side view of greenhouse whitefly eggs. Newly laid eggs are creamy white; older eggs are dark purple gray. *Photo: Lance Osborne*

Fig. 10.5 Greenhouse whitefly adults, eggs, and a few crawlers. Note that the wings are held fairly parallel to the leaf surface. *Photo: John Sanderson*

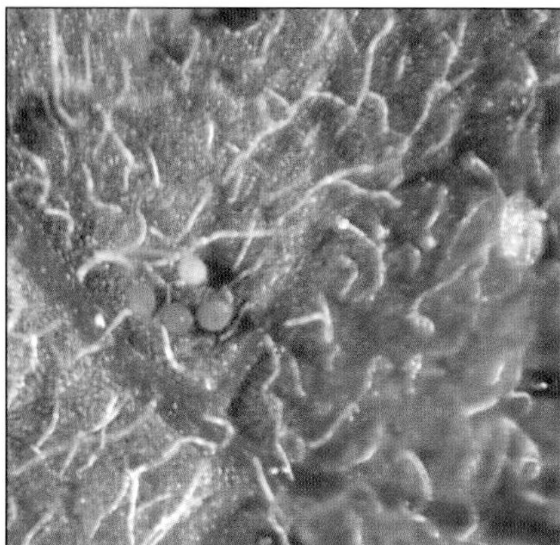

Fig. 10.6 Silverleaf whitefly eggs are often amber to dark brown. *Photo: John Sanderson*

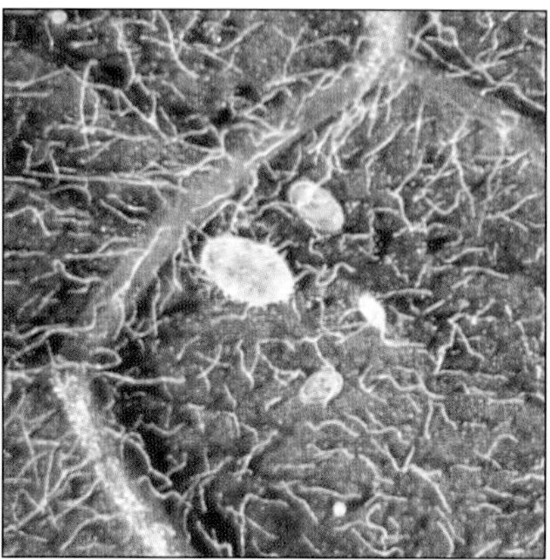

Fig. 10.7 All four nymphal stages of greenhouse whitefly. *Photo: John Sanderson*

Biology

The life cycles of whitefly pests of greenhouse crops are generally similar. A female can begin to lay eggs from one to four days after emerging as an adult. A female may lay up to 200 eggs and live up to 1½ months, but this depends greatly on the whitefly species and environmental conditions, such as temperature and host plant. For example, silverleaf whitefly lays more eggs than greenhouse whitefly on poinsettia, but the reverse is true on gerbera. Eggs are deposited on the underside of leaves, sometimes in a circle or crescent-shaped pattern (see fig. 10.5). At temperatures fluctuating between 18 and 24C (65 and 75F) on poinsettia, the eggs hatch in about 10 days for greenhouse whitefly and 12 days for silverleaf whitefly.

The tiny first nymphal stage (crawler) hatches from the egg, crawls a short distance (a few millimeters), and settles down to feed. It does not move from this spot until adulthood. It first passes through three more nymphal stages. The "pupal" stage (i.e., when the red eye spots of the developing adult are visible through the pupal case (fig. 10.8) lasts five days for both species. At the above temperatures, development from egg to adult takes an average of 32 and 39 days for greenhouse whitefly and silverleaf whitefly, respectively, on poinsettia. Infestations may build rapidly if not detected early, and overlapping of life stages is common.

PEST DETECTION

Monitoring

Whitefly infestations can be monitored with a combination of yellow sticky traps and foliage inspection. The location and relative numbers of adults can be monitored with yellow sticky traps, while nymphs must be monitored by frequent foliage inspection. Though older leaves will have a mix of old and young life stages, older life stages will usually predominate. Eggs and younger life stages are usually on younger leaves.

Sampling procedures are available for nymphs of greenhouse whitefly and silverleaf whitefly on poinsettia. Inspection of whitefly nymphs several days after a foliar insecticide application can aid in determining whether the spray was effective. Dead whitefly nymphs appear to be flattened, shriveled, and very dry (fig. 10.9).

Species identification

Distinguishing the species of a whitefly can be difficult. The best lifestage to use for identification is the "pupal" stage, which is the last nymphal stage before adult emergence. All nymphal stages will commonly be found on the underside of leaves. The pupal stage will

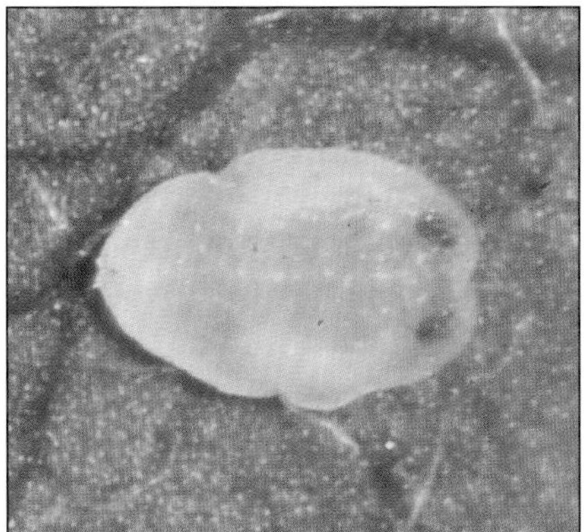

Fig. 10.8 Silverleaf whitefly pupa, top view. Note the red eye spots indicating that this is a pupa. Silverleaf whitefly lack a fringe of filaments around the circumference of the pupa. *Photo: John Sanderson*

Fig. 10.9 Silverleaf whitefly nymphs killed by insecticide. Note the discolored, shriveled appearance. *Photo: John Sanderson*

be the largest nymphal stage, and the insect will usually have two red eyespots near one end of the body (see fig. 10.8). These are the eye spots of the adult developing within the pupa. Careful examination of the pupal case, which is left behind after an adult emerges, can help distinguish between silverleaf and greenhouse whitefly (fig. 10.10). A 10× hand lens or dissecting microscope will be needed to examine pupae closely enough to see these characters and differentiate accurately between the species. Unfortunately, the primary means of capturing adults, yellow sticky traps, inevitably

Fig. 10.10 Pupal cases of silverleaf (left) and greenhouse (right) whiteflies. Note that the fringe of tiny filaments around the circumference of the greenhouse whitefly is lacking on the silverleaf whitefly pupal case. *Photo: John Sanderson*

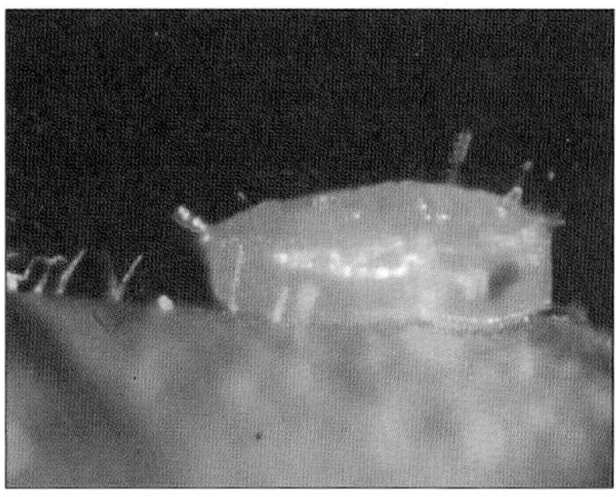

Fig. 10.11 Side view of greenhouse whitefly pupa. Note straight sides that are perpendicular to the leaf surface, giving it a cake-shaped appearance. *Photo: John Sanderson*

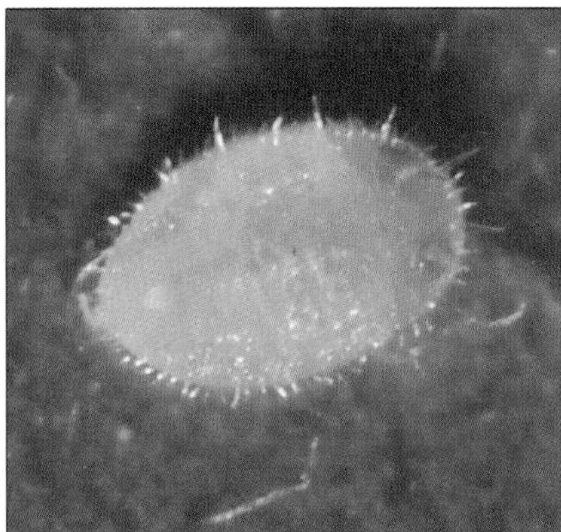

Fig. 10.12 Looking down on a greenhouse whitefly pupa. Note the tiny fringe of filaments around the circumference of the pupa and the whitish color. *Photo: John Sanderson*

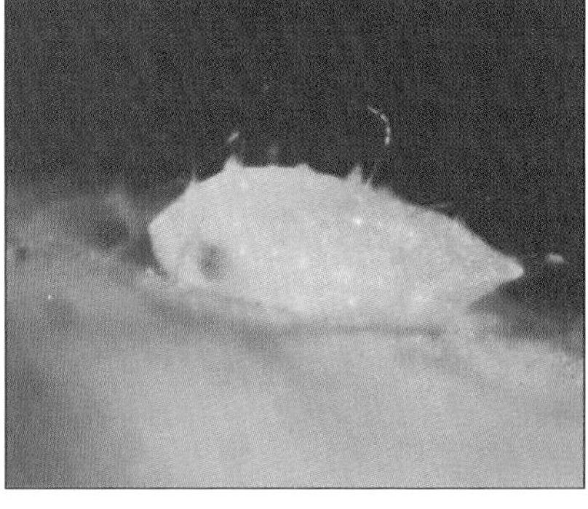

Fig. 10.13 Side view of silverleaf whitefly pupa. Note that the sides are not straight and parallel to the leaf surface as with greenhouse whitefly. *Photo: John Sanderson*

obscure many fine distinctions of appearance and are useful only for identifying one or two species that are rarely serious pests.

Greenhouse whitefly, *Trialeurodes vaporariorum* (Westwood). The pupa of the greenhouse whitefly is oval and has elevated sides that are very straight and perpendicular to the leaf surface (fig. 10.11). This gives it a disklike or cake-shaped appearance from an angle. Seen from above, the greenhouse whitefly pupa has a tiny fringe of wax filaments around the top "rim." (See fig. 10.12.) There are frequently several pairs of longer wax filaments arising from the top surface of the pupa, especially on hairy leaves. Usually, these longer filaments are large and noticeable on the greenhouse whitefly, but this may vary.

On poinsettia, nymphs tend to be whitish. The adult greenhouse whitefly is somewhat larger than the silverleaf whitefly. Wings are completely white, with no bands or stripes. The wings lie fairly flat over the abdomen, almost parallel with the leaf surface (see fig. 10.5).

Silverleaf whitefly, *Bemisia argentifolii* Bellows & Perring (= sweetpotato whitefly, strain B). The pupa of the silverleaf whitefly appears from side view to be more rounded, dome-shaped, or even pointed than a greenhouse whitefly pupae (fig. 10.13). There is no fringe of wax filaments around the top rim of the pupa (see fig. 10.8). Several pairs of longer wax filaments may arise from the top surface of the pupa, but these are usually shorter on silverleaf whitefly than on greenhouse whitefly.

On poinsettia the silverleaf whitefly nymphs tend to be more yellow than the whitish greenhouse whitefly nymphs. The adult silverleaf whitefly is smaller than the greenhouse whitefly, and the body of an adult silverleaf whitefly is slightly more yellow. The wings of the adult silverleaf whitefly are held close and tentlike against the abdomen at approximately a 45-degree angle to the leaf surface (fig. 10.14). This makes silverleaf whitefly adults appear more slender than other species. Wings are completely white.

Bandedwinged whitefly, *Trialeurodes abutiloneus* (Haldeman). This species has been found on poinsettia, geranium, hibiscus, and petunia. The common name for this species comes from the two irregular, smoky brown lines that zigzag across its front wings (fig. 10.15). These bands appear continuous from wing to wing when the wings are folded. The adult also has brown bands on the top of the

Fig. 10.14 Silverleaf whitefly adult and nymphs. Note how the adult holds its wings close to the body, at a very rooflike angle over its abdomen. *Photo: J. Monroy*

Fig. 10.15 Adult bandedwinged whiteflies have smoky-gray bands across their wings. Otherwise they look similar to greenhouse whitefly. *Photo: Ray Gill*

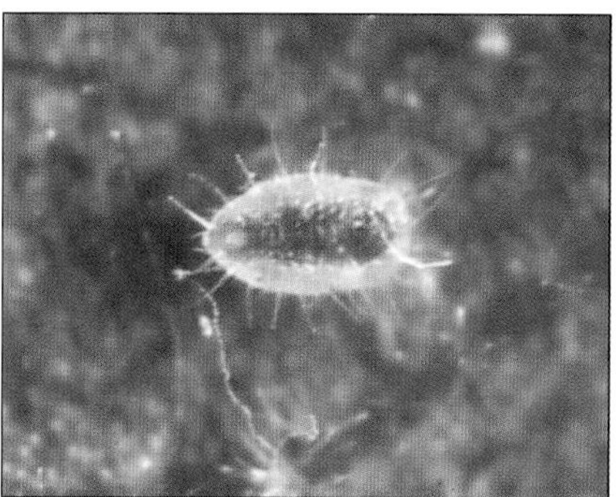

Fig. 10.16 Bandedwinged whitefly pupae have an obvious brown band down the length of the body. *Photo: Avas Hamon*

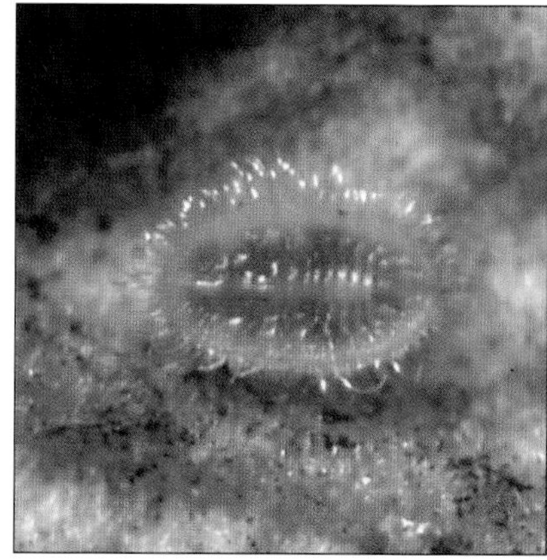

Fig. 10.17 Bandedwinged whitefly pupae have a fringe of filaments around their circumference similar to greenhouse whitefly, but have an obvious brown band. *Photo: Ray Gill*

abdomen. Otherwise, the adult size and shape is very similar to the greenhouse whitefly.

The pupal stage can also be used to distinguish the bandedwinged whitefly from the other species, although these nymphs have only occasionally been found on poinsettia or other greenhouse ornamentals. An obvious dark band that is fairly wide runs down the length of the pupa (figs. 10.16, 10.17).

Cloudywinged whitefly, *Dialeurodes citrifolii* (Morgan). The cloudywinged whitefly infests citrus in Florida and has also been found on gardenia and *Ficus nitida*. It has been observed on poinsettia but is not considered a poinsettia pest.

Adults are larger and broader than greenhouse whitefly, and they have a shaded or cloudy dark area near the tips of the front wings (fig. 10.18). Eggs are dark brown. Leaf color shows through the very thin bodies of nymphs, making them difficult to see. The pupae (fig. 10.19) does not have any filaments around the margins of the pupal case. It is more opaque than the nymph, but the red eyespots of the developing adult are very noticeable. It is difficult to

Fig. 10.18 Adult cloudywinged whitefly. Note the broad wings and slightly shaded area near the wing tips. *Photo: Ray Gill*

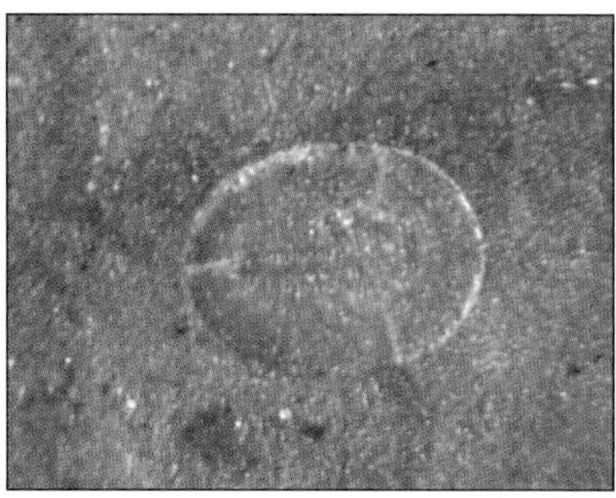

Fig. 10.19 Cloudywinged whitefly nymphs are nearly transparent, but the darker spiracular grooves at the sides and posterior produce an incomplete Y-shape or T-shape. *Photo: Ray Gill*

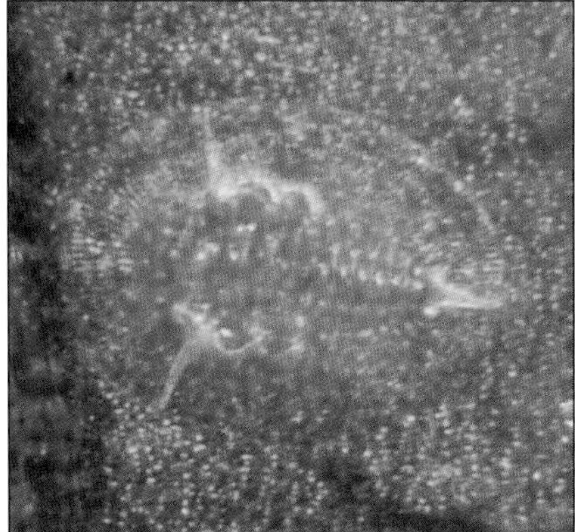

Fig. 10.20 Citrus whitefly nymphs are indistinguishable from cloudywinged whitefly nymphs. *Photo: Ray Gill*

Fig. 10.21 Adult citrus whiteflies resemble cloudywinged whiteflies, but lack the shaded area near the wing tips. *Photo: Ray Gill*

distinguish between the nymphs of cloudywinged whitefly and citrus whitefly.

Citrus whitefly, *Dialeurodes citri* (Ashmead). The citrus whitefly can infest citrus and banana shrub, Boston ivy, chinaberry, English ivy, gardenia, and *Allamanda*. Nymphs do not have any filaments around the margins (fig. 10.20). Nymphs and pupae are very flat, appearing indistinguishable from cloudywinged whitefly. Eggs are beige or light brown. Adults resemble the cloudywinged whitefly, but lack the cloudy spot near the tip of the front wing (fig. 10.21).

Iris whitefly, *Aleyrodes spiracoides* Quaintance. The iris whitefly can infest iris and gladiolus. It has also been found on fuchsia. Colonies of iris whitefly produce a lot of wax, and adults have two faint smoky spots on their wings (fig. 10.22).

Azalea whitefly, *Pealius azaleae* (Baker & Moles). The azalea whitefly is found only on azaleas, but it can infest all species of azaleas. Nymphs and pupae have no wax filaments at all, no marginal waxy fringe, nor any long, wax filaments arising from the top surface of the pupa, even on hairy leaves. The pupa is light yellow to orange yellow, with the margins of the body lighter in color than the center of the pupa (fig. 10.23).

Spiraling whitefly, *Aleurodicus dispersus* Russell. The spiraling whitefly has been reported from plants in 27 families, including citrus and many ornamentals, especially trees, such as black olive, coconut, banana, star apple, and mango. It has been found in southern coastal

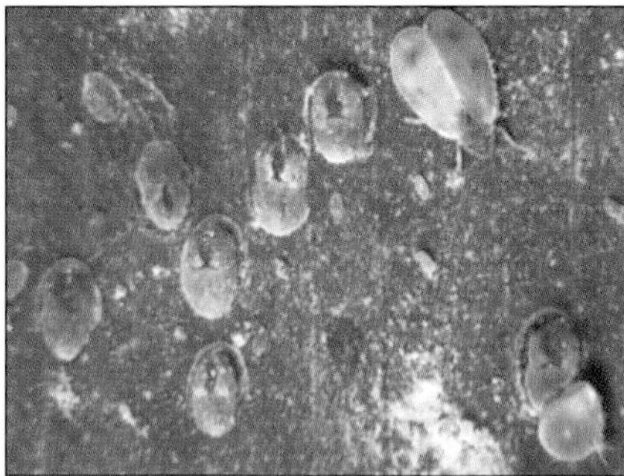

Fig. 10.22 Iris whitefly adults, nymphs, and empty pupal cases. Note their gray waxy appearance and the two smoky spots on the wings. Photo: *Ray Gill*

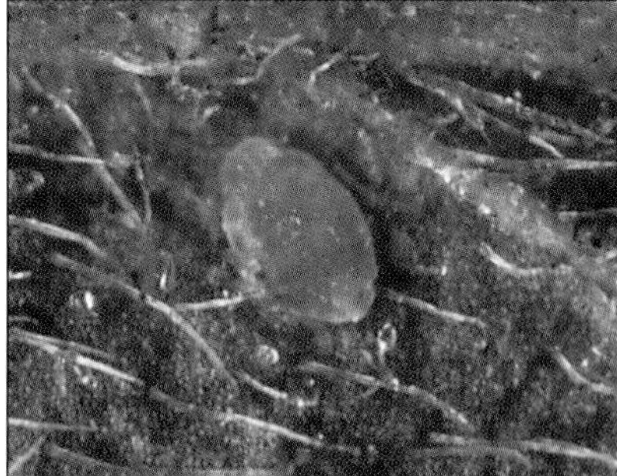

Fig. 10.23 Azalea whitefly nymphs can resemble silverleaf whitefly, but they only infest azalea. *Photo: Avas Hamon*

Fig. 10.24 Spiraling whitefly nymphs are distinctive with large ribbons of wax extruding from the body. *Photo: Stanton Gill*

Fig. 10.25 Ash whitefly adult closely resembles the greenhouse whitefly adult. In California, adults have occasionally been found on poinsettia, but no immature stages have been noted. *Photo: Tom Bellows*

areas of Florida. It is intolerant of cold temperatures. The first three nymphal instars produce wavy bands of wax around the margins of their bodies. The fourth nymphal instar produces a copious amount of white cottony wax (fig. 10.24). Some wax is in long ribbons that are two to three times the width of the body. Mature pupae are colorless to yellowish.

Ash whitefly, *Siphoninus phillyreae* (Halliday). The ash whitefly infests ash as well as fruit and ornamental trees. Heavy infestations can cause wilting and early defoliation of deciduous trees. Honeydew production can be so heavy that it drips from leaves. Adults have been found on poinsettias in California, but no immature stages have been found. Poinsettias are apparently not a good host plant.

The ash whitefly adult looks similar to greenhouse whitefly (fig. 10.25). The pupa is distinctive, with tufts of white wax that run in a band lengthwise down the middle of the body (fig. 10.26). The dorsal surface of the pupa also has numerous (>40) tiny tubes ("hairs") tipped with beads of clear liquid.

Mulberry whitefly, *Tetraleurodes mori* (Quaintance). Adults of the mulberry whitefly have often been found during the fall on yellow

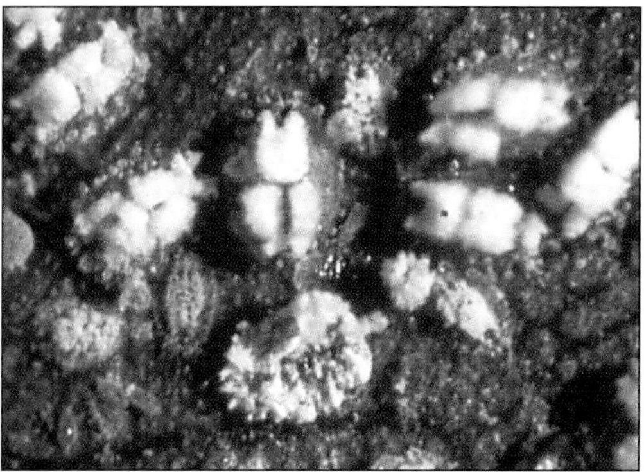

Fig. 10.26 Ash whitefly nymphs have tufts of white wax that run in a band down the length of the body and tiny tubes tipped with beads of clear liquid. *Photo: Tom Bellows*

Fig. 10.27 Mulberry whitefly adults resemble bandedwinged whiteflies, but also have a dark spot near the base and tip of each forewing. They only infest certain tree species, but have been captured on yellow sticky cards in greenhouses in the northeastern U.S. *Photo: Ray Gill*

sticky cards in New York greenhouses. However, nymphs of the mulberry whitefly occur only on certain tree species outdoors and are not pests of greenhouse crops.

The adult has smoky, irregular bands on the front wings similar to bandedwinged whitefly, but it also has a faint spot at the base and tip of each front wing. The abdomen is also completely white, lacking the brown markings that are present on the abdomen of the adult bandedwinged whitefly (fig. 10.27). The pupa is flattened, shiny black, with a fringe of white wax filaments outlining the body.

Biological control

Parasitoids

Certain tiny wasps are specialized parasitoids of whiteflies. These wasps attack whitefly nymphs, killing them in one of two ways. First, the female wasp uses her needlelike ovipositor to lay an egg within or beneath a whitefly nymph. The egg hatches, and the parasitoid maggot feeds on the nymph. Pupation occurs within the nymph. When the adult wasp emerges from the whitefly pupa, it chews a round exit hole through the cuticle at one end of the whitefly pupa. Second, the female wasp punctures the whitefly nymph with her ovipositor, killing the nymph, and feeds from the fluids that exude from the wound, a phenomenon called *host-feeding*.

For whitefly control on short-term floral crops (those grown under eight to 12 weeks), these wasps are usually released weekly in inundative quantities. When used inundatively, the wasps kill whitefly nymphs primarily by host-feeding rather than parasitism, leaving behind dead whitefly nymphs that appear collapsed and dry. Adult whiteflies are not attacked by the wasps.

Several species of whitefly parasitoids occur naturally in the U.S., and these may migrate into unsprayed greenhouses and attack whiteflies. However, the degree of control provided by these parasitoids is usually insufficient for various reasons. Augmentative releases of commercially reared parasitoids are typically more effective.

Encarsia formosa **(Gahan).** This very tiny wasp (0.6 mm, .023 inches) has a black head and thorax and pale yellow abdomen (fig. 10.28). Its wings are transparent. Females normally produce female offspring; males are rare.

Greenhouse whitefly pupae that have been parasitized by *Encarsia formosa* turn black (see fig. 1.35); silverleaf whitefly pupae turn amber brown (fig. 10.29). The adult wasps are rarely noticed. This parasitoid is widely used for biological control of greenhouse whitefly on greenhouse vegetables.

Eretmocerus eremicus **Rose and Zolnerowich.** This is an equally tiny wasp, but it differs from *Encarsia for-*

Fig. 10.28 *Encarsia formosa* adult. Note the black head and thorax and the yellow abdomen. *Photo: M. Hoddle*

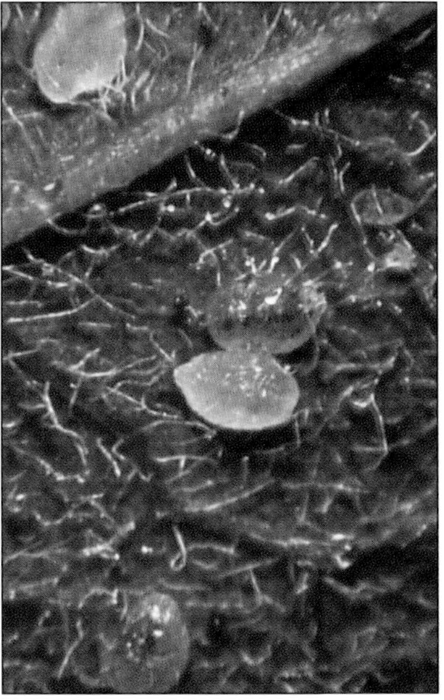

Fig. 10.29 Silverleaf whitefly nymphs parasitized by *E. formosa* turn amber brown, while unparasitized nymphs remain yellow. *Photo: John Sanderson*

mosa in that the adult is entirely yellow (fig. 10.30). It has green eyes and clubbed antennae. Males have longer, more prominent antennae than females. Parasitized whitefly nymphs appear beige in color.

Predators

***Delphastus pusillus* LeConte.** This is a tiny beetle related to ladybird beetles. Adults are shiny black (fig. 10.31). Male beetles have brown on their "faces," while female faces are all black. Larvae are long, thin, and wormlike, with a fuzzy appearance, and have a creamy or ivory color (figs. 10.32, 10.33).

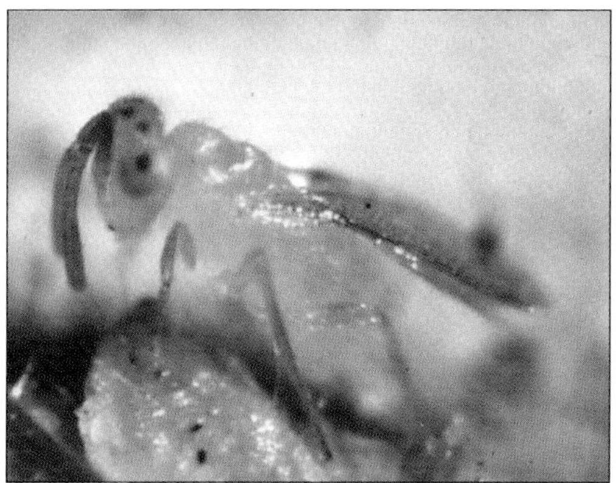

Fig. 10.30 *Eretmocerus eremicus* adult. These wasps are entirely yellow. *Photo: M. Hoddle*

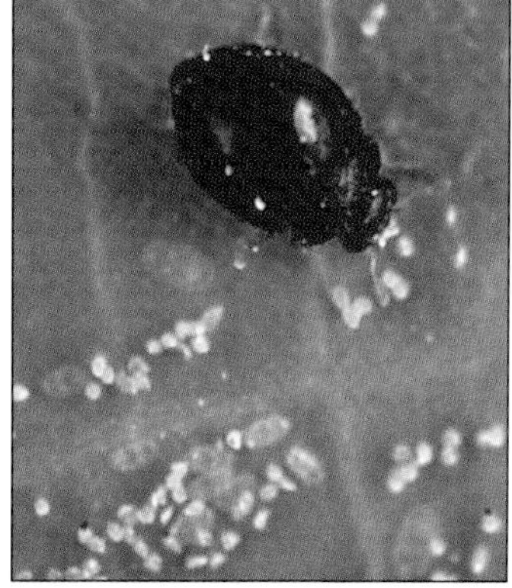

Fig. 10.31 Adult *Delphastus* beetles are very small, shiny, and black, and are voracious whitefly predators. *Photo: K. Hoelmer*

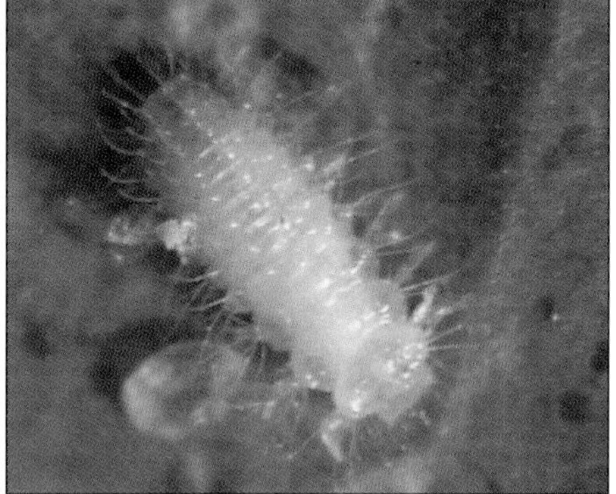

Fig. 10.32 *Delphastus* larvae are tiny, yellowish, narrow and elongated. *Photo: K. Hoelmer*

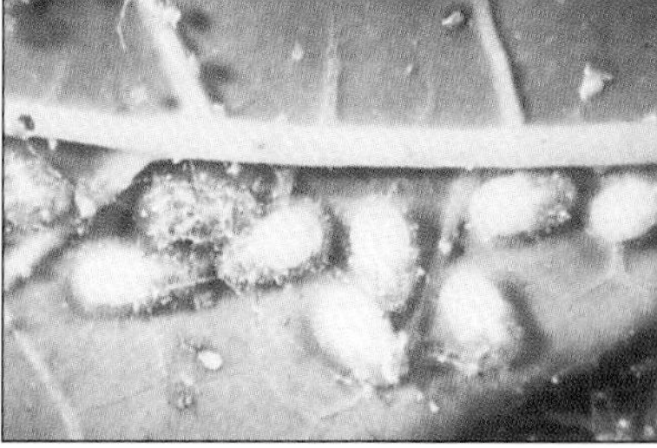

Fig. 10.33 *Delphastus* pupae aggregate near the main leaf veins. Given enough whiteflies for food, they can reproduce in a greenhouse. *Photo: K. Hoelmer*

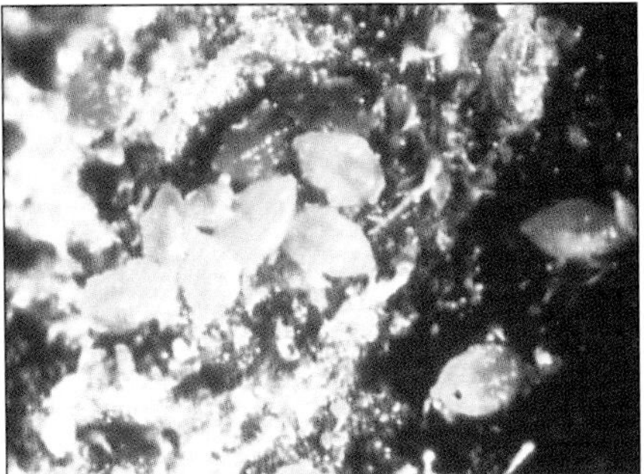

Fig. 10.34 Silverleaf whitefly nymphs infected with *Beauveria bassiana* often turn a reddish color. *Photo: S. Jaronski*

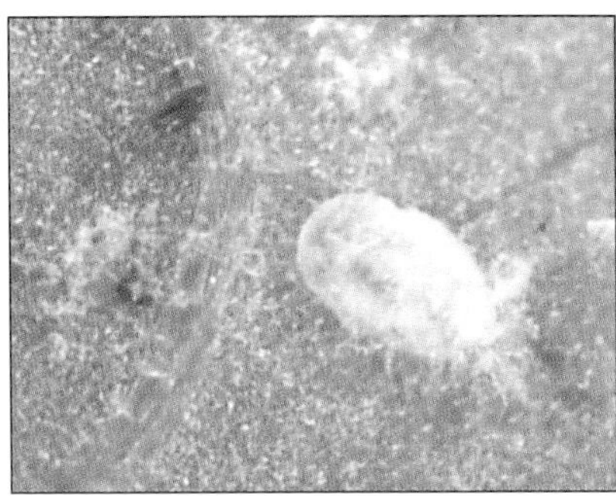

Fig. 10.35 Whitefly nymphs infected with *Paecilomyces fumosoroseus*. *Photo: T. Downer*

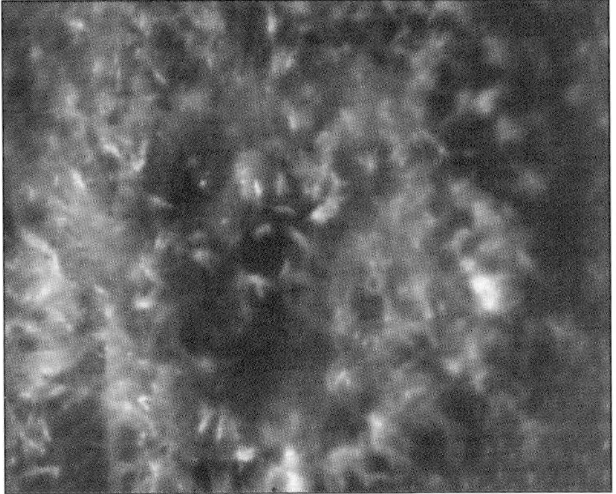

Fig. 10.36 Close-up of a whitefly nymph infected with *Paecilomyces fumosoroseus*. *Photo: Lance Osborne*

***Chrysoperla* (= *Chrysopa*) *carnea* Stephens and *C. rufilabrus* Burmeister.** Known as green lacewings, these insects have larvae that are voracious predators of a wide variety of insects, including whiteflies. Lacewing eggs are found at the tip of long, fragile stalks that keep them suspended off the surface. Newly hatched larvae are tiny (1 to 2 mm, .039 to .078 inches), elongate, pinkish grayish brown, with well-developed legs and prominent sickle-shaped mandibles. They roam leaves fairly quickly, searching for arthropods to eat. They grow to about 8 to 10 mm (.314 to .393 inches) long as larvae.

In nature, pupation occurs within a round, parchmentlike cocoon attached to leaves or stems. Adults are large, 1 to 2 cm long, pale to bright green, with prominent golden eyes, long antennae, and delicate, lacy, transparent wings (see fig. 1.32).

In greenhouses lacewings are usually released in the egg stage or as young larvae.

Pathogens

Several fungal pathogens will infect whiteflies. Two strains of one species are currently available in the U.S., *Beauveria bassiana* (BotaniGard, Naturalis-O) (fig. 10.34). Whitefly nymphs infected with this pathogen will often appear reddish, pinkish, or orangeish, especially if humidity is not high. Other fungi that attack whiteflies but are not currently available commercially in the U.S. include *Aschersonia aleyrodis*, *Paecilomyces fumosoroseus* (figs. 10.35, 10.36), and *Verticillium lecanii*.

CHAPTER 11

Other Pests in the Greenhouse

Some invertebrates that may be found in greenhouses do not fit into the insect and mite classifications as presented in this book. This chapter will cover a mix of insects and other invertebrates that are encountered in many greenhouses. Some of these are plant damaging, while others are present but do not inflict significant damage to plants.

Mollusks

Slugs and snails, class Gastropoda, many families

The moist environment of greenhouses and interiorscapes is ideal for supporting populations of slugs and snails. Several native and imported slugs and snails have been reported damaging foliage of greenhouse plants. All slugs and snails have unsegmented bodies and antennae. The body region that makes contact with the ground is a muscle called a gliding foot (fig. 11.1). These animals produce a silvery, slimy substance that coats surfaces over which they move. Since most slugs and snails are nocturnal in their feeding, the slime trail and feeding injury is noticed before the pest is detected.

Snails have an external shell, and over 700 species of land-inhabiting snails are known in North America (fig. 11.2). There are about 40 species of slugs in the United States. Slugs have no external shell but instead have a protective mantle on the dorsal side. The

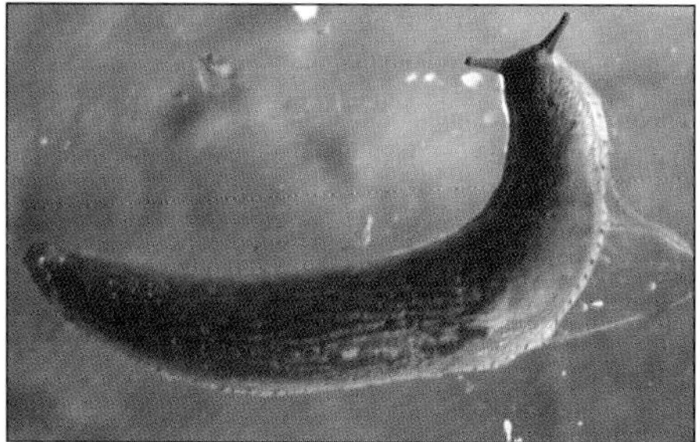

Fig. 11.1 The slug *Arion ater* is found feeding in many greenhouses. *Photo: Charlie Staines*

Fig. 11.2 A snail can consume several times its body weight each night. *Photo: Stanton Gill*

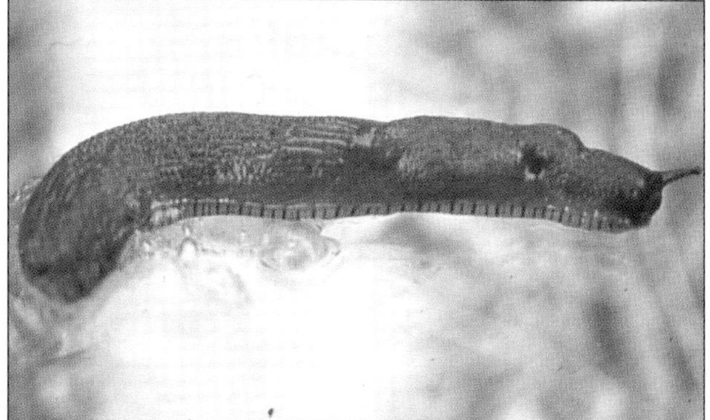

Fig. 11.3 The mantle of a slug is a hardened area on the back which is a remnant of a shell covering. *Photo: Charlie Staines*

mantle is the hump on a slug's back where it can retract its head if disturbed (fig. 11.3).

Both slugs and land snails can withstand lengths of time submerged in water but will drown if held in water for more than a couple of hours. Slugs and land snails have limited protection against water loss and therefore need adequate moisture levels to survive. They can absorb water directly through their skin or drink from puddles. Slugs and snails generally avoid areas with strong air currents since there is a chance of winds drying them out.

Plant damage

Snails and slugs feed on a variety of living and decaying plant matter. Plant damage from slugs and snails occurs by the rasping action of their mouthparts. Damage to leaves appears as irregularly shaped holes with smooth edges (see fig. 12.21). They can chew succulent plant parts and growing tips that are close to the ground. Seedlings are usually killed. A slime trial is nearly always associated with their feeding damage.

Monitoring

Short of finding slugs or snails feeding on plants, the presence of slime trails is the best way to determine that these mollusks are present and responsible for damaged plants. If slime trails are not apparent, yet snails or slugs are suspected, they can be drawn out of hiding. To draw out snails, water the infested area, both on and beneath the bench, in the late afternoon. After dark search them out using a flashlight, pick them up (gloves are handy), and get them to a specialist for identification.

Traps can also be used. A trap can be made from boards (of a size that is easy to handle) or flower pots, raised off the ground by 1-inch (25 mm) runners. The runners make it easy for the pests to crawl underneath. Beer-bait traps have been used to trap and drown slugs and snails; however, they attract within an area of only a few feet. Traps must have vertical sides to keep the snails and slugs from crawling out.

Slugs

Mature adult slugs are *hermaphroditic,* having both male and female organs. Mature slugs twist together to mate, and both adults are simultaneously fertilized. The typical life cycle starts with eggs laid in clusters of 20 to 300 in loose, damp soil in damp locations (fig.

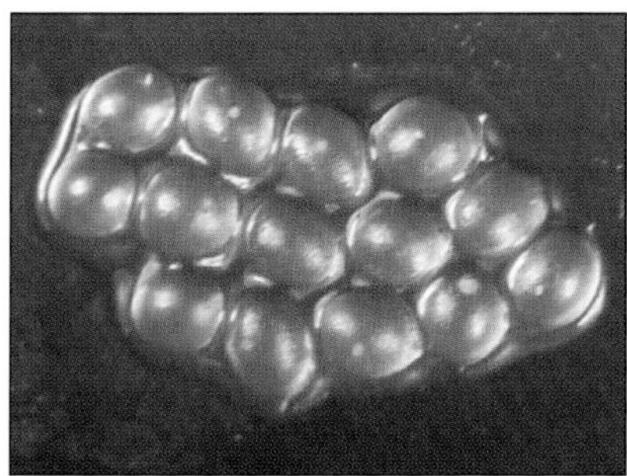

Fig. 11.4 Slug eggs are generally laid in soil or under debris. *Photo: Richard Lindquist*

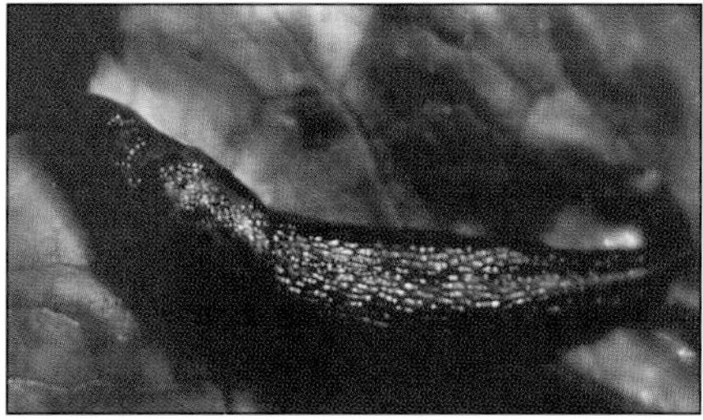

Fig. 11.5 Spotted garden slug is one of the larger slugs found in greenhouses. *Photo: Stanton Gill*

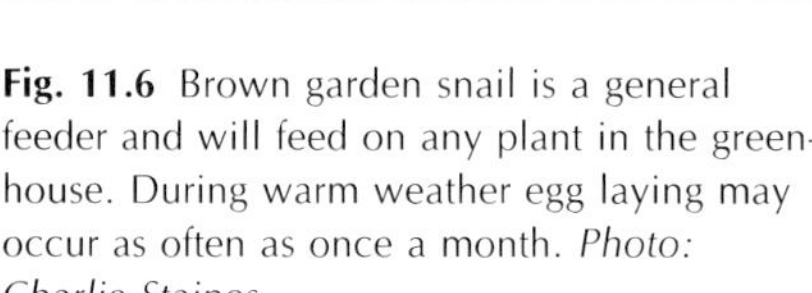

Fig. 11.6 Brown garden snail is a general feeder and will feed on any plant in the greenhouse. During warm weather egg laying may occur as often as once a month. *Photo: Charlie Staines*

Fig. 11.7 Symphylans are white colored arthropods found in soils. *Photo: Mark Ascerno*

11.4). Depending on the species, slug maturation takes several months to over a year (fig. 11.5).

Most feed during the night or on overcast days. Young slugs rasp away plant tissue and eat irregularly shaped holes in foliage as they mature. They generally prefer tender leaves or leaves without hard cuticles. Slugs leave a characteristic slime trail, which can be found on plant parts, bench surfaces, or greenhouse equipment. The slime provides a moisture cushion over rough areas that might damage the foot of the slug.

Land snails

The life cycle of snails is very similar to that of slugs. Snails have a hardened shell that they carry with them and can retreat into when disturbed. Snail genera are often identified by the shape and color of the shell. One of the most damaging snails in greenhouses and nurseries in the U.S. is the brown garden snail, *Helix aspera* (fig. 11.6). This snail is a quarantine pest in some states.

SYMPHYLANS

Class Symphyla, family Scutigerellidae

Symphylans are small arthropods commonly found in greenhouse and interiorscape soils. They are not insects but are related to centipedes and millipedes. A 10× hand lens may be needed for identification of symphylans. Adult symphylans have 12 pairs of legs, long antennae, and 15-segmented bodies (fig. 11.7). They are rapid movers but do not jump like springtails. When exposed to light they move rapidly into crevices or into soil.

They are general feeders and may feed on roots of young vegetable and ornamental crops. When they feed on root hairs, wilting of the plant can occur, as may infection by root rot organisms. In most cases symphyla are simply a nuisance and generally feed on algae, fungi, and decaying organic material.

Females lay eggs in the soil. Newly hatched immatures have only six pairs of legs and 10 body segments. Each time the symphylan molts, it adds a pair of legs, until it has 12 pairs. Adults may live for several years.

Populations of symphylans commonly occur outdoors in compost materials. If using composted materials in your soil mix, make sure it is thoroughly steam sterilized before you move the soil substrate into the greenhouse.

MILLIPEDES

Class Diplopoda, several orders and families

Millipedes are cylindrical, wormlike arthropods with two pairs of legs per body segment and with short antennae. Most are blackish or shades of brown, but some species are red or orange or have mottled patterns. They have many body segments, often with 30 or more pairs of legs.

Millipedes feed on decaying plant material and occasionally the roots of young seedling plants (fig. 11.8). Most species will curl into a spiral when disturbed (fig. 11.9).

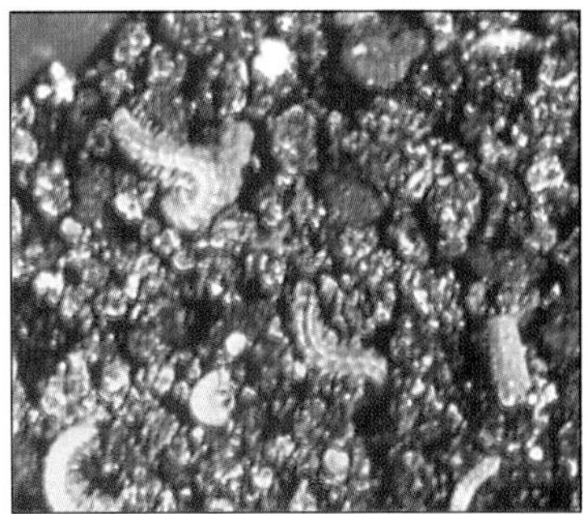

Fig. 11.8 Millipedes are commonly found in the bottom of pots or underneath benches. *Photo: M. Steiner*

Fig. 11.9 Millipedes generally feed on organic material. *Photo: Stanton Gill*

SPRINGTAIL

Order Collembola, several families

Springtails are small (1 to 2 mm, .039 to .078 inches in length), wingless arthropods that live in soil (fig. 11.10). Springtails develop through six to eight instars, and the immatures look similar to adults, except for the size difference. A 10x hand lens may be required for identification.

Most genera of springtails feed on organic matter, algae, and fungi. Some species are plant root feeders (fig. 11.11). Damage can occur to young seedlings, but most species are rarely pests.

These arthropods are worldwide in distribution. Most are white, but different genera can vary in color to purple, red, and brown. Springtails tend to mass together in large populations. They are able to move rapidly with a leaping action by using a powerful, forked, leverlike organ (furcula).

SOWBUGS AND PILLBUGS

Class Crustacea, order Isopoda, several families

Sowbugs and pillbugs are crustaceans that are worldwide in distribution. A common sowbug is *Porcellio laevis* Koch, in the family Porcellionidae. The pillbugs, such as *Armadillidium vulgare*

Latreille, are in the family Armadillidiidae. In Europe the commonly used English name for pillbugs and sowbugs is *woodlouse.* Sowbugs and pillbugs are the only crustaceans that have adapted to life on land.

They are oval in shape, segmented, convex above and flat beneath. They are gray and 5 to 8 mm (.196 to .314 inches) long. Sowbugs have two small, taillike appendages at the rear, and pillbugs do not (fig. 11.12). Pillbugs can roll up into a ball, but sowbugs cannot (fig. 11.13).

Sowbugs and pillbugs generally feed on decaying organic matter but occasionally feed on plant stems and roots of seedlings.

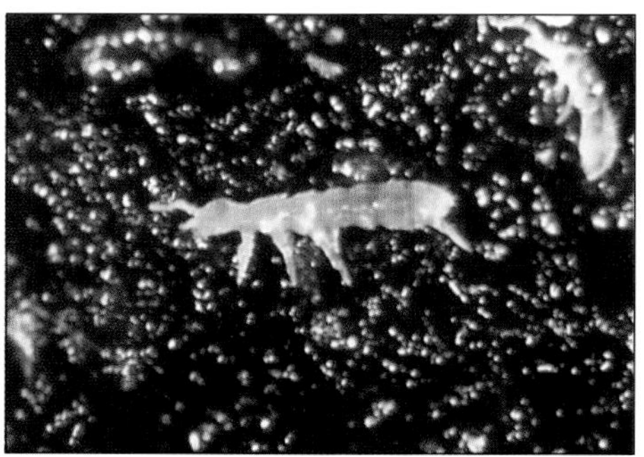

Fig. 11.10 Springtails are common in soils. *Photo: Richard Lindquist*

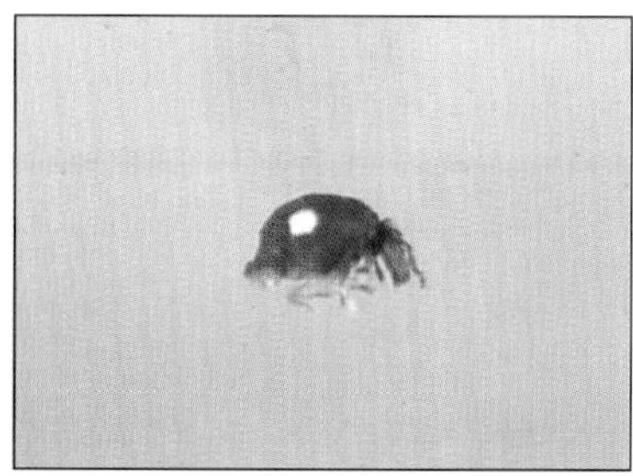

Fig. 11.11 The collembolan, *Bourletiella hortensis*, has been recorded as damaging plant material. *Photo: John Davidson*

Fig. 11.12 Sowbugs have two small, taillike appendages at the rear. *Photo: John Sanderson/Stanton Gill*

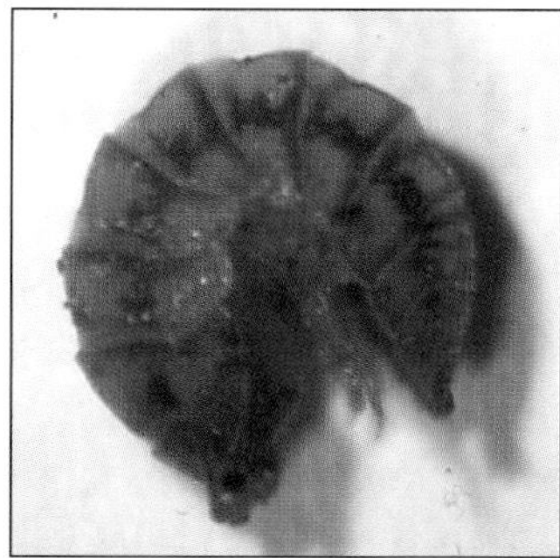

Fig. 11.13 Pillbugs will often roll up if disturbed. *Photo: John Sanderson/Stanton Gill*

CENTIPEDES

Order Scutigeromorpha, several classes and families

Centipedes are not pests of greenhouse crops, but they may be encountered. Centipedes are elongate, flattened arthropods with one pair of legs per body segment (fig. 11.14). When the larvae hatch from eggs, they have four pairs of legs. Depending on the species, the number of legs on adults may vary from 10 to over 100. They have very long, slender, jointed antennae. Centipedes' venom-bearing claws paralyze prey, which includes insects and other arthropods. Centipedes run when disturbed and will not roll into a ball.

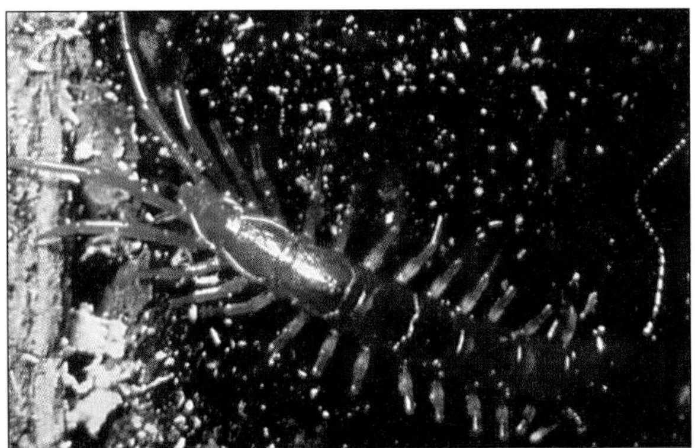

Fig. 11.14 Centipedes are insect predators. *Photo: Bart Drees*

SCORPIONS

Class Arachnida, order Scorpionida, several families

Scorpions are not plant pests but may be hiding in greenhouses in warmer regions of the U.S. The general body form and thornlike rigid stinger of the scorpion is easily identifiable. Like spiders, scorpions have two body regions, the cephalothorax and the abdomen. However, the abdomen is segmented, with a taillike posterior that terminates in a telson bearing a venomous stinger.

Scorpions' nocturnal habit and tendency to inhabit shady crevices may surprise greenhouse growers. Scorpions emerge from their hiding places at night and prey upon ground-inhabiting insects and other small animals, such as mice. They may occasionally move into a greenhouse, especially in the southwestern United States.

Females do not lay eggs but give birth to active young. These climb upon the back of the mother and remain fastened by their pincers until after the first molt. All scorpions are venomous, but most species are not dangerous. In the U.S., two species are known to be lethal: *Centuroides sculpturatus* and *C. gertschi*.

WHIP SCORPION

Class Arachnida, order Pedipalpida

Whip scorpions are not greenhouse pests but may be found under flats or pots. They occur in the southern United States from coast to coast. This arthropod is an occasional visitor in southern greenhouses.

These harmless arachnids are nocturnal, hiding during the day in damp places. The body length varies from 2 to 6.5 cm (.787 to 2.55 inches). The principal genus found in the United States is *Terantula,* although it is not a tarantula, which is a large spider. The whip can be twice as long as the body.

OCCASIONAL INSECT PESTS, CLASS INSECTA

Cockroaches, order Blattaria, families Blattellidae and Blattidae

Four common species of cockroaches found in greenhouses and interiorscapes are German cockroach, *Blattella germanica* (Linnaeus) (fig. 11.15), brown-banded cockroach, *Supella longipalpa,* American cockroach, *Periplaneta americana* (Harris), and oriental roach, *Blatta orientalis* Linnaeus. A

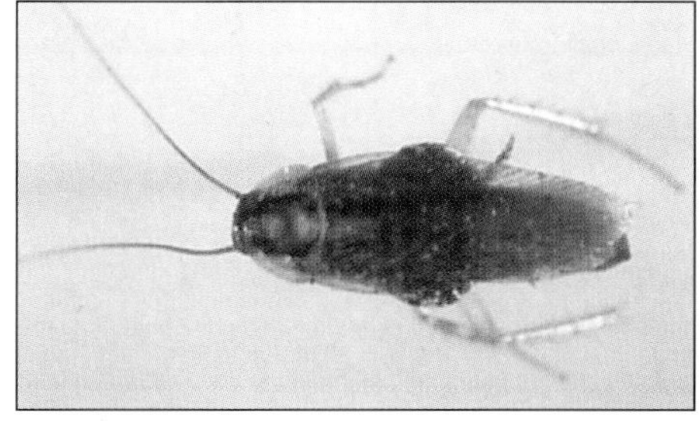

Fig. 11.15 The German cockroach has distinct dark striping on the thoracic region, just behind the head. *Photo: Stanton Gill*

fifth cockroach species, wood cockroach, *Parcoblatta pennsylvanica* (De Geer), is an occasional pest in greenhouses and interiorscapes.

Cockroaches may cause some injury to plants but hide in the moist, warm environment of the greenhouse. Cockroaches are *thigmotactic,* that is, they like tight places. They are also nocturnal, coming out of their hiding places at night in search of food and water. If cockroaches are spotted during the day, chances are the infestation is very heavy or they have been poisoned by a previous pesticide application. Working areas should be kept clean of food residue and trash to prevent buildup of large cockroach populations.

Crickets, order Orthoptera, family Gryllidae

Crickets are a nuisance pest that usually move from outside into greenhouses or interiorscapes in the fall. Crickets have long, filiform antennae that are longer than the body, and the *tegmina,* the front wings, lie flat on the back. The field cricket, *Gryllus assimilis* (fig. 11.16), and the house cricket, *Acheta domesticus,* are two species commonly found in greenhouses. Crickets can be attracted to lights and will often migrate during the first cold days of fall, through cracks and crevices. Excessive rainfall may cause an invasion of crickets into a greenhouse. House crickets can maintain themselves indefinitely indoors if they have found food and water, whereas the field cricket generally needs to complete its life cycle outdoors.

The field cricket can be solid black to straw colored. The house cricket is generally brown. The females for both species have three conspicuous appendages extending from the tip of the abdomen, the middle one being the sword-like ovipositor. Males of both species have only two caudal appendages.

Fig. 11.16 Field crickets are black and often can be heard "singing" in the greenhouse in the evening and early morning. *Photo: Bart Drees*

Earwigs, order Dermaptera, family Forficulidae

Fig. 11.17 Earwigs hide under pots and flats and have distinct pincers at the tips of their abdomens. *Photo: Stanton Gill*

Earwigs range in size from 5 to 25 mm (.196 to .984 inches) in length. These are elongate, flattened insects with a shiny exoskeleton of brown to black. Earwigs live in dark, moist places, such as under benches or under flats. They are nocturnal but may be active on heavily overcast days.

The most distinct characteristic of earwigs is the paired, forceplike *cerci,* or pincers, at the tip of the abdomen (fig. 11.17). The common name *earwigs* is based on a European superstition that these insects enter sleeping people's ears and bore into their brains. They are harmless to humans. Earwigs are omnivorous, mainly feeding on live and dead insects, decaying plant material, and occasionally flowers of plants.

Adults have two pairs of wings. The front pair are short and leatherlike. The hind wings are membranous and folded under the front pair. Even though earwigs have wings, they prefer to move by crawling. The pincerlike cerci on the tip of the abdomen are straight on the female, while the male has curved cerci.

Fig. 11.18 Fire ants are a major nuisance, causing a "burning" sensation as they bite then spray a liquid from their abdomen. *Photo: USDA*

Fire ants, order Hymenoptera, family Formicidae

Fire ants, *Solenopsis* spp., are native to South America. This species now ranges throughout the southern portion of the United States and south to Brazil and Peru. Fire ants are largely a ground-nesting ant. They have been found nesting in soil in nursery pots. Many states quarantine against introduction of this pest (fig. 11.18).

Fire ants get their name from the severe reaction caused by their stings. The workers have two nodes in the petiole and two segments in the antennal club. The body, especially the abdomen, is usually very hairy.

Leafhoppers, order Homoptera, family Cicadellidae

Leafhoppers are fast-flying, slender insects with short, bristlelike antennae. Leafhoppers have piercing mouthparts and suck plant juices from green parts of plants. Feeding causes a stippling of foliage and, in some cases, curling and distortion of new growth.

Both the adults and the nymphs are strong hoppers, but they often move sideways on a stem when first disturbed. Most of the species are wedge shaped, but they vary in coloration, shape, and size. Leafhoppers lay eggs into leaf tissue and go through incomplete metamorphosis. The adult holds the wings rooflike over the abdomen. Nymphs resemble adults except they lack wings, developing wing pads as they mature (figs. 11.19, 11.20).

Plant bugs, order Hemiptera, family Miridae

There are a few plant bugs that damage plants in greenhouses. The tarnished plant bug, *Lygus lineolaris* (Palisot de Beauvois), is

Fig. 11.19 Potato leafhopper nymphs are narrow and bullet shaped. *Photo: Ward Tingey*

Fig. 11.20 Adult potato leafhoppers are similar to nymphs but have wings. They will rapidly leap away if disturbed. *Photo: Ward Tingey*

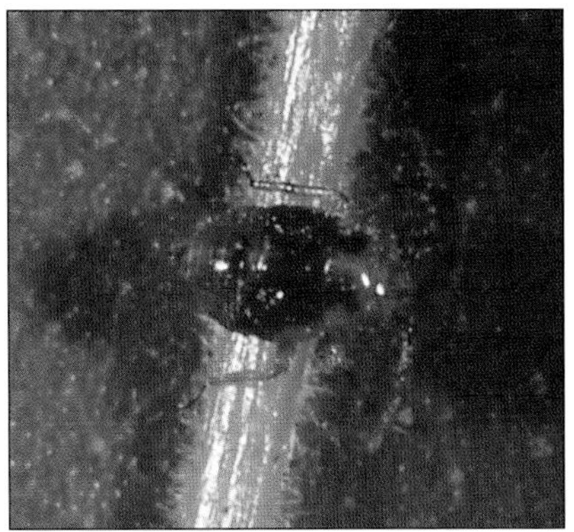

Fig. 11.21 Tarnished plant bug nymphs are found feeding on tender new growth of plants. *Photo: John Davidson*

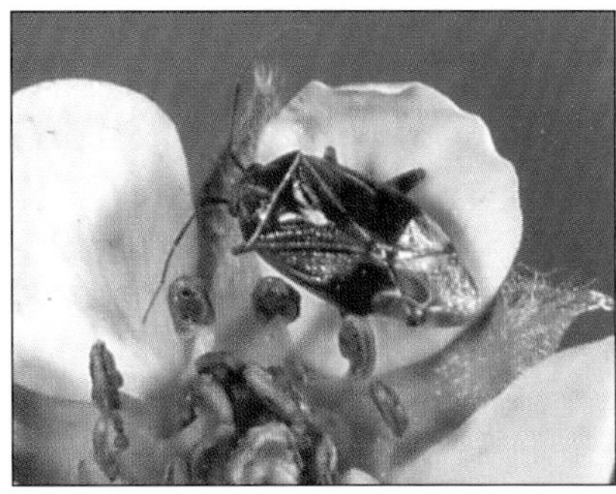

Fig. 11.22 Tarnished plant bug adults move rapidly if disturbed. *Photo: Richard Lindquist*

Fig. 11.23 Four-lined plant bug has distinct black and yellow striping on its back. *Photo: Richard Lindquist*

among the most damaging of the Miridae family (figs. 11.21, 11.22). This insect, found throughout the continental United States, attacks asters, basil, mint, chrysanthemums, dahlias, impatiens, goldenrod, and marigolds.

Newly hatched nymphs are yellowish green and about 1 mm (.039 inches) long. Older nymphs are yellow green to green and are wingless. As nymphs mature they develop yellow, green, or black spots. Older nymphs have four black spots on the thorax and one on the abdomen. The head is light green. The full-grown adult is about 4 to 5 mm (.157 to .196 inches) long.

The tarnished plant bug damages plants by inserting its needle-like mouthparts (stylets) into plants and extracting juices. Toxins may be injected during feeding. Females prefer to insert eggs into young leaf tissue, tender stems, or flowers. Eggs laid in the leaf veins cause swelling to tissue. Nymphs pass through five instars, causing feeding damage in all stages. Feeding causes terminal growth to be distorted and yellow.

Most tarnished plant bugs migrate into the greenhouse from outdoors. Microscreening can help exclude this pest. Once established in a greenhouse, however, multiple generations can occur, with the average life cycle being 21 to 28 days. Greenhouses near farms growing forage crops may suffer most from invasion after crops have been harvested.

Another Mirid that causes damage to greenhouse crops, especially mints and several other herbs, is the four-lined plant bug, *Poecilocapsus lineatus* (Fabr). The bug is yellow, with four black stripes on the wing covers (fig. 11.23). The damage to plants is similar to the injury caused by tarnished plant bug, but on some herb species a characteristic brown spotting occurs on the leaf surface. Eggs are inserted into the plant tissue, and the nymphs go through five instars. It has a short life cycle, and the adult's activity outdoors is over by the end of spring.

Part 3

Identification of Plant Damage of Specific Crops

CHAPTER 12

Diagnosing Causes of Plant Damage

Insects and mites can damage greenhouse plants in many ways. Sometimes the damage caused by one species can be confused with that of another, leading to misidentification of the real problem and possibly the use of inappropriate and ineffective control tactics. Pest damage can also be confused with disease symptoms, nutritional imbalances, or many other causes. Finally, combinations of several kinds of plant damage can produce symptoms concurrently, making it difficult to pin down a single cause.

Experience aids tremendously in diagnosing plant damage. Experienced managers learn which crops are damaged by which pests and what the damage looks like. Experienced growers know that to acquire such knowledge, it is helpful to keep mental and preferably written records of growing practices, scouting observations, and pest management tactics, such as irrigation dates, plant growth regulator applications, fertilization regimes, results of soil and water tests, ambient temperatures, and pesticide application information (e.g., exactly what was applied, how much, where, when, by whom, with what equipment, and under what environmental conditions). Referring to this historic information or providing it to a crop consultant aids in diagnosing plant damage, which may have originated days or weeks prior to first observation.

The following discussion is intended to aid in distinguishing among types of damage caused by various insects and mites as well as assorted other sources.

Fig. 12.1 Dieffenbachia with spider mite injury that has resulted in leaves with brown edges. *Photo: John Sanderson*

Fig. 12.2 Look for spider mites on the underside of injured foliage. *Photo: Stanton Gill*

LEAF STIPPLING

Leaf stippling is defined as small to tiny white spots on leaves or petals that may be grouped in patches or that may cover an entire leaf or plant.

Spider mites. Spider mites have very tiny mouthparts that remove green chlorophyll from individual leaf cells. Removal of chlorophyll and other plant cell contents causes very tiny white specks to appear on the upper surface of leaves. Stippling caused by spider mites tends to be very fine, first showing through to the upper leaf surface on only a small portion of the leaf surface. More of the leaf will be covered with this fine stippling as the mite colonies grow, and the leaf and even the whole plant may become bronzed or grayish and defoliated (fig. 12.1). If you turn over a leaf that has been damaged by spider mites, it will usually have very fine webbing, on which the tiny mites run around, and their spherical eggs may be found (figs. 12.2, 12.3). Broad

Fig. 12.3 Lewis mite webbing on tip growth of poinsettia in the bract stage indicates that mites have gone past the early damage level for most poinsettia plants. *Photo: Stanton Gill*

Fig. 12.4 Broad mite damage to lower surface of begonia leaves. *Photo: Margery Daughtrey*

Fig. 12.5 Leafminer feeding injury on chrysanthemum. *Photo: John Sanderson*

mites can cause bronzing of the lower leaf surfaces on some plants (fig. 12.4).

Serpentine leafminers. Adult leafminers cause white dots on leaves from the punctures they make when laying eggs or feeding (fig. 12.5). If adult leafminers are numerous, they may produce many punctures on the same leaf (fig. 12.6). There may also be some tiny young mines issuing from some of the punctures, caused by newly hatched larvae beginning their mines in the leaf.

Each puncture is much larger than the pinpoint stippling caused by spider mites. The punctures are generally not clumped together on a leaf, but are usually spread over the upper leaf surface.

Thrips. When feeding on exposed plant surfaces, most thrips found in greenhouses damage the surface cells of the leaf or petal in small patches, rather than in stipples. Damaged patches on leaves appear as "silvered" scars (fig. 12.7), which may eventually turn straw

Fig. 12.6 Many adult leafminer females have punctured marigold foliage, causing the leaves to appear stippled. *Photo: Dick Lindquist*

Fig. 12.7 Thrips injury to chrysanthemum leaves causes foliage to have a stippled to silvery appearance. *Photo: John Sanderson*

Fig. 12.8 Typical thrips injury to a chrysanthemum leaf. *Photo: John Sanderson*

Fig. 12.9 Thrips feeding causes discolored patches on flower petals. *Photo: John Sanderson*

colored or brown. Damage to petals can result in light or dark patches, depending on the flower (figs.12.8, 12.9). Patches damaged by thrips are also usually accompanied by small, dark specks, which are the fecal waste of the thrips (fig. 12.10, see also fig. 8.2).

Planthoppers/leafhoppers. Planthoppers and other plant bugs also can cause white stippling from their feeding on the lower surface of leaves. Their stipples are generally of similar size as that caused by leafminers, but they tend to be clumped together or in erratic lines, because they often feed as they crawl over the leaf surface (fig. 12.11). Gently turning over a leaf that has planthopper stippling may or may not reveal a planthopper.

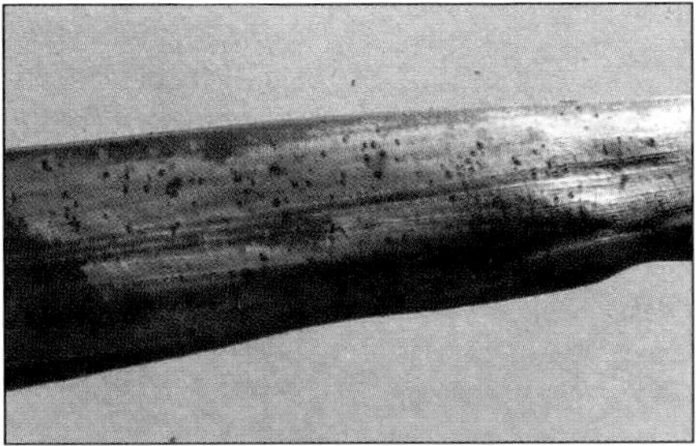

Fig. 12.10 Thrips injury and fecal droppings on orchid foliage. *Photo: Stanton Gill*

Fig. 12.11 Leafhopper stippling to rose leaf and cast skins of leafhoppers. *Photo: Stanton Gill*

Lacebugs. Lacebug stippling is similar to planthopper stippling (fig. 12.12), but it often also has dark fecal spots from the lacebugs. Also, lacebugs are more likely to be found in the vicinity of the damage.

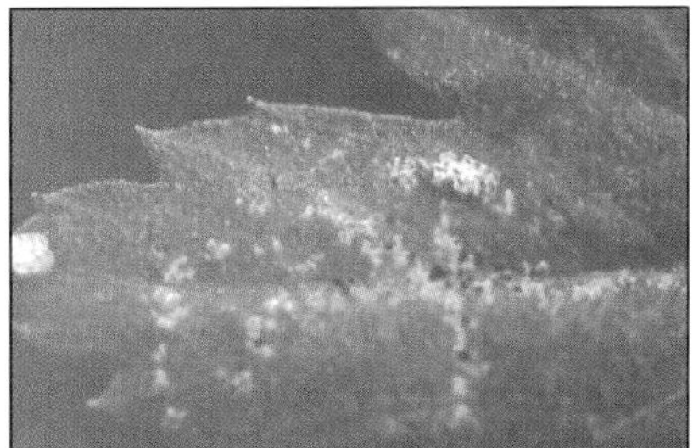

Fig. 12.12 Stippling caused by lacebugs on chrysanthemum. *Photo: Margery Daughtrey*

Nutrient deficiency. Magnesium deficiency can sometimes produce symptoms that appear as stipples or specks.

LEAF AND FLOWER DISTORTION

Leaf and flower distortion is defined as leaves and flowers that are misshapped, crinkled, distorted, and/or stunted.

Aphids. The toxic saliva and feeding activity of some aphids can cause leaves of certain plant species to become stunted and distorted (fig. 12.13, see also fig. 2.4). When aphids are the cause of such distortion, other signs of their presence are usually apparent, such as white cast skins, sticky honeydew, and possibly sooty mold, as well as the aphids themselves, which may be found on the lower surfaces of the leaves or on new, growing tips. Some viruses that are transmitted by aphids may also cause distorted plant growth (see fig. 2.7).

Thrips. When thrips, such as western flower thrips, feed on and destroy some of the cells of young buds or terminal shoots, the

Fig. 12.13 Heavy aphid infestations can cause distorted leaves. *Photo: John Sanderson*

Fig. 12.14 Thrips feeding on developing poinsettia leaves can cause this type of injury. *Photo: John Sanderson*

Fig. 12.15 Rose midge feeding on the tip flower shoot can kill it, causing what is called a "blind shoot." *Photo: Stanton Gill*

Fig. 12.16 Thrips injury to newly expanding leaves causes distorted growth on this impatiens plant. *Photo: Stanton Gill*

resulting leaf or flower can be distorted. This type of damage usually cannot be noticed when it first occurs, but it becomes apparent as the leaf or flower expands and becomes distorted because of the death of some of the cells (figs. 12.14, 12.16). Colonies of Cuban laurel thrips cause *Ficus* leaves to curl and discolor in a very characteristic manner (fig. 12.17).

By the time the damage is observed the thrips will probably not be in the damaged area but may be feeding on new tissue in other protected leaf or flower buds. It is usually impractical to sample young plant buds and foliage for thrips because of their tiny size and the unlikeliness of finding them. Sometimes thrips can be detected by tapping shoots or buds onto a white surface. The best way to detect the presence of thrips is through diligent monitoring with yellow or blue sticky cards. If sticky card records indicate that thrips were abundant at about the time that damaged plant tissue was young and developing, then thrips are a likely culprit.

Cyclamen and broad mites. Both of these tarsonemid mites can cause leaf or flower stunting and distortion. Broad mites are recorded from ivy, impatiens, New Guinea impatiens, clematis, and peperomia, among others. Cyclamen mites are recorded from ivy, African violet, cyclamen, fuchsia, geranium, gloxinia, snapdragon, and azalea, among others. Damage caused by these mites will tend to be localized, confined to one or several plants in a small area, rather than widespread.

Both these mites are extremely tiny. Cyclamen mites commonly infest the growing tips and young leaflets of host plants, and damage appears as the tissue expands (figs. 12.18, 12.19). Broad mites occur more generally over the plant, where they feed on the undersurface of the leaves, causing them to curl and become brittle (see fig. 12.90). Damaged leaves must be inspected with a minimum of a 14× hand lens or dissecting microscope to confirm the presence of either species. Protected areas on damaged leaves should be examined for the tiny mites, their eggs, and/or the skins

Fig. 12.17 All stages of Cuban laurel thrips can be found in curled and twisted tip growth of ficus plants. *Photo: Stanton Gill*

Fig. 12.18 The leaf and shoot buds in the axil of kalanchoe plants are damaged by broad mite feeding. *Photo: Stanton Gill*

Fig. 12.19 Leaf distortion on African violet has been caused by cyclamen mites. *Photo: John Sanderson*

that remain after molting. Inspect the inside of curled leaves, leaf axils, terminals, and other protected areas.

Leafhoppers. Leafhoppers, such as the potato leafhopper, can cause stunting and curling of infested plants. "Hopperburn" is caused by toxic saliva injected by potato leafhopper. There is a distortion of the leaf veins, which results in yellowing around the margin of the leaf. The leaf eventually curls inward. Flower development may be reduced or ceased.

Viruses. Various plant viruses can cause distortion in leaves and flowers. Some of these viruses may be transmitted by insects.

Nutrient deficiency. Trace element deficiencies (e.g., boron and copper deficiencies) may result in distortion of new growth.

Chemical injury. Applications of pesticides or other chemicals (herbicides, plant growth regulators, fungicides, or insecticides) can sometimes cause deformities, usually if used inappropriately or under adverse environmental conditions.

Leaf Chewing or Skeletonizing

Leaf chewing or skeletonizing involves leaves and petals that have been damaged with notches, holes, patches of leaf tissue removed between veins, or leaves that are entirely missing.

Snails and slugs. Damage appears as irregular holes in foliage and tends to be more severe on foliage nearest the ground (figs. 12.20, 12.21). Seedlings and young plants can be entirely defoliated.

Because damage is done at night and these pests hide in moist, dark, protected places during the day, they are not likely to be found feeding. However, slugs and snails move on a shiny slime trail (fig. 12.22), and this telltale trail can dry and remain on foliage, soil or growing media, or on the sides of pots. During the day, snails and slugs may sometimes be found under pots and flats, beneath benches, or in other hiding places.

Caterpillars. Chewing damage can be done to the leaf surface as well as to the edge of a leaf (fig. 12.23, see also fig. 3.1, fig. 3.23). Damage by young larvae is often made to the leaf surface; the leaves are not completely eaten through but remain damaged with a thin,

Fig. 12.20 Slug damage to hosta appears similar to damage from caterpillars. *Photo: Stanton Gill*

Fig. 12.21 Small holes in caladium foliage are caused by feeding activity of slugs. *Photo: Stanton Gill*

Fig. 12.22 The slime trails left by slugs and snails help to determine if they are the cause of chewing damage *Photo: Charlie Staines*

Fig. 12.23 Cross-striped caterpillars feed on ornamental cabbage and cause holes in the foliage. *Photo: Stanton Gill*

transparent layer of cells (a "window") (fig. 12.24). Older larvae may eat entire leaves and petals. Some species damage the growing points, causing unwanted branching. Fecal pellets, called frass, are eliminated as the caterpillar feeds and may fall onto leaves or the soil below the feeding site.

Damage tends to be localized, not widespread, in a greenhouse. Cutworms are night feeders and hide in the growing media at the base of the plants or under pots during the day. They may feed on leaves, buds, or flowers or chew through the stem of a young plant, cutting it off near the soil line. They will not be found on the plant during the day. Some caterpillar species roll or web leaves together

Fig. 12.24 Early instar caterpillar feeding causes skeletonized damage to dahlia foliage. *Photo: Stanton Gill*

Fig. 12.25 Light foliar injury results from Japanese beetle feeding on a zinnia. *Photo: Stanton Gill*

Fig. 12.6 Japanese beetles cause a skeletonizing injury of rose leaves. *Photo: Stanton Gill*

and may be found within the rolled leaves unless they leave to pupate. Pheromone traps may be used outdoors to monitor for adult (moth) activity.

Beetles and weevils. Adult beetles can damage foliage and flowers (fig. 12.25). They tend to skeletonize the leaf, leaving many holes between veins, rather than completely consuming the entire leaf or large sections of it (fig. 12.26). It is common to find the adults eating the leaves or flowers. Larvae feed on roots, not foliage.

Notches on the edges of leaves of certain plant species are a common sign of damage by adult black vine weevils (see fig. 9.3). Because the damage occurs at night, the adults are not often found on the plant, but they may be discovered hiding in the soil or under pots. Larvae do not damage foliage, but they feed on roots and can be a severe pest of some ornamentals.

Grasshoppers. In some regions of the U.S., grasshoppers may invade greenhouses and feed on plants with their chewing mouthparts. They can consume significant amounts of foliage or entire plants. If damage by grasshoppers is suspected, they will usually be abundant outside the greenhouse at a time when vents and doors have been recently opened. Damage may be most common near vents and doors, where they have entered the greenhouse.

When stationary, their color can help them blend into the foliage, but they readily jump or fly if they are disturbed. They usually consume leaf tissue from the edge, rather than in the middle of the leaf.

LEAF SPOTS AND BLOTCHES

Leaf spots and blotches are defined as patches of leaf tissue that are damaged, necrotic, or discolored.

Leafminers. Most leafminers in greenhouses do not produce true blotch mines. There is usually at least some portion of the mine that has a serpentine shape. On some outdoor-grown annuals and herbaceous perennials, it is possible for a blotch mine to occur. Check whether the blotched area of the leaf appears to be made up of an upper and lower thin membrane, with the inside of the leaf mined empty (see figs. 5.4 and 12.63).

The immature form of the insect may still be within the mine. If present, it should be visible by holding the mine up to the light. If not present, then look for a slit or hole where the insect emerged from the mine. This exit point is usually found on the lower surface of the leaf. There may also be frass or other fecal material left behind in the mine.

Plant bugs. Four-lined plant bug and other plant bugs can inject toxic saliva into a leaf during feeding, which can result in a small, dark, fairly circular spot at each site where the bug fed. There are usually at least several spots on each leaf (see fig. 12.65). These spots can eventually decay and leave holes in the leaves. These leaf spots can be confused with fungal or bacterial leaf spots.

In the Northeast, the plant bugs are usually active in the summer and into the fall and may become fairly common in unsprayed greenhouses. Plant bugs should be noted on sticky cards, as well as on leaves or flowers, and may be correlated with the appearance of the leaf spots.

Fungal or bacterial infections. Discolored spots on leaves caused by plant-pathogenic fungi or bacteria may sometimes be mistaken for insect feeding injuries. Because many insects remove plant tissue as they feed, holding a leaf up to the light often allows you to discriminate between disease symptoms and insect feeding injury. Although fungal and bacterial leaf spots may appear water-soaked under high-humidity conditions in a greenhouse, they will remain fairly opaque. Occasionally, if leaf tissue is infected by a plant pathogen, the killed tissue may be walled off and drop away from the leaf, producing a "shot hole" symptom, which might be mistaken for feeding injury.

Fungal leaf spots often develop fruiting bodies, which aid in their identification. A hand lens will facilitate viewing evidence of fungus infection. Spore containers sometimes appear as tiny, dark bumps, either in rings or scattered across a leaf lesion. *Botrytis cinerea,* a very common greenhouse fungus, produces distinctive "gray mold" when it sporulates on dead plant tissue.

A plant disease diagnostic laboratory should be consulted if the cause of plant symptoms is unclear after careful examination of the injured plant.

Physical and chemical injury. Excessively bright light and overly cold irrigation water may cause leaf spotting on some sensitive plants. Materials applied to crops for the purpose of disease or insect control, growth regulation, or fertilization may all, under some circumstances, produce leaf spots or blotches, particularly if an excessive dose is accidentally applied. Plants under water stress at the time of a treatment are more likely to be injured.

If you suspect a chemical injury, recheck your records for both rates of application and environmental conditions in the weeks preceding the appearance of symptoms. If injury is due to an event such as a pesticide application, subsequently expanding leaves will be symptomless unless the material is systemic within the plant, so you may note that only a few leaf pairs show symptoms.

YELLOWING

Scale insects. Scale insects can cause general leaf yellowing, especially on foliage plants (fig. 12.27). If soft scale is present, look for honeydew, ants, as well as the scale themselves on leaves or branches.

Mites. Severe feeding by spider mites and flat mites can cause a leaf to become bronzed or grayish. These leaves may eventually fall off the plant (see fig. 12.3).

Fungus gnats. Fungus gnat feeding damage to roots can disrupt nutrient and water uptake.

Poor root health. Poor root health caused by poor drainage or root rot diseases can result in yellowing.

Insufficient fertilizer. Insufficient nitrogen can cause yellowing. Imbalances in soil pH and in trace elements can also cause yellowing, especially in young leaves.

Fig. 12.27 Large populations of brown soft scale will cause yellowing and dropping of foliage on ficus plants. *Photo: Stanton Gill*

Wilted Foliage

Fungus gnats. Damage to roots by fungus gnat chewing can reduce water uptake and result in water stress (fig. 12.28, see also fig. 4.1, fig. 4.4). The damage can also provide a wound for entry of plant pathogens, which can affect root health and eventually water uptake.

Fig. 12.28 Fungus gnat larvae can bore into the stems and roots of poinsettia causing the plant to collapse. *Photo: Margery Daughtrey*

Boring caterpillars. Certain caterpillar species, such as the European corn borer, can tunnel into stems of chrysanthemums, gladiolus, geranium, dahlia, and other thick-stemmed plants, disrupting the flow of nutrients and causing wilting of

Fig. 12.29 European corn borer larvae injury to chrysanthemum. The stem is cut open to reveal frass that is excreted by the larvae feeding within the stem. *Photo: Stanton Gill*

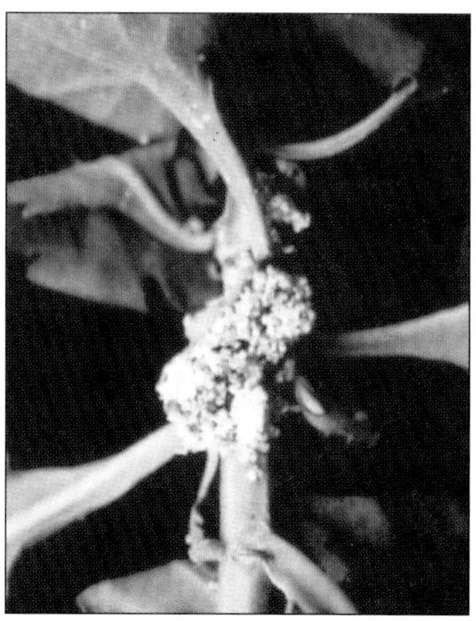

Fig. 12.30 Frass accumulating on the outside is caused by the European corn borer larvae feeding within the chrysanthemum stem. *Photo: Stanton Gill*

the foliage above their tunnel (figs. 12.29, 12.30). If the plants are single stemmed, the entire plant may become wilted.

Evidence of the insect tunneling appears as a pile of frass near or below the obvious hole where they entered the stem. The caterpillar may sometimes be found within the stem.

Root rot and stem rot diseases. Such fungi such as *Pythium, Rhizoctonia, Thielaviopsis,* and *Fusarium* spp. may attack the roots and/or stem base of plants and cause wilting of the aboveground portions. To find evidence of fungus infection, examine root tips for darkly discolored tissue, which is frequently softened. Also look for discolored (sometimes sunken) tissue or fungus mycelia or sporulation at the base of the stem.

Excessive soluble salts. Plants grown at excessive soluble salt levels may wilt. Close inspection of roots may show desiccation of the root tips. Conduct regular soil analyses during crop production to keep abreast of soluble salt levels resulting from your fertility program.

Irrigation problems. Plants need adequate amounts of water. On the other hand, overwatering can also result in poor root health and wilting.

Honeydew

Honeydew is a sticky sugar-containing secretion produced by aphids, soft scale, and whitefly.

Fig. 12.31 Honeydew, sooty mold, and cast skins on this hibiscus are produced by aphids. *Photo: John Sanderson*

Homopteran pests. Most insects in the order Homoptera, including aphids, whiteflies, mealybugs, and scale insects, produce honeydew as a waste product as they feed on plant sap. Honeydew falling from an infestation can coat foliage below, leaving a sticky, shiny residue. The honeydew often attracts ants. A grayish black sooty mold may then grow on the honeydew, which makes the plant even more unattractive (fig. 12.31).

Leaf Drop

Spider mites and other mites. Severe feeding by large populations of these mites can cause leaves to become yellow, dry, and fall off the plant. Such a high population of spider mites will create very apparent fine webbing on the leaves. Large populations of tarsonemid mites will not have webbing, but a hand lens will reveal the tiny reddish mites or their cast skins, eggshells, and other evidence of their infestation.

Scale insects. Feeding by scales can cause chlorosis, leaf drop, and stem dieback. The insects can become so numerous that they encrust a stem. Soft scale infestations will produce honeydew.

Poor root health. Water stress, root rots, and excessive soluble salts can all eventually lead to leaf drop.

Flower Shatter and Petal Drop

Plant bugs. Tarnished plant bug and related bugs may feed on flower buds, causing them to abort. Damaged flowers may also fail to develop on one side. Such damage can occur before the insects are noticeable. This injury is more common out of doors than within the greenhouse. On crops such as chrysanthemum, aster, and other composites, careful scouting of foliage and yellow sticky cards should be done, especially near flowering. The bugs might be detected on sticky cards. Look for them in outside sources, such as weedy fields, and be aware that they may enter the greenhouse through unscreened vents and doors.

Pesticide damage. Pesticide damage can result in damage to petals, including petal drop.

Atmospheric pollutants. Atmospheric pollutants, such as ethylene, can cause flower shatter and petal drop.

Plant Damage

Aeschynanthus

Fig. 12.32 INSV on aeschynanthus. *Photo: Ethel Dutky*

Ageratum

Fig. 12.33 This white spotting on ageratum foliage is caused by the piercing and sucking of leafhoppers as they feed. *Photo: Stanton Gill*

Anemone

Fig. 12.34 Poppy-type anemone with green peach aphids feeding on the flower. The green peach aphid has a characteristic notch between its antennal base. *Photo: Stanton Gill*

Antirrhinum (Snapdragon)

Fig. 12.35 This leaf distortion on a snapdragon is the result of thrips feeding on developing foliage. *Photo: Leanne Pundt*

Azalea
(*See* Rhododendron)

Beaucarnea (Ponytail Palm)

Fig. 12.36 Mealybugs look like snow covering the foliage of this ponytail palm. *Photo: Stanton Gill*

Fig. 12.37 Mealybugs produce a white wax, as seen on this ponytail palm foliage. *Photo: Stanton Gill*

Begonia

Fig. 12.38 INSV on begonia causes leaves to become mottled and show dead spots. *Photo: Ethel Dutky*

Boston ivy (See Parthenocissus)

Brassica (Ornamental cabbage)

Fig. 12.39 Harlequin bug nymphs use their stylet mouthparts to pierce the leaf tissue of ornamental cabbage causing a white stippling injury to the foliage. *Photo: Stanton Gill*

Browallia

Fig. 12.40 Browallia plant shows severe leaf injury from thrips feeding. *Photo: Stanton Gill*

Cabbage, ornamental (See Brassica)

Capsicum (Pepper)

Fig. 12.41 Aphids feeding on newly emerging pepper leaves can distort foliage. *Photo: Stanton Gill*

Fig. 12.42 Caterpillars damage the foliage of peppers with their chewing. *Photo: Stanton Gill*

Celosia

Fig. 12.43 Green peach aphids often gather in large numbers on flowers as seen on this crested celosia. *Photo: Stanton Gilll*

Fig. 12.44 Aphids are clearly evident as they cluster on this celosia stem. *Photo: Dan Gilrein*

Fig. 12.45 Thrips feeding has caused a stippling injury on a wheat celosia plant. *Photo: Stanton Gill*

Cineraria

Fig. 12.46. Green peach aphids are clustered on the tip growth of a cineraria. *Photo: Stanton Gill*

Fig. 12.47 INSV on cineraria causes leaf mottling and distortion. *Photo: Ethel Dutky*

Citrus, ornamental

Fig. 12.48 Aphid populations tend to build up on the tip growth of ornamental citrus plants. *Photo: Stanton Gill*

Fig. 12.49 Two-spotted spidermites cause a fine chlorotic speckling of ornamental citrus foliage. *Photo: Stanton Gill*

Cleome

Fig. 12.50 Thrips will feed on cleome foliage producing a stippling injury. *Photo: Stanton Gill*

Chrysanthemum (*See* Dendranthema)

Codiaeum (Croton)

Fig. 12.51 This injury to croton foliage is caused by two-spotted spider mites. *Photo: Stanton Gill*

Coleus

Fig. 12.52 The citrus mealybug's white wax is very noticeable, especially on plants with dark foliage. *Photo: Stanton Gill*

Fig. 12.53 The piercing mouthparts of four-lined plant bugs and the toxin they inject into plant parts cause necrotic spots which will coalesce, as seen in this coleus foliage. *Photo: Stanton Gill*

Fig. 12.54 INSV on coleus. *Photo: Ethel Dutky*

Cyclamen

Fig. 12.55 Heavy populations of two-spotted spider mites lead to discoloration and browning of cyclamen foliage. *Photo: Stanton Gill*

Fig. 12.56 Western flower thrips have damaged this cyclamen leaf. *Photo: John Sanderson*

Croton
(*See* Codiaeum)

Dahlia

Fig. 12.57 Distorted dahlia foliage is caused by foxglove aphid feeding. *Photo: Stanton Gill*

Dendranthema (Chrysanthemum)

Fig. 12.58 Aphids are massed together on a chrysanthemum stem. *Photo: Dick Lindquist*

Fig. 12.59 Aphid cast skins on chrysanthemum leaves have a ghost-white color and are useful for detecting aphids. *Photo: John Sanderson*

Fig. 12.60 Cabbage loopers are occasional pests on chrysanthemum foliage. *Photo: Stanton Gill*

Fig. 12.61 Corn earworms feed on chrysanthemum flowers and foliage. *Photo: Stanton Gill*

Fig. 12.62 Greenhouse whitefly adults can be found on the lower surface of chrysanthemum leaves. *Photo: John Sanderson*

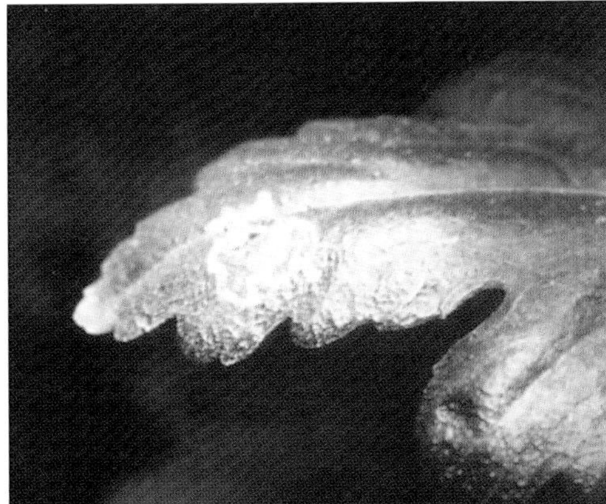

Fig. 12.63 Leafminer injury is revealed on chrysanthemum leaf. *Photo: John Sanderson*

Fig. 12.64 Mealybugs are very mobile and can migrate to and feed on chrysanthemums. *Photo: Stanton Gill*

Fig. 12.65 Plant bugs feed in spring through early summer, producing spotting of chrysanthemum foliage. *Photo: Dick Lindquist*

Fig. 12.66 This chewing damage to chrysanthemum leaves is caused by salt marsh caterpillar. *Photo: Stanton Gill*

Fig. 12.67 This chewing damage to chrysanthemum flower petals is result of spotted cucumber beetles. *Photo: Stanton Gill*

Fig. 12.68 Thrips injury is revealed by dimpled and distorted patches on chrysanthemum leaf. *Photo: John Sanderson*

Fig. 12.69 The two-banded Japanese weevil causes a notching injury to the flowers and leaves of chrysanthemum. *Photo: Stanton Gill*

Dracaena

Fig. 12.70 Aphids are often found on new tip growth of dracaena foliage. *Photo: Stanton Gill*

Fig. 12.71 Mealybugs tend to accumulate at the base of dracaena foliage. *Photo: Stanton Gill*

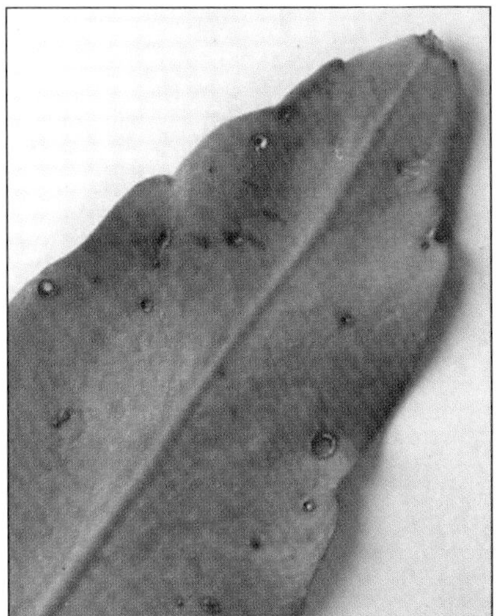

Epiphyllum

Fig. 12.72 The small, necrotic pit areas produced by false spider mite feeding could easily be mistaken for pathological disease symptoms on this epiphyllum plant. The small mite may be found in the damaged pit areas. *Photo: Stanton Gill*

Euphorbia (Poinsettia)

Fig. 12.73 Poinsettia with small leaflets formed on undersides of leaves—a genetic problem combined with greenhouse environmental stress. *Photo: Stanton Gill*

Fig. 12.74 Poinsettia with darkened stem from too high a soluble salt level. *Photo: Stanton Gill*

Fig. 12.75 Lewis mites cause a fine, stippled appearance to poinsettia foliage. *Photo: Stanton Gill*

Fig. 12.76 If Lewis mites attack poinsettia at the bract stage, the injury can look like this. *Photo: Stanton Gill*

Fig. 12.77 Though rather rare, brown soft scale can be found on poinsettia stems. *Photo: John Sanderson*

Fig. 12.78 Large infestation of shore fly adults can leave black fecal spots on foliage. *Photo: John Sanderson*

Fig. 12.79 Bleaching effect of bract is caused by feeding injury of silverleaf whitefly. *Photo: John Sanderson*

Exacum

Fig. 12.80 INSV on exacum. *Photo: Ethel Dutky*

Fuchsia

Fig. 12.81 Whiteflies are common pests on fuchsia plant. *Photo: Stanton Gill*

Geranium (See Pelargonium)

Gerbera

Fig. 12.82 A white serpentine leafminer mine is evident on the margin of this gerbera daisy leaf. *Photo: Stanton Gill*

Fig. 12.83 Leafminer mines are very noticeable on this gerbera. *Photo: John Sanderson*

Gladiolus

Fig. 12.84 Gladiolus thrips—larvae and adults—feed on gladiolus flowers and foliage. *Photo: Stanton Gill*

Fig. 12.85 Damage from gladiolus thrips produces a silvery stippling of the foliage. *Photo: Stanton Gill*

Gomphrena

Fig. 12.86 Thrips pierce leaves and cause necrotic tissue on gomphrena foliage. *Photo: Stanton Gill*

Hibiscus

Fig. 12.87 Hibiscus is highly attractive to greenhouse and silverleaf whitefly. *Photo: John Sanderson*

Fig. 12.88 Mature longtail mealybug females are easily recognized by their long, white wax appendages projecting from the rear of the insect. Hibiscus plants are very susceptible to mealybug infestation. *Photo: Stanton Gill*

Impatiens

Fig. 12.89 Aphid cast skins are clearly seen on impatiens. *Photo: Dan Gilrein*

Fig. 12.90 Broad mites cause distorted, twisted tip growth injury on garden impatiens. *Photo: Stanton Gill*

Fig. 12.91 Leafhopper injury on garden impatiens looks similar to thrips injury. With thrips feeding, round fecal drops will often be found on the foliage, but this is not true of leafhopper injury. *Photo: Stanton Gill*

Fig. 12.92 Spider mite injury on New Guinea impatiens in hot, dry growing conditions. *Photo: Stanton Gill*

Fig. 12.93 Thrips injury to fully expanded leaf of garden impatiens has a silvery, stippled appearance. *Photo: Stanton Gill*

Kalanchoe

Fig. 12.94 Broad mites or cyclamen mites produce stunting and distortion of tip growth on the terminal buds of kalanchoe. *Photo: Stanton Gill*

Lactuca sativa (Lettuce)

Fig. 12.95 Thrips and spider mite injury on greenhouse grown lettuce plant causes foliage to become silvery, then turn to yellow. *Photo: Stanton Gill*

Lantana

Fig. 12.96 Stippling injury on fully expanded lantana leaf is result of thrips. *Photo: Stanton Gill*

Lettuce (*See* Lactuca sativa)

Lilium

Fig. 12.97 Melon aphids are often found feeding on tip growth of Oriental lily. *Photo: Margery Daughtrey*

Fig. 12.98 Lift Easter lily foliage to spot aphids that feed on the undersides of leaves. *Photo: Stanton Gill*

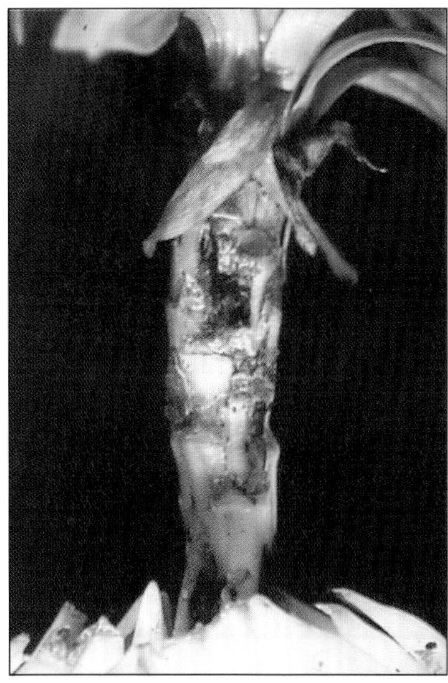

Fig. 12.99 Bulb mite injury can cause necrotic cankers on Easter lily stems. *Photo: Mark Ascerno*

Marigold (*See* Tagetes)

Nasturtium

Fig. 12.100 Serpentine leafminer injury on nasturtium leaf does not kill the plant but may reduce its marketability. *Photo: Stanton Gill*

Fig. 12.101 A large thrips population causes death of leaf tissue and makes this nasturtium plant unattractive. *Photo: Stanton Gill*

Fig. 12.102 Thrips will feed on nasturtium flowers as well as foliage. *Photo: Stanton Gill*

Pansy (*See* Viola)

Parthenocissus (Boston ivy)

Fig. 12.103 Boston ivy growing in hot, dry conditions is often host to the two-spotted spider mite. *Photo: Stanton Gill*

Pelargonium (Geranium)

Fig. 12.104 Foxglove aphid feeding damages geranium foliage. *Photo: Stanton Gill*

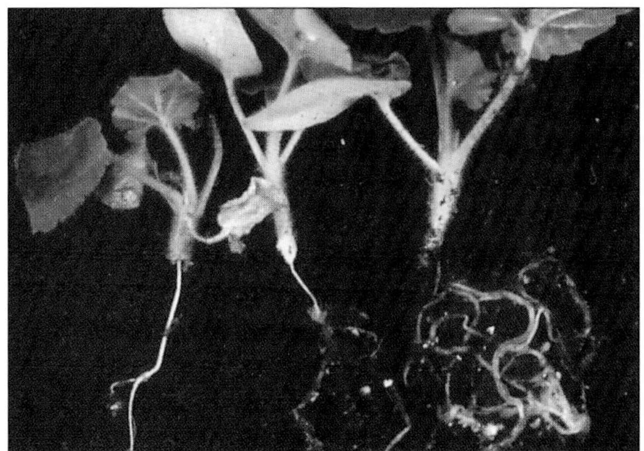

Fig. 12.105 Fungus gnat larvae feed on the roots and bore into the stems of geraniums. *Photo: Margery Daughtrey*

Fig. 12.106 Silken webbing on geranium leaf is evidence of spider mites. Feeding damage by spider mites can resemble oedema. *Photo: John Sanderson*

Fig. 12.107 Mottling of geranium leaf has been caused by thrips. *Photo: Stanton Gill*

Fig. 12.108 Geranium flower reveals injury from thrips feeding. *Photo: Stanton Gill*

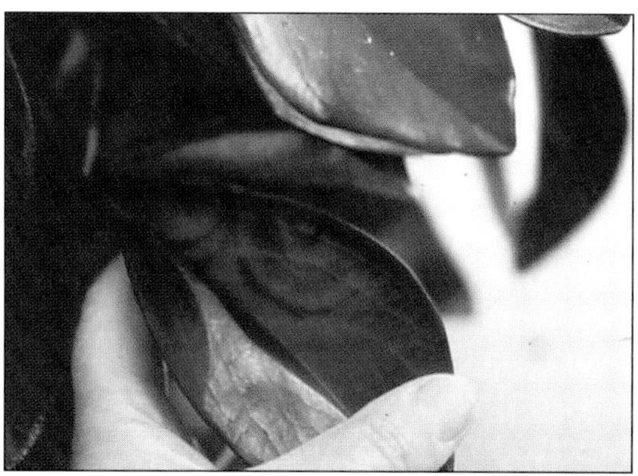

Peperomia

Fig. 12.109 INSV on peperomia. *Photo: Ethel Dutky*

Pepper (*See* Capsicum)

Periwinkle (*See* Vinca)

Petunia

Fig. 12.110 Thrips produce spotting injury on petunia flowers. *Photo: Stanton Gill*

Pittosporum

Fig. 12.111 Two-spotted spider mite feeding results in silvery, faded appearance of pittosporum foliage. *Photo: Stanton Gill*

Poinsettia (*See* Euphorbia)

Ponytail Palm (*See* Beaucarnea)

Portulaca

Fig. 12.112 Aphids are clearly seen on dark green portulaca leaves. *Photo: Margery Daughtrey*

Fig. 12.113 Portulaca foliage has a silvery, stippled appearance produced by thrips feeding. *Photo: Stanton Gill*

Primula

Fig. 12.114 Aphid feeding injury on primula results in distorted new growth. *Photo: Stanton Gill*

Rhododendron (Azalea)

Fig. 12.115 Azalea lacebug feeding causes stippling damage to this azalea foliage. *Photo: Stanton Gill*

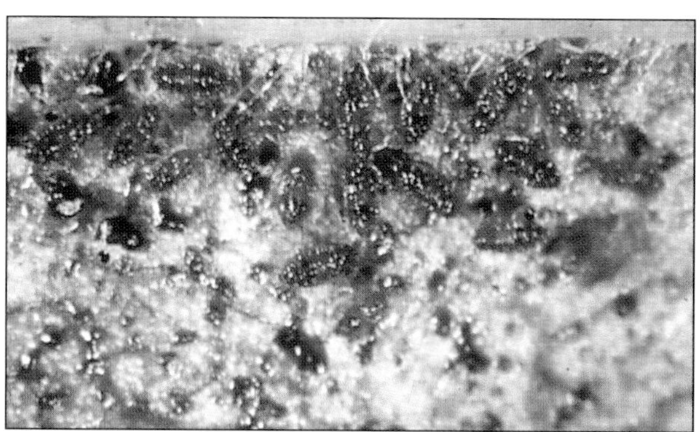

Fig. 12.116 Azalea lacebug nymphs are found on the undersides of foliage and are brownish with small spines on their bodies. *Photo: Stanton Gill*

Rosa

Fig. 12.117 Green peach aphids cluster in large numbers on flower stem and bud of rose. *Photo: John Sanderson*

Fig. 12.118 Aphid skins and eggs on this rose leaf are easy to spot. *Photo: John Sanderson*

Fig. 12.119 Thrips can damage the edges of rose petals. *Photo: John Sanderson*

Fig. 12.120 Thrips damage to rose foliage can cause distorted leaves. *Photo: John Sanderson*

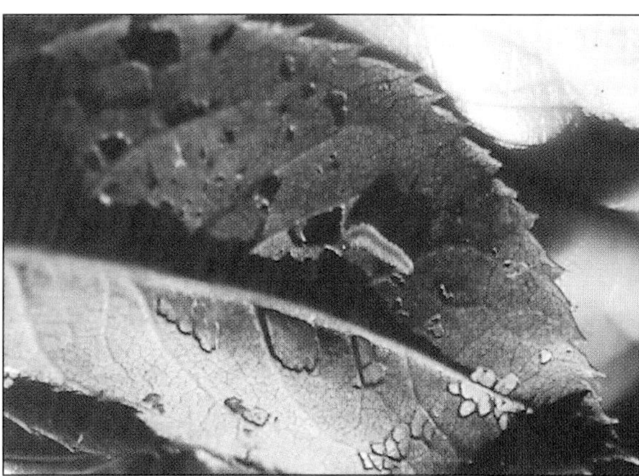

Fig. 12.121 Bristly rose slug, *Endelomyia aethiops*, which is the larval stage of a sawfly, damages rose foliage by skeletonizing it. *Photo: Stanton Gill*

Salvia

Fig. 12.122 Leaf curling on salvia is produced by aphid feeding. *Photo: Stanton Gill*

Fig. 12.123 Holes in salvia foliage are caused by caterpillar feeding. *Photo: Stanton Gill*

Fig. 12.124 Injury to salvia foliage is the result of thrips feeding. *Photo: Stanton Gill*

Schefflera

Fig. 12.125 Schefflera can have large, yellow-brown patches on foliage produced by feeding of false spider mite. *Photo: Stanton Gill*

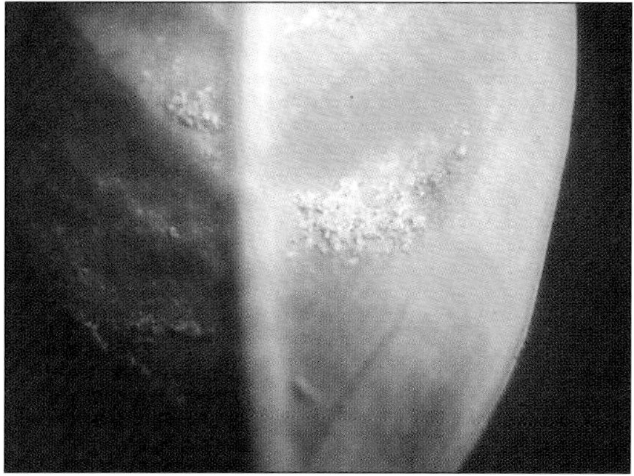

Stephanotis

Fig. 12.126 Damage from flat mites is evident on this stephanotis leaf. *Photo: Dan Gilrein*

Fig. 12.127 INSV on stephanotis. *Photo: Ethel Dutky*

Streptocarpus

Fig. 12.128 Streptocarpus with flat mite feeding injury shows leaf edge browning, which looks like a phytotoxic leaf burn. *Photo: Dick Lindquist*

Tagetes (Marigold)

Fig. 12.129 Thrips cause a silvery, stippling injury on marigold foliage. *Photo: Stanton Gill*

Fig. 12.130 The severe damage to the lower leaves of these marigolds was caused by the mines of the leafminer, *Liriomyza trifolii. Photo: Michael Parrella*

Verbena

Fig. 12.131 Thrips cause yellowing of verbena foliage. *Photo: Stanton Gill*

Vinca

Fig. 12.132 Thrips feeding on periwinkle flowers cause a white bleach area on petals. *Photo: Stanton Gill*

Fig. 12.133 INSV on vinca vine. *Photo: Ethel Dutky*

Viola (Pansy)

Fig. 12.134 Spider mite stippling damage is clearly seen on these pansy leaves. *Photo: Margery Daughtrey*

Fig. 12.135 Thrips piercing mouthparts cause spot injury of pansy flower. *Photo: Stanton Gill*

Zinnia

Fig. 12.136 Aphids are evident on lower surface of zinnia leaves. *Photo: Dan Gilrein*

Fig. 12.137 Feeding injury to zinnia flower is caused by cucumber beetle. *Photo: Michael Hoffmann*

Fig. 12.138 Leafhoppers can cause stippling injury to zinnia foliage. *Photo: John Sanderson*

WATER PLANTS

Fig. 12.139 Water plants are now being grown in greenhouses and have several specific pest problems. The following slides are of some of these problems. *Photo: Stanton Gill*

Fig. 12.140 Aphids are very evident on the open pink flower of a water lily. *Photo: Stanton Gill*

Fig. 12.141 Aphids and sooty mold growing on honeydew on water lily foliage can make the plant unattractive and unmarketable. *Photo: Stanton Gill*

Fig. 12.142 Water lily with feeding injury of China mark moth. Moth is concealed in the center of the hole in the lily leaf. *Photo: Stanton Gill*

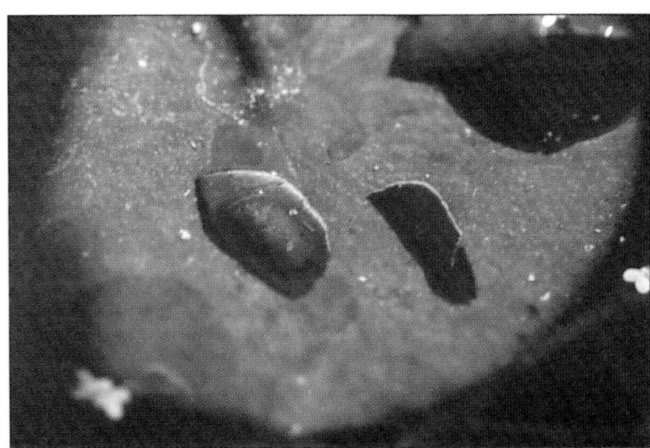

Fig. 12.143 Water lily with two leaf surfaces webbed together by the larvae of China mark moth. *Photo: Stanton Gill*

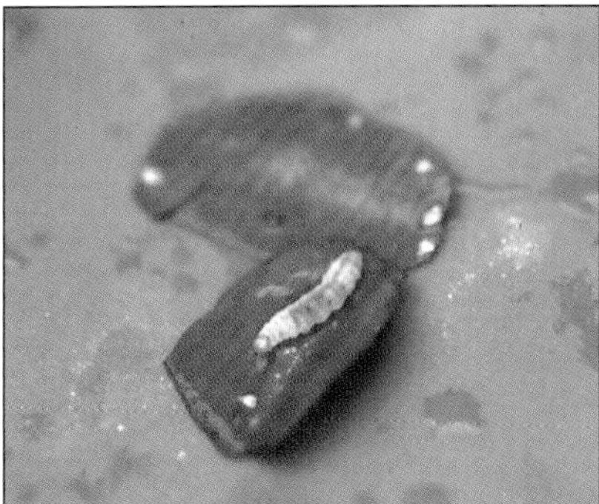

Fig. 12.144 Water lily leaf pieces are pulled apart to show larvae of China mark moth. *Photo: Stanton Gill*

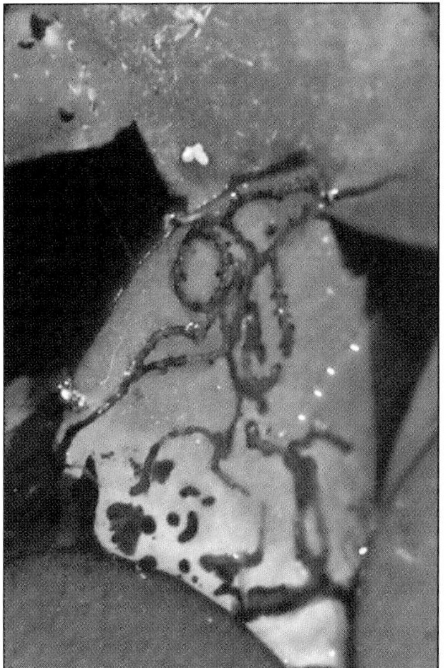

Fig. 12.145 Water lily foliage can be heavily injured by leafminer midge. *Photo: Stanton Gill*

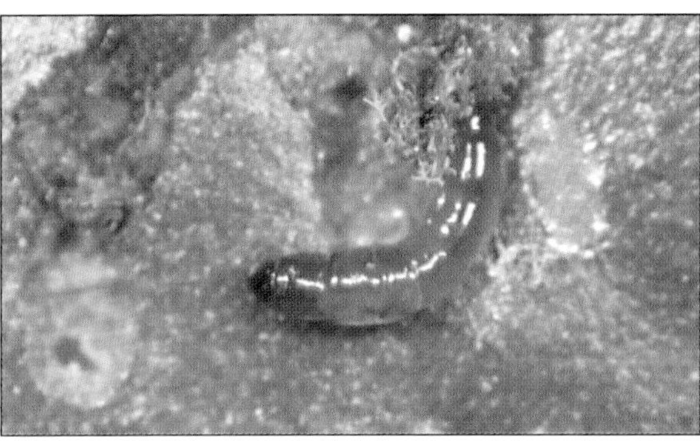

Fig. 12.146 Water lily leafminer midge larvae are yellowish to brownish in color. *Photo: Stanton Gill*

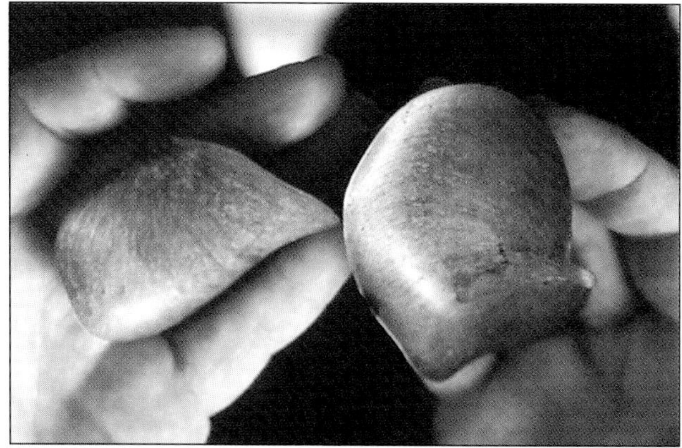

Fig. 12.147 Water hyacinths in production greenhouses often develop problems with spider mite injury of foliage. *Photo: Stanton Gill*

Fig. 12.148 Spider mite feeding damage is common in water pickerel grown in aquatic plant greenhouses. *Photo: Stanton Gill*

Glossary

alate—a winged aphid

antennae—prominent sensory organ on the head of an insect

aptera—a wingless aphid

arthropod—an organism with an exoskeleton and joint appendages, such as an insect, mite, spider, centipede, or crustacean

caterpillar—larval stage of butterflies and moths

cauda—the tail section of an insect

classification—All creatures are classified in a hierarchical system (phylum, class, order, family, genus, and species) to keep information orderly and help us determine their relationships with each other. This universal method of biological nomenclature prevents confusion among geographic regions of the world. Common names can vary from location to location, but the Latin names are universal. For example, the western flower thrips is classified as follows: phylum: Arthropoda; class: Insecta; order: Thysanoptera; family: Thripidae; genus: *Frankliniella;* species: *occidentalis.* Also, knowledge of one insect species may provide information on how the larger group such as its genus or even the family, feeds or damages plants.

cocoon—a silken case formed by an insect for pupation, within which metamorphosis from larva to pupa to adult occurs

conidiospores—asexually produced fungus spores

crawler—first-instar nymph of a scale insect or other related Homoptera, such as first-instar whitefly

cuticle—insect skin made of chitin

deutonymph—the second nymphal stage of a mite, after egg, larva, and protonymph

diapause—a physiologically induced period of prolonged rest or dormancy in insects and mites

entomopathogenic—a disease organism that kills insects

exuviae—the skin or exoskeleton covering an arthropod's body, after it has been shed in order for the arthropod to grow

exoskeleton—the external skeleton of an insect, composed of hard cuticle; also called the skin

frass—fecal material and food fragments produced by an insect in feeding

hermaphrodite—animal with both male and female reproductive organs

honeydew—sticky, sugar-containing secretion produced by aphids, soft scales, and whiteflies

instar—An instar is the form (made up of size, color, and shape) of a nymph or larva between molts. The first-instar nymph or larva hatches from the egg. It feeds, grows, expands its skin to full size, then molts. The newly emerged individual is larger and is called the second instar. This process is repeated. Most insects have between three to six nymphal or larval stages.

insectary—commercial facility for rearing insects, usually beneficial organisms for sale for biological control

larva—(plural larvae) the immature stage between egg and pupa of an insect with complete metamorphosis. The common names for the major pest larval types are: *grub* = soil dwelling beetle larva; *maggot* = fly larva; *caterpillar* = butterfly or moth larva

mandibles—structures that function as both jaws and teeth

membranous—filmy, often transparent

metamorphosis, complete—Insects with complete metamorphosis have four life stages: egg, larva, pupa, and adult. Growth occurs in the larval stage, which is represented by a series of successively larger forms called instars. Plant damage may be done by the larva and/or the adult stage, depending on the pest family. Larvae and adults that go through complete metamorphosis, such as caterpillars, beetles, leafminers, fungus gnats, shore flies, and humpbacked flies, usually do not feed on the same plant in the same manner.

metamorphosis, gradual—Insects with gradual metamorphosis have three life stages: egg, nymph, and adult. Growth occurs in the nymphal stage, which is represented by a series of successively larger forms called instars. Similar plant damage is done by nymphal and adult stages. Nymphs resemble adults but lack fully developed wings, and both stages usually feed in the same way on the same plant. Insects with gradual metamorphosis include thrips, aphids, whiteflies, leafhoppers, scales, and mealybugs.

molting—Insect molting or shedding is the process in which a fully expanded skin (exuviae) is split, crawled out of, and left behind. This may take about an hour. The new skin quickly hardens to become the new protective body covering, also serving as the skeleton to which muscles are attached, since there is no internal skeleton. Molting must occur for an insect to grow. Each new skin is larger than the previous shed skin. Most species have genetically determined adult size limits. Molting and growth only occur in nymphal and larval stages. In most insects no growth occurs after the adult stage is reached. Therefore, small beetles, moths, and flies do not grow into larger individuals. Adult female scale insects are a notable exception.

mycelium—a mass of hyphae (hyphae are threads of a fungi)

necrotic—dead or dying tissue

nymph—the immature stages between egg and adult of an insect with gradual metamorphosis

ovipositor—organ with which eggs are laid

parthenogenesis—reproduction without mating

pheromone—a substance secreted by an organism that causes a specific behavioral reaction by other individuals of the same species; often used in traps to lure insects for pest monitoring

phytophagous—describes an organism that feeds on plants

polyphagous—eating several different types of food

polymorphism—the occurrence of two or more different forms (morphs) within one species; common in aphids

proleg—the fleshy, unsegmented abdominal leg of a caterpillar

protonymph—the first eight-legged stage after the egg and six-legged larva in a mite

pupa—the resting stage between larva and adult of insects with complete metamorphosis. Pupae do not feed, and they are usually hidden under leaves, in soil, or in debris. Many caterpillars encase their pupae in silken cocoons. The pupal casing of a butterfly is called the chrysalis.

puparium—a case created by the hardening of the larval skin, in which a fly pupa and adult is formed

species—a group of interbreeding individuals or populations, similar in structure and physiology, that are different from all other groups and produce fertile offspring

spiracle—hole in the side of an insect through which it breathes

stages—stages are the periods of an insect's life that are usually much different in appearance and behavior; e.g., egg stage, larval stage, etc.

vector—a carrier and transmitter of disease-causing organisms

viviparous—giving birth to live young

INDEX

Page numbers for photographs are in italics.